A gun in a b

The sto

Yoel Gat

A gun in a battle of knives

The story of Gilat

Yoel Gat
A gun in a battle of knives

Translation: Avi Aronsky

To my beloved children, Yonatan and Orit,
who paid the dear price of having spent little
time with dad for many, long years and to my
dear wife Simona, who was and will be the
source of my power.

Table Of Content

Prologue

Although I have set out to tell the tale of but one Israeli company, **Gilat Satellite Networks**, the book can also be viewed as the story of the Israeli high-tech industry in its entirety — an industry built by dreamers and visionaries. Many of these individuals realized their dreams of having an Israeli company reach lofty heights by dint of introducing Israeli *chutzpah* (audacity) to the big world, which enabled them to compete against giants and succeed.

• • •

What is it that attracts so many people to high-tech like moths to light? To comprehend the industry's allure, you must first acquaint yourselves with those exceptional people who are known as 'entrepreneurs.' In most cases, entrepreneurs are individuals between the ages of 35 and 40 who understand that half of their lives— or at least half of their careers — are already behind them, and they are looking for a change.

The next question is what motivates the entrepreneur to marshall all of the forces and the intensive focus needed to drive his new enterprise? It is not the financial incentive, for money is merely a by-product of success, not the goal. In fact, as far as the entrepreneur is concerned, money is the least important factor at the start of a new undertaking. More than anything else, the entrepreneur wants to make an impact on the world. Perched on the wings of his imagination, desire, and dreams, he searches for the 'next big thing.'

A company — and in our case, an Israeli company — is the means for realizing those ambitions. At first, all you hope for is to develop your own product. Once the product is ready, you make an effort to try and sell it. Thereafter, you do everything in your power to establish a reputation on the world market, and then you strive to become the world leader in your field. All this, however, is not enough. You want the company's ascent to continue: You want to reach the stars.

If any entrepreneur knew beforehand the effort that starting up a company entails, he or she probably would not have chosen this path. However, the entrepreneur believes against all odds. The entrepreneur wants to establish, influence, take off, and achieve. This passion for success is stronger than any other part of his or her personality. It is the raison d'etre and fate of the entrepreneur.

Like any enchanting fairy tale the story of Gilat consists of a united team with a strong culture, blind faith in the righteousness of its way, and uncompromising willpower. It is the story of a company that came out of nowhere to become a corner stone of its industry and, following a series of decisive and judicious moves, assumed the role of global leader. However, once Gilat began to dream of reaching places that only the huge companies dare to roam — the American home consumer market — it fell flat on its face.

Gilat had clear competitive advantages. Its technology completely outclassed the competition; they fought with knives while Gilat had a gun in each hand: A unique technology that was reliable and inexpensive; satisfied (and at times ravingly happy) costumers; an aggressive culture; and, exceptional people skills — nearly everything. The company was driven by a vision and a loyal founding team — an extensive group of veterans from the 'Unit' (in the Israeli army) — that spearheaded the discovery of a large market and quality opportunities.

However, sources of strength always bear the seeds of their own destruction. The glare of success momentarily blinds the entrepreneur and he fails to notice the warning signs .The world conditions that led to success does not stand still; changes in the big picture glide by unseen and, it seems that in an instant, the marketplace is already clamoring for something else. Undaunted, the entrepreneur and his team continue to forge ahead with the old dream until momentum suddenly stops. But by then it's too late, as the organization has blindly followed the entrepreneur into the abyss, still convinced of the rightness of its way and still imbued with that fervent faith.

Lastly, this is the story of five entrepreneurs who set out together on a long trek: Shlomo Tirosh, the former commander of "the

Unit"—a straightforward, aggressive, dedicated, and energetic man with a merciless tongue; and Gidi Kaplan, a talented engineer who fathered many of the main technological ideas that Gilat developed and ran its development and technology group for many years.

It is also the story of a pair of brothers who are about as different as can be: Joshua and Amiram Levinberg—the sons of Zalman Levinberg, the long-time manager of *Maariv* (one of Israel's largest daily newspapers). Joshua, the older brother and a mythological figure, was the only one of us with previous experience in the high-tech world. He was responsible for the marketing and business development and also handled all administrative matters. Short and skinny with piercing eyes that scrutinize five dimensions simultaneously, Joshua is a sharp strategic and complex tactical thinker who had a profound influence over all the primary directions the company considered. Amiram, the younger yet more solid of the two brothers, was my comrade-in-arms. Before the establishment of Gilat, we worked side by side, at adjoining doors, for ten years. Dubbed "Mr. Common Sense" by the founding team, Amiram is an alert individual with a knack for piecing together a puzzle and comprehending the big picture in a visible and coherent manner. He is curious with strong technical skills and a rare understanding of the mysterious ways of the market. Moreover, he is more than willing to burn the midnight oil in order to learn a new subject. It is hardly surprising, then, that Amiram was responsible for all of Gilat's successful products.

This is also my story. The defining event of my life occurred at the age of sixteen. As a group leader in the Scouts (in Israel the Boy/Girl Scouts are co-ed), I made up my mind that my team was going to win the city Leadership Cup and dedicated a half a year of my life to that goal; I dreamt about the competition every night and planned for it every day. I motivated my groups and they too were swept up by the vision. The preparations were long, difficult and exhausting, but the actual triumph was a walk in the park because all the steps were mastered ahead of time during the drills: **a gun in a battle of knives**. This lesson has remained etched in my mind to this very day.

At Gilat, I served as a player-coach, although too much of the time was spent as a player. I lacked any business background, save for my business management studies before Gilat was founded, but I was born for marketing and sales. I have the ability to rally people — employees, customers and investors — around me and convince them that my ideas are worth pursuing, occasionally beyond what is desired…

The five of us enjoyed working as a tight, entrepreneurial team. We would focus on a specific objective and, immediately after achieving it, we would turn to a new and bigger goal. The magic word was **momentum**—a fast-paced, step-by-step building process, which involved an immense and occasionally heroic effort on our part. We firmly believed that we would ultimately reap the fruit of our labor.

Furthermore, we considered our enterprise a modern form of Zionism; namely, a promising model for the Israeli economy, which would provide us with a deep sense of satisfaction.

The competition over world markets was waged on a daily basis and was often ruthless. We set out for battle against giants and bested them. We competed against anyone, anywhere, under any conditions and did not concede so much even on a single battle – even after the top analysts in the world proclaimed that we had realized our dream of global leadership in our field. And let me remind you that we started out as a small Israeli company, whose name no one could even spell.

1

And I called her name "Gilat"

Gilat was born on November 17, 1986, and I didn't even know it. The company's origins date back to an unforgettable meeting at the office of my Unit's commander, and attended by the head of Israeli Military Intelligence, Then General Amnon Lipkin-Shachak. Over the course of the meeting, I attempted to convince General Shachak how important it was to include the project that I was heading in the Military Intelligence's technological unit (the "Unit") in the next year's plan, but the intelligence chief rejected my every word.

The project derived from a brilliant idea that was conceived several years earlier by a select coterie of people; I beg the reader accept this characterization since, for security reasons, I cannot actually describe the project or the "brilliant idea". After devoting several years to getting it off the ground, we believed in the project and wanted to see it come to fruition. By then, I was already a veteran manager, thirty-four years old, directly and indirectly responsible for hundreds of employees, but I suddenly found myself backed into a corner.

The conversation was tough and unfriendly. In fact, some of General Shachak's statements still echo in my mind to this very day. I tried to push the project and Shachak blocked it. When I asserted, among other points, that the project would employ hundreds of people, he railed that, "We will not have any workers' 'unions' dictate our plans to us". I glanced over at Colonel Shlomo Tirosh, the previous commander of the Unit, who was also involved in the project; he looked towards the ground. I saw that he too was hurt by the words of the intelligence chief.

My hands trembled, and I felt that the general was unwilling to even listen to reason. "This type of project", I repeatedly attempted to explain, "requires the establishment of extensive infrastructure, and we must implement it swiftly…"

"No", Shachak passed judgment. "I am sorry, but it will not be in next year's plan".

I was frustrated and irate. That very minute, I made up my mind to leave everything behind: Military Intelligence, the Unit, the IDF (Israeli Defense Force — i.e. the Israeli army). I was unable to conceal my feelings, and Shachak immediately realized what had come over me. "Its not so bad Yoel", he tired to console me. "You have made more difficult decisions in your life…"

"I respect your decision", I answered, "but I am afraid that if you shelve the project, you won't need my services any longer".

"Think it over", Shachak concluded. "We both know that you still have a lot to contribute".

Until that day, my Unit was the center of my life. The Unit is a unique, intimate, and focused body with impressive technological capacities and wonderful people whose names are engraved in the intelligence community's honor roll. It is an organization that has adopted a culture of achieving the mission under any circumstances, with the dedication and motivation for supreme concentration and effort. I was assigned to the Unit as a young *atudai* (a soldier who is sent to university by the army to acquire an advanced military vocation before enlisting) who had just completed an undergraduate degree in electrical engineering. At the Unit, I came across many of the qualities — determination, power, and faith in one's abilities — that I have since strived to emulate. I was entrusted with a tremendous amount of responsibility over vital matters. In return, I devoted every last drop of energy that I had to the Unit. No less important was the deep sense of satisfaction that I received from being a member of a body that significantly contributed to Israel's defense. It is very difficult to leave such an organization and such people, especially after thirteen long years of vigorous work.

I left the Unit and drove straight home, knowing that I was in for a long, sleepless night. As is my custom, I wanted to "sleep on it", but the verdict was already made. All that remained was to formulate a justification for my own peace of mind and overcome my deep sense of disappointment.

The very next morning, I reported to the Unit Commander and notified him of my decision. Then, I went to tell Shlomo Tirosh; he was not surprised, for he had personally witnessed what had transpired at that fateful meeting. He nonetheless tried to persuade me to stay and not to throw everything away, but soon realized that I was dead set on leaving. Towards the end of our brief conversation, Shlomo smiled and asked, "Well, so what's next?". Shlomo indeed understood that something was in the making. He would soon be at my side.

Gilat was off and running. That very same day, I spoke with Amiram and Gidi, who were my partners on the project. I told them about the meeting with General Shachak and my decision to leave the army. "I want you to join me", I said. "We are going to found a company that creates its own products. We'll be able to take advantage of our skills, experience, and desire to work together as a select team".

Amiram and Gidi were intrigued. I immediately sensed that the concept had found a rapt audience. I knew that I was no longer alone: there was a team and an objective. We agreed to meet a few days later in order to exchange ideas and start articulating a plan. Amiram recommended that we add his brother Joshua to the team, for the latter was someone with what Amiram described as "a sense for what is going on in the world outside of the IDF". I was elated, for we were already a foursome, and I had a hunch that a fifth, Shlomo Tirosh, was on his way.

There was a team, excitement, and a strong desire to forge ahead and succeed. All that remained were two minor details: how exactly do we start up a company from scratch and what the hell would this company actually do?

We obviously did not have offices, so the founding meetings of the new, as of yet nameless, company were convened in our homes, each time in another living room. Both then and now, I considered these meetings, which lasted well into the night, to be romantic and naïve. Everything was discussed with unbridled passion and the belief that we were on the verge of something big. However, we were still uncertain of exactly what we wanted — whether to establish a consultancy or develop our own unique products — what the market wanted, and what would be the division of responsibilities among the founders.

We were only certain of one thing — that we were made of the right stuff. The four of us had experience working together and felt that we complimented each other well: Shlomo Tirosh, who joined later on, brought passion and military ideas; Joshua, the skeptic, was the one to ask the questions; and Amiram and Gidi contributed creative technological ideas.

From the kitchen, my wife Simona overheard the ideas that were being bandied about and the millions of dollars that were piling up. She was convinced that we had lost our minds. However, given the fact she had already seen what we were capable of doing together — Simona and I met in the Unit and got married during the course of our service there, and she was still serving in the Unit and involved in the aforementioned project when I left — she decided that it was best to keep quiet...

We did not have our minds set on any particular idea. Our meetings were a sort of pot in which everyone threw in ideas, and perhaps at the end of the day something would come out of all that brainstorming. For example, at one of the first meetings, we noticed that Joshua arrived with a somber look on his face. "That's it", he explained, "our future has been cut off. I heard that a group of guys have left a corresponding unit...and are founding a communications company of their own...called NICE (which eventually became a leading Israeli high-tech company). They won't leave us any room to maneuver..." Shlomo, on the other hand, recommended that we develop a product called 'Mister' that would provide satellite communications to mobile military units; for another concept I could leverage the work I had done my MBA thesis on couriering express mail in Israel. Among the many topics that we considered was the field of cable television, which was then making its first steps in Israel.

At the end of the day, we had an excess of ideas and were unfocused. However, we had a strong desire to work together and knew that we would ultimately find the fields of operation that were right for us.

Notwithstanding our lack of a clear direction, we decided that we had to come up with a name for the company. A name always signifies a beginning or a new direction and points to a willingness to seek fulfillment and meaning. Moreover, it endows its owner with a face and character. Since I have always attributed a mystical or magical importance to names and have thus invested quite a bit of time to finding appropriate names for projects, products, and even my car, I volunteered for the job. It was an interesting challenge, coming up with a name for a new company that might not even be established and whose *raison d'être* was still up in the air. All

I knew was that I wanted an elegant Hebrew name. After playing about with the abbreviations of our first and sir names, I hit the bullseye : G (*the Hebrew letter gīmel*) for Gat or Gidi; I (*yōd*) for Yoel; L (*lamed*) for Levinberg; and T (*tāw*) for Tirosh. G I L A T. Our Gilat.

In the meantime, until a game plan and the company were established, we also had to earn a living. A few weeks after we officially founded the company, I was contacted by Itamar, a good friend from the army, who told me that he had just been appointed assistant director of business development at Dankner Investment Corporation (one of the top investment firms in Israel). The company was planning to enter the field of cable television, and the first government bids for franchises were scheduled to be released towards the end of 1987. Consequently, Dankner were searching for a consultancy that would help them learn the technical and business aspects of the field.

"But we don't understand much about cable television…", I told him.

"Learn at our expense", Itamar responded. "It's a piece of cake for you guys". Itamar then drafted a bid for a consulting company and helped us prepare the offer that obviously won the bid. Given the fact that I had only recently left the army and this was my first experience in the business world, the bid was an important lesson on how big business operates: if you first lay eyes on the bidding documents after they have been released to the public, your chances are slim because the one that lands the contract usually helped write the documents to begin with.

I would not be stretching the truth if I were to say that Gilat owes its existance to Dankner Investment. Gilat soon found itself immersed in the world of cable television. We felt like pioneers and were involved in nearly everything the field had to offer: technological and economic consulting, choosing equipment, and designing cable television networks in the different Israeli cities of Rehovot, Bat Yam, Holon, Haifa, and Kiryat Shmonah. In essence, MATAV and Tevel (the leading Israeli cable television providers) underwrote the first days of Gilat and enabled us to develop our initial products, which ultimately triggered our stunning breakthrough.

Although we were planning and consulting on how and why to stretch coaxial cables underground, our heads were in the clouds — or to be more precise, beyond the clouds, where satellites orbit the earth. The field of communication satellites was hardly new to us, as we dealt with this field over the course of our military service; we were captivated by this cable-less, constraint-free technology that allows for mobility and rapid deployment. Moreover, no Israeli companies and, for that matter, very few companies throughout the world were seriously involved in this emerging field at that point. Consequently, we decided that this was our direction and focused on learning the field in an attempt to see whether we were capable of planning a product. During Gilat's early stages, we believed that the primary applications of our product would be entirely for military purposes: communications between mobile forces, tanks, headquarters, combat units, and more.

The satellite communications industry dates back to the launching of the Russian satellite Sputnik in the autumn of 1957, which was the first time that mankind had demonstrated the ability to transcend beyond the boundaries of the Earth and enter into space. In 1965, the first communication satellite, Early Bird, was launched with the objective of proving that communications could be established between an artificial object floating 22,000 miles above Earth's equator and any location on the planet. This possibility was first raised by Arthur C. Clarke in an article published in 1945, twenty years before the launching of the Early Bird. In that same article, Clarke claimed that as few as three communication satellites could connect any two points on the globe.

The modern communication satellite is a box about the size of a large refrigerator, and is powered by about thirty feet of solar panels fitted into its sides. Antennas, each approximately the size of a large umbrella, are fastened onto the satellite. The antennae project beams onto the surface of the Earth which are called 'footprints'; these beams radio signals that are transmitted to and from the earth. The signals are relayed by the satellite back to the dishes on Earth (named "earth stations"), which are installed at various locations and are permanently pointed towards the communication satellite. The smaller the dish, the easier it is to install and operate.

It was indeed the "VSAT" (Very Small Aperture Terminal), or small dish market, that we were interested in. By definition, VSATs are dishes with diameters of less than six feet. There are basically two types of dishes: one way or two way systems. The one way dishes are only used for receiving signals (reception) and are thus most suitable for broadcast applications, such as television and distribution of business information. In contrast, two-way dishes allow for reception and transmission and can thus be used for interactive applications such as credit card verification, and (then, in the future) broadband internet access.

The essence of VSATs is obvious: the smaller the dish, the less information that can be transmitted and received. Therefore, our challenge was to develop technical concepts that would enable us to use smaller dishes while maintaining reasonable throughput, while focusing on achieving a low price. This was Gilat's vision.

In May 1987, some two months before Gilat was registered as an Israeli company, I traveled to the United States. The purpose of my visit was to conduct an in-depth study of the satellite industry, which included identifying our potential competitors and establishing initial contacts with appropriate companies that could perhaps help us identify and market our products. Our premise was that we could blaze a path to the market by harnessing creative Israeli engineering with the marketing muscle of an American giant. Only today do I realize just how naïve we really were…

By the time I set out on my trip, the idea of Mister had already begun to take form, so I took along detailed sketches of the product concept: a mobile unit — exclusively for military use — with a small antenna that enables motorized armed forces to communicate from various locations. We had reached the conclusion that there was no point in producing the entire product by ourselves. The best course of action, as far as we were concerned, was to hook up with an American company and integrate several systems — some of which were to be manufactured by top international suppliers — into our final product. Our first target was Spacenet.

Spacenet was a division of GTE, then among the largest telecommunications companies in the United States that was later integrated into Verizon. Spacenet specialized in building and launching satellites into space establishing data-communication networks for the telecommunications needs of GTE. Later on, Spacenet also became a major provider of small dishes (VSATs). Spacenet was not a technology company that actually developed products; its niche was designing and delivering new services using its satellite. Accordingly, it purchased most of its technology from other companies, primarily the Japanese company NEC. Spacenet thus appeared to be the perfect potential partner for a small, Israeli start up like Gilat.

My first contact with Spacenet's senior management was attained with the help of Haim Davidi. Davidi was among the first engineers at the Israeli Ministry of Communications and subsequently worked for Bezeq (Israel's telecommunications monopoly and still the country's leading company in that field). In addition, Davidi was one of the founders of the Emek Ha'ela Station, Israel's principal satellite communications earth station. After the system was up and running, Haim started working for the American company that built the station, a subsidiary of GTE, and presided over its sales in Israel.

I met Haim — a robust, well-connected redhead, who is pleasant but appropriately aggressive as well — in 1983, while setting up a project for the Unit. Davidi's company was competing over part of the project, and he made it clear to us that his company was going to win the contract "with or without us". I learned to respect him over the course of the bid, as he did everything that was needed in order to ensure that his company would win. Haim indeed won the contract — incidentally, against my recommendation — and we have since become good friends. It is also worth noting that his company did an outstanding job.

Haim arranged a king's welcome for me at his company's headquarters in the United States, and from there it was smooth sailing to Spacenet and a meeting with the company's top team. The first Spacenet official I met with was Tom Shimabukuro, an engineer who was in charge of new technologies. Tom, who was dubbed *Abakushkah* at Gilat — simply because we had difficulties pronouncing his Hawaiian name — was an older, stout man. A teacher by nature, Tom had a passion for technology and an innate curiosity for people and new ideas. We got along well, and Tom became our first mentor in the field of small dishes, as he provided us with solid advice on technology, competitors, and the market. To this day, I am perplexed as to why Tom helped us for so many years. Perhaps, he was the first to believe that Gilat would develop a resounding technology that would eventually change the industry.

The most important advice that Tom gave us was to develop a one-way product. Such a product would both prove our ability and fill the needs of a key market which Spacenet did not cater to at the time.

In order to burst forth with a new product beyond the borders of Israel, we initially required a strategic partnership. An Israeli technology company that totals five people must have a global market focus due to the limited local market. Thus, from the outset Gilat had no choice but to cater to the international market from the moment it had something to offer. In fact, an endless amount of possibilities stood before us, and it was thus imperative that we determine which markets were most suitable for our product; the countries to market to at the outset; and last but not least who our potential first costumers were.

The ability to sell the first system is crucial to the development of a start-up, as a fledgling company that lacks a reputation, reference customers, and a brand name. Save for its technological ability and boundless desire to succeed, it basically has nothing. Often, the only way for a start-up to realize its aspirations is to find a strategic partner with a reputation in the industry, who is prepared to sell the company's products in the target markets and to become the proverbial "reference account". In return, the start-up has no choice but to worship its partner and agree to all its demands.

This sort of partnership is not forged at a single senior level meeting in which the start-up persuades the established company to purchase its goods. The development of such a relationship entails a long, demanding, and at times depressing process of building a continuous, daily, and extended relationship with decision makers on all levels all aimed at one goal: convincing their engineers that your technology is superior. This task is all the more difficult, if not impossible, if you happen to be offering a substitute for a technology that has been developed in-house. You have to prove to their marketing people that the product definition is top rate, meets the demands of the market – and overcome the inevitable "not invented here" syndrome. The product must also be put to the test of their quality control staff, who will determine whether it meets their standards. Obviously, you have to persuade their finance people that the product is economically viable and better than the existing alternatives. Moreover, it is crucial that their management believes that your people are of the highest caliber and that your own management is strong and well-versed in all the requisite fields. Finally, you have to convince them that your company will last for the foreseeable future, despite the fact that your existence depends on their ability and **willingness** to sell your product.

Does this sound complicated? In reality, it is much more difficult.

Managing alliances is indeed an art form, not an exact science. It is predicated on the ability to build personal relationships at the appropriate levels — in our case, engineers versus engineers, marketing people versus marketing people, financial people versus financial people, and management versus management. Naturally, you must also attain an in-depth understanding of the organization that you are attempting to penetrate: to identify its character and organizational structure, both formal and informal, and decipher their internal politics.

Above all, the start-up management must ceaselessly pamper the targeted organization with attention, even if this comes at the expense of many other important activities. This principle is quite clear, but is not always carried out. As in war, victory depends on amassing soldiers and resources in the right place and at the right time. You do not necessarily need a larger army, but a general must deploy more soldiers and materiel in a timely fashion at the pivotal engagements of the battle.

We internalized these principles, and I departed for the United States knowing that we were prepared to do everything in our power to win Spacenet over. I returned from the trip with the requisite product definition, and we began to prepare for the next step: to prove our technological capabilities to Spacenet.

2

First Steps

By November 1987, Gilat was a registered company with five full-time employees and three consultants. Business with Dankner Investment continued to go well; and no less importantly, we had a product definition for a one-way satellite system which was already in its development stages, and had made a commitment to deliver a finished product to Spacenet within six months. These challenges necessitated the immediate establishment of development infrastructure from scratch, while simultaneously continuing our full-time consultancy work for the cable companies. Our guiding principle was "tunnel vision": Gilat was in a closed tunnel and looked neither right nor left. We simply forged ahead until several months later we came out at the other end with a working product that could be shipped to the United States.

We set up shop at two venues: the basement of my father's construction company, from where we conducted our cable business; and a cheap, rented apartment in north Tel-Aviv's Neve Sharett neighborhood. We moved all the laboratory equipment that was previously kept in private homes to the small apartment and augmented our new 'research center' with cheap, used equipment.

Amiram, the team's natural leader, assumed control over the development, together with Uzi, an engineer that served with us in the Unit, and Hanoch, a computer engineer who entered the pages of Gilat's rather short history as our first employee who did not hail from the Unit (several thousands were to follow in his footsteps). The documentation was written by Haim Bechor, who was contracted as an external consultant. We worked in the apartment some twenty hours a day and the neighbors were positive that we were running a brothel, as young men were entering and leaving the premises around the clock.

We regularly invited people who were likely to take an interest in the product to the apartment. For example, I brought Scientific Atlanta's top sales person, John Bucket, over for a tour. He was selling transmission systems for cable networks and, with our assistance, sold quite a bit of equipment in Israel, which was used to lay down the infrastructures of Israel's then developing cable-television industry. John was very impressed by the system: "You can feel the energy in the air", he told me again and again. "This can be a lethal product..."

On April 26, 1988, five months after entering the tunnel, we packed the equipment for a trip to Spacenet. I can't help but smile when recalling the metal cases that we built — a special delivery from the Mazuz Brothers — for three transmitters, three receivers, three computer cards, a computer equipped with all the requisite software (so that we would not have to rely on local computers), and all the accompanying documentation, including our first ever user manual (look Spacenet, we even thought about that). All the equipment was ready and appeared to constitute a "real" finished product.

Amiram and I arrived at Ben-Gurion Airport (Israel main International Airport), and El-Al's ground staff couldn't believe that we actually intended on boarding the plane with the equipment in hand. They vehemently objected, but we refused to give in. After a long, heated debate, we reached a compromise: they allowed us to take the crates on to the plane with us, while Amiram and I agreed to put the equipment in the bathroom during take-off and landing and to sit in the next to last row and watch over the equipment, which would be stored behind the last row throughout the duration of the flight.

On Wednesday morning, we touched down at Dulles International airport for the short ride to McLean, Virginia, an upscale area that is the home of Spacenet's posh offices. Despite the jet lag, we immediately set out for Manassas VA, a thirty minute drive from McLean, where Spacenet's logistical center is located. If McLean is the Park Avenue of Virginia then Manassas is the local shanty town, but this did not bother us. We rushed to the building where our presentation was scheduled to be held in order to check and install our equipment.

Fortunately, we were accompanied by one of the Spacenet's

technical personnel, who explained to us what was going on and which antenna to hook up to. Despite this gentleman's good intentions and those of several kind souls at the Manassas complex, everything was out of whack and one mishap led to another: the device that we brought from Israel had never actually been connected to a satellite before; the synthesizer malfunctioned; the American power system used (obviously) different voltage than the Israeli system; and the measuring equipment that they used was inappropriate for our equipment. We finally managed to connect to the network, but then a fuse burnt in the computer and we had to start all over again.

Less than five hours remained until our crucial presentation — the one that we had toiled over for nearly six months — and nothing was going right. We felt as if we were going to make fools of ourselves before the dignified forum of engineers who were coming to check out the guys from Israel. Even while Amiram and I were working out the mess, I made note of several lessons that could be drawn from the incident: First and foremost, you can't take chances with such critical events. You can't just waltz in at the last moment, for there always will be unforeseen problems. Therefore, you always have to give yourself an adequate safety net. If we had come a day earlier, we would have saved ourselves a great deal of heartache.

In the end, it all worked out, and we solved the problems the only way we know how: one at a time. After two and a half hours, all the systems were up and running. We still had time to rush to the hotel, shower, change into suits, and get back on time for the meeting. A second before the presentation, Amiram scrambled up to the roof to fix yet another unexpected problem, and I discovered that in all the excitement I had lost my voice and could barely speak. Notwithstanding these two scares, the presentation went smoothly. I spoke in a near whisper, but the audience was enraptured: "Magicians", someone remarked; "These guys are going to sweep out the competition from the market", said another. We had come a long way from Israel to Virginia, but it was well worth it. We proved to Spacenet that we were made of the right stuff and that this small company from Israel could deliver the goods. Furthermore, we showed that the dishes for receiving satellite signals could be a whole lot smaller — down to 12 inches. This was truly revolutionary from their standpoint, and we believed that the ticket to Spacenet was in our hands.

Despite the fatigue — the flight from Israel to Virginia, the nerve wracking installation, and the long presentation — we accepted a dinner invitation from C.T. Wu, the manager of Spacenet's advanced engineering group. C.T., an energetic Taiwanese, is a highly technical engineer as well as a seasoned corporate politician. He was extremely impressed with our abilities and decided to give us a free, comprehensive, and riveting lesson on the politics and decision-making process at Spacenet.

At the time, Spacenet employed over a thousand people. Its staff was divided into several groups, each of which responsible for its own field. The most important group from our standpoint was the domestic sales team, which was run by Joe Barna, an older Hungarian-American who was risk-averse and well-connected to the Japanese company, NEC. "Don't expect him to help", C.T. warned us. "Barna will do whatever he believes is good for NEC. Try to penetrate the level below him".

The international sales team consisted of two groups, which were constantly immersed in power struggles against each other. One group was based in McLean and the second — ISC, the group that Haim Davidi worked for — was near Boston. We obviously hoped that that Davidi's group would best their rivals, as they were then our closest allies in the company, and C.T. also crossed his fingers for us.

The third group, the engineering and development team, was split into three main groups and a variety of small bands, that no one quite knew to whom they belonged. Over the course of what was becoming a lengthy dinner, our distinguished host explained to us that the development group would vehemently object to any external development; in other words, to any products offered by outside companies. However, his advanced engineering group would gladly support us, as would the third sub-group: the technology team that was headed by our acquaintance *Abakushkah*. "Tom is a nice guy", C.T. Wu dampened our enthusiasm, "but his influence is limited. They don't listen to him, and he is no politician. You must search for more formidable sources of political power within Spacenet..."

"And what about the marketing group?" we asked.

"They will be attentive", he reassured us. Moreover, he informed us that the Finance Department was absolutely irrelevant insofar as our objectives were concerned.

Above and beyond all the departments and figures stood Spacenet's legendary president, Jerry Waylan. "The man is considered God in the corridors", C.T. explained. "He is very technical, smart, knows everything, and is a wonderful sales person. He never commits himself and allows all his people to plead their case before him. And when he feels like it, he decides. It will be very difficult for you to gain his attention and even harder to gain his support, but the road to winning over Spacenet passes through him. Look for any way to endear yourselves to Jerry. The picture you have received may be complex and seemingly impenetrable, but you can succeed. Display the same determination that you guys did in developing the products, and pray".

C.T. had provided us with valuable information, which we would fall back on in the future before making strategic decisions that pertained to our relations with Spacenet. By the end of dinner, we were completely worn out and confused. We returned to the hotel and tried to fall asleep, but without much success.

The next day, Thursday, we met with many groups at Spacenet, most of which we had never heard of before and tried to place them using the information C.T. had provided us with. However, the sales people and department heads were unwilling to meet with us, and it took us quite some time to get over that hurdle. On Friday, we installed a receiver unit in *Abakushkah*'s office and got to meet the legendary Jerry Waylan for the first time. He was affable and intrigued, but — true to C.T.'s description — did not commit to anything.

That same day, we were already invited to a product meeting at Spacenet. It was an excellent meeting. We laid the foundations for a subsequent, preliminary meeting on the two-way product that we were planning to develop. Moreover, we discussed a myriad of other possibilities, including jointly developing products, attracting external funding; and getting Spacenet to help us define the marketing plans and strategies. It was as if we were dreaming. We felt as if we had infiltrated Spacenet, but we still had no idea of what laid in store for us.

We hurried back to Israel, intoxicated with euphoria. As soon as we landed, we received a call from the Unit. They informed us that our last project — the same one whose rejection led to my resignation from the army — was in the running for the Israel

Defense Award and asked us to prepare a proposal. The project had successfully ended a while ago, but since I was its former head, I was called up for two weeks of reserve duty in order to push the process along. We were undoubtedly on a roll. During such periods, you are immersed with work, but all your efforts appear to be right on target and everything falls into place. In the best periods of life, you have time for everything.

In mid-1988, we indeed received the Israel Defense Award. We were proud of the fact that seven of the twelve winners were already working at Gilat. One of the judges was Dan Tolkovsky, the former commander of the Air Force and among the founders of Israel's high-tech industry. Our paths crossed again two years later when we decided to raise our first round of financing. Tolkovsky stood at the head of what was then the only venture capital fund in Israel, and the fate of our fundraising was in his hands. Tolkovsky looked at us and said, "You don't have to tell me a thing about yourselves, guys. I was on the judges' panel of the Israel Defense Award in 1988, and I know exactly what you guys did and what your are capable of doing…" As the old Hebrew proverb puts it, "The work of the righteous is done by others".

We started working like mad on development plans for the two-way product. Towards the end of 1988, Joshua entered my office with a rather strange proposal: "I heard that there is an office for rent on Barzel Street in Ramat Hachayal" (an industrial area in northeast Tel-Aviv). What do you think about moving there and basing all the company's operations from there?"

My immediate reaction was against the move: "It will cost us a fortune. Is it that bad here?"

Joshua refused to relent. "We can get a whole floor with four thousand square feet. We'll start with three thousand and rent the rest to a company that designs printed circuit boards (PCBs), which perhaps we can do business with (so typical of Joshua). Eventually, we will all have to sit together, so let's start now. You'll see how slowly but surely, Gilat will take over the entire building…" Joshua, the man behind the vision, took Amiram and me to see the place.

The Barzel Street of 1988 was not the Barzel Street of 2008. Today it is lined with state-of-the-art buildings that house the top high-tech companies. However, back then, it was more reminiscent of Bombay: an old-tech manufacturing district brimming with old buildings, garages, smoke, and soot. On the way to the building, we maneuvered past the streams of sewage that stretched across the entire length of the road. At first glance, the site was rather seedy: forklifts greeted us at the entrance; the steps were narrow; and there was only one bathroom per floor. Joshua ignored the décor and immediately took us to the third floor, which consisted of a large entrance hall; a conference room (only upon seeing it did we realize how sorely we needed one); ten inner rooms; large open spaces by the kitchenette and in the back which Joshua already earmarked for R&D and the cable television group, respectively…

We loved the place and took it within days. Unlike today's standards, we did not renovate the offices. Joshua brought a heap of used furniture from a company that went bankrupt, and we assembled the furniture ourselves. The conference table — half round, half rectangular — barely fit into the room. There was no semblance of uniformity between the desks, chairs, and the rest of the equipment, but all this did not disturb us. From our standpoint, the new offices were a real step up and were akin to a royal suite in our eyes. Following a most dignified ceremony, we left the apartment in Neve Sharett and the basement in my father's construction company and moved to the new venue. We could not resist a modest celebration to mark the dedication of our new abode. For the first time since the founding of Gilat, we began to feel like a real company.

The breakdown of duties at Gilat, which had remained intact since the company's establishment, was clear: Shlomo was in charge of the finances; Gidi and Amiram handled the engineering, technology, and development; and Joshua and I were responsible for the marketing and sales. As the CEO of the company, I also took upon myself two other essential tasks: to lead amongst equals and to be the "chief visionary" in the company.

During this period, a plethora of characters wandered around Gilat's corridors, checking out the company, offering advice, and taking an interest. Perhaps the strangest of the lot was Robert Bontzek, a kind-hearted Australian Jew and a strong supporter of Israel. Bontzek — an aging bachelor, full of energy and ambition, with a sense of humor, curly hair, and dancing eyes — owned a business that supplied audio-video systems to various companies. He had come to Israel in search of two things: interesting companies to represent in Australia and a nice Jewish bride.

When Robert first arrived, we couldn't stop cracking jokes about Australia in the corridors: "Where is it on the map" or "A dish for every kangaroo". However, Robert had his mind set on representing us in Australia and persisted with his lobbying until we realized that it is indeed an interesting country: a continent with sixteen million people in 1990 and vast communications needs. He also tried to pressure me into exhibiting our product at Australia's largest telecom fair. To this day, I am still unsure of whether I relented to Robert's pestering because I believed that it was a good opportunity, or because I was unable to withstand his pressure.

In February 1990, I got on a plane for Australia, but this time I traveled alone. I took along samples of the one-way equipment, in the same metal crates that we took to Spacenet several months earlier. However, this time I had the crates put in the cargo and spent a small fortune on overweight charges. After twenty-four hours of continuous flying, I finally landed and headed straight for the exhibition site in order to install the sample equipment. I went up to the roof to point the dish to the satellite as I had done so many times before, but for some reason I couldn't get it straight, even after hours of trying.

A young Aussie, who had watched my futile attempts to establish a connection, came up to me and asked what I was doing. "Isn't it obvious", I replied, "I am trying to find the satellite".

He smiled and said, "Laddie" — despite the fact that I was at least ten years older than him — "the satellite in Australia is to the North and not to the south like you're used to…"

I had finally gotten the picture. Communication satellites are positioned on the equator, so that in the southern hemisphere — to which, I may add, this was my maiden voyage — the satellite is located to the north, in contrast to Israel, Europe, and the United States where you always point the dish to the south.

For three days, I stood in the booth with Robert and met with potential customers. I was impressed by the country and the will of its people to party and avoid working too hard — namely, the pursuit of the good life. Although I marketed the product quite aggressively, I was surprised to find that only a few people were interested in our one-way product. Most of the demand was for two-way systems, which we were still developing. The most intriguing visit was by the representatives of the Equatorial Satellite

Systems Australia Company, which was co-owned by Equatorial — an American firm that was the first start-up in the field — and a local company that held the majority of the shares. Their first representative to stop by our booth was an Israeli engineer, followed by a technical group, and finally the company's CEO. Needless to say, they were very impressed with our product. After the exhibition, they took me to their impressive facilities outside of Melbourne and gave me a presentation of their company. It was as if I had fallen straight from heaven into their laps, as I quickly discovered that they were unsatisfied with Equatorial's equipment and were searching for an alterative. They conducted thorough test procedures on our product and were pleasantly surprised to find that it worked flawlessly.

I ended up staying in Australia for two more days and received an order worth over $400,000 for three hundred receivers and three transmitters. I was in the clouds. Our first business trip and I had bagged a huge order. We had a company, a building, and now an order. The heavens were smiling down upon us. I rushed back to the hotel to notify the guys and sent them a fax of the historical contract — Gilat's first order ever. They, too, were overcome with joy. When I returned to Israel after another exhausting trek, all the founders were waiting for me at the airport with a bottle of champagne. We toasted *le'chayim*, took pictures to commemorate the moment, and drove home with the feeling that the sky's the limit.

I promised the Aussies that we would finish the units within four months, and the entire company thus started working on the order immediately. When we were about done — after having already invested nearly $200,000 — we decided, as is customary in every large international transaction, to insure the order before we shipped the goods to Australia,. The export insurance company conducted a check and got back to us with an unequivocal answer: "There is nothing to insure; Equatorial Australia is on the verge of bankruptcy".

The shocking news reached me while I was in Joshua's home in New Jersey (as noted, Joshua had moved with his family to the United States in order to be close to Spacenet and our future customers). I immediately called the Israeli engineer who had established the initial contact between me and the company, and he confirmed the bad news. The company had indeed gone under and the deal was off. Furthermore, there was no one to reimburse us for the hundreds of thousands of dollars that we had invested until now. Minutes later, I rang up our controller to check up on our financial situation. As if the cancellation was not enough, he informed me that the cash reserves were dangerously low and that soon there wouldn't be enough cash to pay salaries. We had counted on the Australian money, which had obviously not panned out.

We were all stunned and felt that Gilat was on the brink of collapse. When I was at Equatorial's offices, I didn't notice any signs of trouble. The company appeared to be strong and sure of itself. It had a magnificent building, a robust and satisfied staff, and seemed to be backed by serious investors. Who could have fathomed that they would flop within three months? Our first order turned out to be our first major setback. We learned our lesson well: in any large transaction, you have to insure the payment in advance. In this instance, I had simply acted recklessly.

For a company like ours, which did not have outside capital and at this stage counted on internal funding and income from our consulting business, this could have been a fatal blow. The cash flow figures painted a morbid picture, as by August we would not have the money to make payroll. This left us with two months to raise capital. During those trying days, I received yet another captivating lesson on the role of a corporate CEO. One of his or her primary functions is to bring in money any way possible: selling equity in the company, consulting, or sales. However, none of these possibilities seemed realistic in the immediate aftermath of the Equatorial fiasco. The situation was truly catastrophic. I was still in the United States and planned on traveling to a trade show in Singapore, but Shlomo imposed a firm veto: "Yoel, I am sorry, but we don't have money. If it's up to me, I'll lay down on the runway so that you won't be able to take off…". I understood the hint and packed my bags. But instead of getting on a plane for Singapore, I returned home in a dejected mood.

An important business principle states that you raise money whenever you can and not when you need to. Nevertheless, we were forced to execute our first round of financing with our backs to the wall. Successful fund raising entails the formulation of a coherent story with the following components: a market, a product, sales, a strong management team, and a reliable plan. You also need time, which is exactly what we lacked. Plans are not enough. To build this story you have to be able to point to deeds as well. However, in our predicament, how could we put a positive spin on the Australian deal, when we were saddled with hundreds of thousands of dollars of equipment that no one needed?

At that very time, the venture capital fund era was just getting underway in Israel, and there was only one fund in the entire country, Athena Venture Partners (named after the hopelessly elusive and exotic Greek goddess). Venture capital funds raise capital from various sources and invest it in start-up companies. All these funds are predicated on the same idea: although most start-ups eventually fail and the money goes down the tubes, there are always some companies that succeed and return between ten to thirty dollars for every dollar invested in them. Another investment company that could have considered our sort of operation in those days was the Discount Investment Corporation. However, since its investment in Scitex (an Israeli high-tech firm specializing in digital printing and graphics) five years earlier, it had steered clear of the high-tech sector. Who else, then, could we have possibly turned to?

We first met Lori Kaufmann in early 1989. Lori is an American who has prepared many business plans over the course of her career and had already seen it all. She is a brilliant strategic thinker, who graduated from the Harvard Business School. At our first meeting with her, we presented Gilat's vision, which was followed by an unexpected and captivating lesson on what Lori refers to as "focus". From her standpoint, focus is the basis for all company operations. She sat with us for hours, asked all the right questions, and opened our eyes to the future. In addition, Lori made us realize just how unfocused we were. In her estimation, we had invested too much energy on cable television, all of which came at the expense of Gilat's main cause: satellite communications. We tried to explain to her that the company would have never survived without cable television and the money from Dankner Investment, but she refused to concede the point. It was the first time in my life that I heard the adage, "Decide what business you are in, who your costumers are, and what value you are providing them with…" Lori claimed that we should have raised money and concentrated on the satellite market from the very outset. "You are too small to be dealing with everything", she gingerly reprimanded us. "Choose what you want to focus on".

Lori Kaufmann is indeed a person graced with incredible abilities. Decisive, quick, and well-versed in a broad range of areas, she reads and digests material at the speed of a paper shredder. Moreover, she does not chose words carefully even when what she has to say is likely to annoy the ears of her listener.

We met with Lori and her husband Yadin — a managing partner at the Athena Fund — several times, even before the Australian setback. Yadin was captivated by our vision. On several occasions, he let us know that we could turn to him if we wanted to raise money. We had rejected his hints, with childish naiveté, and made it clear that we did not need the money. However, after the Australian disappointment, we were in dire need of cash. Consequently, we asked Lori to prepare an updated business plan, which would encompass all of our operations as of May 1990, and we turned to Yadin.

Raising money is nothing short of an art form. You have to know how to present a rosy picture, even though you are quickly running out of money. We made quite an effort to fashion together an enticing story: a gang of ex-intelligence officers from an elite unit; Israel Defense Award winners; a broad technological background; a new and intriguing market; a relationship with Spacenet, an American giant; faith and passion burning in our eyes. Gilat was quite a compelling story, a company that had funded itself for three years, developed all its technology on its own, and concurrently provided comprehensive services to several of the largest cable companies in Israel. The story was quite impressive, but even this was not enough.

In order to spread the risk, Yadin recommended that we also turn to American venture capital funds. As far as he was concerned, we were an Israeli company that foreign funds would be willing to invest in. We turned to several of these firms, and they dispatched representatives to our offices in order to evaluate the company and its products. At the time, a fair share of the rooms and open spaces were still unoccupied. So in order to impress our distinguished guests, we filled them with people who had no connection to the company whatsoever. The visitors saw a company bursting with enterprise; its rooms were full of employees diligently toiling away at their jobs. I could only imagine the look on their faces were they to have discovered that some of those vibrant offices had emptied out several minutes after they had left the building.

We invested quite a bit of energy on impressing the representatives of the venture capital funds. Our engineers and the company's managers met with them and described the breakthrough that we were hoping to bring to the exciting VSAT market. We made quite an impression, but to our regret the American companies were averse to investing in an Israeli company during a period in which there was still uncertainty over the prospects of the country's high-tech industry.

Gilat's turnaround came in the form of our close acquaintance Micha Angel. In my opinion, Micha fully deserves of the name "the architect of the Israeli communications industry". He founded Tevel (the aforementioned Israeli cable television company) and Cellcom (one of Israel's leading cellular phone companies) and handled those accounts on behalf of Discount Investment. Micha and I both participated in discussions between our respective companies about Israel's incipient cable television industry. Every time he popped over for a visit at our offices, he would sneak off to the lab where he would interrogate our engineers on all that concerned the progress of our product. He always asserted that our line of work was exceedingly more interesting than cable television, and swore that one day he would eventually get in on the action.

That day eventually arrived, without any advanced notice. During a conversation with Amiram and me in Gilat's corridor, Micha said, "You know what? We also have to get in as investors".

We laughed and reminded him that, "You guys haven't invested in high tech for years".

"That's right", he replied, "but the time has come".

"Will you be able to do something in the next few weeks?" we asked, cautious not to reveal so much as a bit of excitement.

"Yes. We'll try to get in at once and with the same conditions as Athena", Micha concluded. As the saying goes, it's either 'all or nothing…'

The road to the investment was paved, and the partners that we acquired were excellent. Amiram represented us in the negotiations along with a bright American attorney named Gene Kleinhandler, who would accompany us for many years to come and me until today. Our relations with Gene constituted an incredible synthesis between an American and Israelis. Moreover, Gene was the perfect partner for adopting a hardline approach. During the negotiations, I sat next to Amiram and was stunned at how he managed to navigate his way through the thicket. Every time it seemed as if the negotiations were about to go up in smoke, I whispered the following plea into Amiram's ear: "How can you fight over this point when you know that in two weeks, we won't have enough money for salaries?"

However, Amiram maintained his composure: "Don't worry. They want the deal just as badly as we do. With a bit of patience, we'll get what we want". And as usual, he was right.

The investment agreement was signed in August 1990, some three months after the crisis, and the money came in a week after the signing. Gilat raised $1.5 million in August, with an option for an additional $1.5 million a year later. In return, we provided them with 50% of the company's shares. We took a deep sigh of relief, for we could now pay the salaries with a clear conscience, while the investors didn't quite understand how half of their initial transfer had instantly vanished into thin air. We were thrilled, as without the money Gilat would have been forced to close down, and we also proved our ability to raise capital. Arik Keshet, among the company's senior engineers, then came up with an ingenious remark that has remained etched in my mind to this very day: "Gilat is the only company I know whose strategy is predicated on a set of miracles…"

In any event, the first chapter of our 'miracles strategy' had come to a successful close.

3

Behind Enemy Lines with a Knife between the Teeth

A penetration, by its very definition, is executed at only one particular point of entry.

Companies, big and small firms alike, operate in many areas because they cannot foresee where they will succeed and where they will fail. Consequently, despite the fact that the key to a successful market penetration is total, uncompromising focus, most companies lack the focus needed for a pinpoint attack.

Gilat essentially focused on Spacenet for lack of a better choice. They were the only company that we managed to build some sort of relationship with, and the only ones who were willing to consider outside technology.

For all the emotion expended and its disappointment ending, in the final analysis the Australian adventure was marginal. We wanted the deal and needed it to survive and prove our ability to sell, but we knew that the focus had to remain on Spacenet. This was the company we wanted to take off with. Faithful to our gospel, we devoted all our resources to Spacenet enabling us to blaze a path to market by harnessing our engineering skills to the marketing prowess of an American giant.

The installation of our one-way system at Spacenet in April 1988 constituted a turning point. Gilat — a miniscule company from Israel, with only twelve employees whose engineers tripped over their tongues whenever they tried to speak English — proved its ability and stirred up interest in its products and technology. Our faces lit up with pride as we swallowed every word of an article that appeared in Spacenet's internal newspaper under the following title: "USATs—the Wave of the Not-so-Distant Future". The article glorified and extolled the work of the dedicated engineers at Spacenet who were developing new satellite applications. It also noted, as a side note and in fine print, that a company called Gilat was the manufacturer of the new technology. Only an alert reader could have discerned that such an entity exists. All the credit went to them — they initiated, invented, and planned it all. Nonetheless, there was no reason for us to lose sleep over this, as we knew that our future customers would always understand that the product belonged to the disheveled Israeli engineers in t-shirts and not Spacenet's sales executives dressed in their suits and ties.

We read every single word of that article and scanned between, above, and below the lines. Although it was merely the internal newspaper of a single company, for us it was a big deal. It was the first time that anyone had taken the trouble to write about our company or that the name Gilat had appeared in print.

After reading the article, Amiram had only one thing to say: "Spacenet has boundless potential. They could be truly great if we were running it".

Due to the successful installation, we received our first visit to Israel that same month from a Spacenet representative: Pete Nielsen — who later became Spacenet's manager of the joint project with Gilat and could be counted among our strongest supporters in the organization — was sent to Israel to find out exactly what stood behind the group that promised to steer Spacenet to a brighter future. He was astonished to find a band of twelve young men who were preoccupied with deploying cable television systems. We were frank with him and admitted that without Spacenet's contribution to the shared project, especially its sales capabilities, Gilat would be forced to concentrate on other topics.

Pete swallowed hard and wrote what in American terms, was a glowing report, which was then distributed to all the members of Spacenet's management: "They are an impressive and very unique group", he wrote. "I recommend that we strongly consider the possibility of developing a joint product with them".

In July 1988, two months after Nielsen's visit, Amiram and I met with Ed Mlavsky, the founding manager of the BIRD Foundation, a joint Israeli-American fund that invests in projects involving both Israeli and American companies. The objective of the foundation (which offers a corresponding funding track to that of the Office of the Chief Scientist of Israel) is to encourage technological and subsequently marketing cooperation between Israeli and American businesses. The main idea, which was perfectly aligned with our objectives at the time, was for the American company to provide the market and the Israeli company to supply the technology. For the most part, Ed supported collaborations between Israeli firms and mid-sized American companies, but the prospects of working with a giant like GTE — Spacenet's parent company — was quite tempting.

The three of us engaged in a lengthy discussion on the topic. I told Ed that we were thinking of developing a two-way satellite product for data communications that could be used for specific applications, such as credit card verification for retail and restaurant chains and other businesses with numerous sites. We would develop the hardware and Spacenet would develop the software. Whereas we had innovative ideas for building a cheap and simple product that could compete with any of the systems that were currently on the market, Spacenet's part of the product would be based on software that it had already developed with the Japanese company NEC. Moreover, we told Ed that Amiram and Uzi had already filed a patent on the idea. In fact, this patent turned out to be one of our principal intellectual-property assets, as it blunted Gilat's competition in the field for many long years.

"What's your budget for the project?" Ed asked.

I took a deep breath: "About $3 million".

"And how many people are there in the company?"

"Eight people who are relevant to the topic".

Ed nearly fell over in his chair when he absorbed the numbers. "We'll give you half the money. How are you going to come up with the rest?"

"Spacenet", I replied without hesitation.

Ed — a very experienced businessman who had seen it all and was well familiar with all the scheming that goes on behind the scenes — explained to us why having Spacenet co-fund the project would be a big mistake: "It's a bureaucratic and tired company", he said. "You have got to be the ones sitting on the driver's seat. You can't concede your rights to the product because of their contribution to the cost of development. And you certainly can't give them extensive marketing rights because then they will completely dominate your company and become its true owners".

Ed was absolutely right. He had brought into focus a course of action that perhaps, given our miniscule size, we did not have the courage to consider. Gilat may have had innovative ideas and a knife between its teeth, but we didn't dare think that we could interact with a giant like Spacenet as equals. We accepted Ed's advice and behaved accordingly. The joint proposal that we eventually drafted for the BIRD Foundation was completely symmetrical: two equals—Gilat and Spacenet—doing business together.

Following our conversation, Ed paid a visit to Spacenet, where he received a royal welcome. Even Jerry Waylan, the all-powerful president, invested more time in him than we ever received. Ed explained to them what the BIRD Foundation was all about and encouraged them to enter the process with Gilat. He promised them his assistance and coaxed them into submitting a joint proposal. On September 15, 1988, Gilat and Spacenet indeed submitted a joint proposal with the following title: "A Proposal to Develop an Ultra Small Aperture Terminal - Satellite System".

In the memorandum to the proposal, the two companies described the project's commercial potential. "Our market research suggests that Gilat and Spacenet will be able to sell over 50,000 units by the project's tenth year and control a 25% share of the product's international market, which amounts to cumulative sales of $162 million". It is worth noting that the numbers that were thrown into the air were far from over-optimistic, By 2001, ten years after the product was launched, we had sold about 400,000 units, reached a market share of 50%, and grossed over one billion dollars in total sales.

Given the impressive assets that Spacenet brought to its business relationship with Gilat— being one of the world's leading suppliers of satellite communications and a wholly-owned subsidiary of the communications giant GTE (with some $15 billion dollars in annual sales) — we were not surprised that the BIRD Foundation's approval arrived in January, less than three months after its submission. The BIRD Foundation allocated a two-year budget of $2.37 million to the project, and the agreement was signed by Joshua Levinberg of Gilat and Spacenet's Joe Barna.

In October, well before the Bird Foundation approved the project, we flew to Virginia to begin working with Spacenet on the development plan for the new product. We informed them that we intended to press ahead with both the one-way and the joint development of the two-way products. Each side clarified what they expected out of the joint project, including their respective roles and the timetables. We believed that Spacenet was entering the partnership in good faith and that the two of us would start working together in earnest.

Unfortunately, Spacenet's performance fell far short of our expectations. We had hoped that after such a convincing declaration of intentions, Spacenet would storm forward with all its might, but in practice only a small and initially marginal group, headed by Pete Nielsen, began to work on the topic. As far as Spacenet was concerned, the project was peripheral and barely merited any attention within the organization. We were forced to be creative and strategize how to motivate Spacenet to pick up its pace. The mere fact that development was underway was not enough. We wanted progress. We wanted to see the Spacenet marketing people pitching the project so that the relevant players would know that a new product was slated to hit the market soon. We wanted momentum, but were disappointed.

In late 1990, when it appeared as if we were on the right track, Joshua suddenly offered to move to the United States. "Gilat's vice-president of marketing and sales has nothing to do in Israel", he explained. "I have to move to the United States in order to be as close as possible to Spacenet…and the other companies that we want to do business with".

Today this step seems like a no-brainer, but in 1989 it was nothing short of revolutionary. Joshua was certain that he would have to sweat it out in order to convince me that it was absolutely vital for him to move to the United States, and he began to devise a list of arguments: efficiency, savings, and better relations with the decision makers at Spacenet. To his surprise, I immediately agreed and Joshua was on his way. Following a short adjustment period with his family in New Jersey, where his wife's sister lived, Joshua moved to McLean, Virginia and rented an office within walking distance (with an umbrella when it rained) of the Spacenet building. Joshua was an exemplary commando soldier: a strategist but a wonderful tactician as well. Working alone, Joshua lit a fire under all the ranks at Spacenet, from the lowliest engineer up to its president. He was not above — or so the legend goes — surprising Spacenet's vice-presidents in the bathroom stalls, where he would not give in until he attained everything he asked for. Joshua spearheaded the infiltration of Spacenet. He was the commander in the field and thus responsible for Gilat's relationship —both with the technical and marketing teams — with our American partners.

I loved the way Joshua fearlessly managed the battlefront. The moment he identified an opening, he did everything in his power to steadily widen the breach. He ferried over and bombarded it with new and fresh forces. Engineers regularly arrived from Israel for technical discussions, including occasional visits from Gidi and Amiram; I intermittently joined the fray. Given the presence of our senior commanders on the front lines, the ranks of Spacenet's participants rose as well. During my trips, Joshua and I would try to get past the door to Jerry Waylan's office, but with only moderate success. We also occasionally visited the international group in Boston. The general strategy was to conduct a continuous dialogue at all levels and create a dynamic plan of operation, which both companies would have to react to and that would remain firmly rooted throughout the Spacenet's organization. We persistently collected daily intelligence in the hallways in order to learn the terrain and keep abreast of what was going on with our competitors. The more we became familiar with Spacenet and the way it operated, the greater were our doubts about the fledgling partnership between the two organizations.

That said, Spacenet had their own doubts. These mutual concerns had an impact on the progress of the joint project. After the initial enthusiasm wound down — remember the day of, "Those guys are magicians…" — suspicions began to surface. Spacenet was primarily worried over whether a small company like Gilat would be able to persevere and survive in the long run. Moreover, there was grumbling that taking a gamble on Gilat might damage Spacenet's hard-earned relations with the other companies who developed technology on its behalf, especially NEC with which Spacenet had a long and intimate relationship. In fact, NEC's budget for entertaining the Spacenet people that came to Japan was larger than Gilat's entire 1990 budget. We had heard stories of the black limousines, outfitted with young, long-legged Japanese women, waiting for Spacenet's senior executives when they arrived for a visit.

Not surprisingly, we also had our own doubts about Spacenet. Although it was indeed a huge company with a rich, dignified parent in the form of GTE, Spacenet proved to be a cumbersome, unprofitable, and lazy company. It lost most of the deals that it competed over to superior competitors, foremost among them the Hughes Network Systems, which was then part of the powerful General Motors Corporation.

We wavered quite a bit over the choice of our partner and the appropriate business model; we were merely the equipment vendors while all marketing and sales efforts were essentially in Spacenet's hands. We weren't sure if this was the model that suited us. Our product, which was already at an advanced stage of its development, was slated to hit the market at a revolutionary price of $4,500 per unit, as the cost of our competitors' equipment was $9,000 to $10,000. As a result, we were far from certain that we had bet our money on the right horse and worried that we had surrendered too much authority to them.

At this juncture — several weeks before raising our first round of financing, when we were still desperate for money in order to continue paying salaries — we were mired in this "identity crisis". If that weren't enough, we started hearing rumors from across the sea that Spacenet had received a much better offer than our own from NEC, and the Virginians were thus leaning towards canceling our project. As it happens in such scenarios, all the communication lines were disconnected, and even our closest allies at Spacenet were unable to provide us with straight answers. One evening, the terrible news arrived through the fax (only good news arrives over the phone; the bad news is always sent via fax). The transmission stated that we would soon receive an official notice of the project's cancellation in the mail.

Outraged, I called Glen Sacra, the head of the international group that worked from Boston. He confirmed that it was already a done deal and not just a rumor. We felt as if our entire world had come apart. After the Australian blow, which left us on the ropes, the knockout punch had apparently arrived. Our large strategic partner — without whom there was no chance for a company like ours to spread its wings — was dumping us.

We decided to put up a fight. What other options did we have? We launched a formidable campaign using all the tools at our disposal. Our final offensive was a strident message that we forwarded to Spacenet's management via Glen Sacra: "If you cancel the project, you won't be able to do any more business in Israel (then an important market for Spacenet), and you will also suffer the consequences in the United States on account of the BIRD Foundation's involvement on this matter". We asked them to reconsider and raised the option of keeping the project as a peripheral product, strictly for the international market. In other words, we offered to cede the entire domestic American market to the Spacenet-NEC team. I told Sacra that, "You and I will run this project".

It is difficult to describe the somber mood that had settled over the company. Every morning, our hands trembled as we checked the mail for the fatal news. Let there be no mistake about it: had the cancellation notice arrived, it would have spelled our end. No investor in his right mind would touch a company which relied on a primary American distributor that subsequently stopped working with it before the product even hit the market.

In any event, the threats and pressure apparently worked, as Spacenet never sent the official notice. They decided to carry on with the project in order to avoid rocking the boat, but placed it on the backburner as a secondary project that was solely intended for the international market. We knew that we were living on borrowed time and that we were wedded to a company that could easily change its mind in the future. However, we also knew that we lacked the time and the wherewithal to develop other partnerships. The lot had fallen on Spacenet and we would have to concentrate all our efforts on winning over its trust. From hereon in, every employee of Gilat knew that he or she had to give top priority to anything that was connected to the joint project with Spacenet. The laser beam that was aimed at the point of penetration was slowly heating up.

In August 1990, immediately after the vital seed money came in, I went to Korea. ETRI, the Korean high-tech sector's leading research organization, was requesting proposals for technology transfers in the field of VSATs on behalf of the large Korean companies: Samsung, LG, Hyundai, and Daewoo. Since it was clear from our understanding with Spacenet that the American market was off-limits to us, we had no choice but to investigate other options around the world.

Upon my arrival, I was immediately drawn into meetings with senior executives. The first meeting was with the organization's director, Dr. Jung. He was forty-seven years old, and awe-inspiring.

We sat in his office together with a group of young, energetic engineers. The environment reminded me of the Unit, as they began to strafe me with technical questions on frequencies, antenna sizes, and suppliers. Jung presided over the discussion in an authoritative manner, jumping from topic to topic — back and forth between technical and business issues — like a seasoned merchant:

"Are you prepared to give exclusive marketing rights to Korean companies?" he asked.

"Look, not exactly…", I replied.

"Are you willing to send your people to Korea?"

"It depends on the payment, of course…"

"Look", Jung told me in a direct manner, "we want to turn into the world's leading power in this field of VSATs and nail the Japanese and American industries. We are interested in collaborating in the technological and marketing fields and are looking for companies that will help us realize our vision".

As he talked, I tried to analyze the scenario: What would be left for us? What did we stand to gain? In the meantime, I just listened, but soon I would be the one having to provide the answers and make decisions.

Korea is a unique country in which everything is geared towards promoting the local industry. The four largest companies cooperate with one another and the government. In fact, some of the companies' representatives sat in on these meetings, while I — the representative of both a small company, which still did not have a product, and a somewhat larger company, GTE — was left to contend with these sharks all by myself.

In my estimation, the group that I encountered is indicative of the Korean business sector to this very day: heavy-handed people for whom clarity is not among their most cherished qualities. Their business culture is completely different than that of any of the other countries that I have come across.

That night, they took me to a night club for what was referred to as dinner, but it was obvious that they had something entirely different in store. The establishment was extravagant and exorbitantly priced. Seated at the tables of this sumptuous trap were many other western business men wrapped in local girls, who conveyed one single message: sex. I was but one person surrounded by an entire team. They went on and on about how profitable it would be to do business with them and what a strong nation Korea was, so that any company that bound its business future to them would ascend to the skies. The entire time, the Korean girls were wandering about the table transmitting clear messages of 'good time'.

I felt as if I was in a psychedelic movie. I didn't engage in either the situation or the place. I listened patiently and occasionally told them a little about Israel and Gilat, but I couldn't wait to get out of there, return to the hotel, and rest before the next day.

After two hours, I put my glass down on the table and asked them to take me back to the hotel. They couldn't believe it. Apparently, they were not accustomed to having western businessmen reject the exciting entertainment that they had arranged for them in such an emphatic manner. Perhaps, they interpreted my behavior as being rude, an insult and a sign that I didn't want to do business with them.

I returned to the hotel room with the sense that I had blown an opportunity. I had failed to nurture a more intimate relationship with a group with whom I was going to be conducting tough negotiations. My behavior did not quite accord with the guidelines I had set for myself at the outset of my business, to attain maximum penetration by building personal relationships with the people on the other side of the table. Before I went to sleep, I spoke with Amiram and Glen Sacra from Spacenet. I told them what had happened and shared my feelings with them. Together, we tried to figure out exactly what the Koreans wanted and what, in essence, we wanted. We agreed that I would make a decision following the more in-depth negotiations the next day. The decision on whether to advance the deal was ultimately in my hands. Our management strategy, which we inherited from the army and the Unit, was clear: the commander in the field is the one who makes the decision, right then and there.

If the night club was the Koreans' carrot then their stick was brandished the next day in the form of aggressive negotiations over the amounts of money and specific rights that would be exchanged. The tone was vastly different. They wanted it all for a pittance, and the negotiations were rapid and replete with blatant threats: "You are not the only one coming to us. People from all over the world want to work with Korea. If we don't work with you, we'll stand against you".

I understood that a fair deal was not going to come out of

all this. "We did not come all the way to Korea", I responded, "in order to hand over all our rights for royalties. I assume that we will meet again as competitors". I left the room disappointed. It was yet another failure on our long trek. In any event, it is worth noting that the Koreans' threats never made it past the conference room door. Throughout our years in the field, we never encountered any serious Korean competitor.

After my trip to Korea, we decided to focus our marketing effort on Europe. We really had no other choice as the American market was sealed off to us at that point; Spacenet, however, was neglecting Europe. Nissan Leviathan, an experienced sales person who had learnt the nuts and bolts of the European market, joined our staff. He set up shop in Paris, from where he coordinated Gilat's European marketing operations. Nissan is practical, focused, and has a good grasp of what it takes to sell a product to an organization. He quickly earned a reputation as a sales person who promises the customers much more than the company can offer. Our engineering people, who were often unable to meet his expectations, dubbed the products he sold as "NiSATs" (rhymes with VSATs).

Nissan quickly landed two significant deals. The first was a French company called Ingenico, which was a small but leading supplier of point-of-sale equipment in France. Among its products, Ingenico supplied large retail chains with point-of-sale devices for verifying credit cards. It also sought to develop satellite communication services in order to expedite the verification process. Our business relationship with the French progressed nicely. The company forwarded us an analysis of the amount of traffic that was transmitted between each store and the main computer center, which enabled us to design the system according to their exact specifications. This was the first time that an end-user customer presented us with actual figures from the field which enabled us to determine their true needs.

The second customer that Nissan reeled in was the Italian company Olivetti, which had originally made a name for itself as a manufacturer of typewriters and had subsequently become a major supplier of office automation equipment in Italy and all of Europe. Nissan expended a great deal of energy on identifying the precise group at Olivetti that was likely to be interested in our products. Once he had tracked it down, the group indeed took an interest. After we agreed to give them extensive marketing rights in Italy and other parts of Europe, they proceeded in the direction of an order.

In October 1990, during one of our many visits to the Spacenet fortress in Virginia, Amiram, Joshua, and I started to sense that there was a change in the air. We always made sure to visit Spacenet as often as possible in order to see and be seen; hold numerous conversations in the corridors; get a feel for the company's pulse; and sniff out developments. During that same visit, we felt that something was up. The ground was beginning to shift beneath a seemingly stable structure; a wave of significant events, both external and internal, had apparently washed over Spacenet transpired in a short time frame.

Several external events influenced our standing, included Gilat's success with Ingenico, especially the company's willingness to submit precise traffic patterns and confirm their plans to work with us. Additionally there were persistent rumors that Hughes — Spacenet's top competiton — was about to launch a new product that was similar to Spacenet's existing system, but much cheaper. According to those same rumors, Hughes was on the verge of closing a giant deal with Chevron. Their product was going to be installed in six thousand gas stations at a price of 4,000 dollars per unit, which stood in sharp contrast to the 12,000 dollars that Spacenet was currently charging.

Yet another significant event was unfolding at the time. GTE had acquired a large telephone company named Contel towards the end of 1990. The merger included a subsidiary, Contel ASC, which also dealt in satellite communications. The subsidiary was much larger than Spacenet, but since GTE was the acquirer of Contel ASC parent company – Contel - Spacenet took over Contel ASC. This was the first time that we had witnessed a merger and acquisition transpires right before of our eyes. We were astonished by the dramatic process, which also provided us with a valuable lesson for the future.

In the immediate aftermath of the acquisition, Jerry Waylan headed up a transition committee — a rather subtle name for a dictatorial transfer of power — which was charged with spearheading the merger. Urgent decisions had to be made regarding what product lines the merged organization would continue to support. A sizeable portion of its products would have to be discontinued in order to avoid confusion, cut superfluous expenses, and send a coherent message to the market. The original Spacenet staff obviously wanted to prove that their products were superior to those of Contel. However, the product that was being designed with NEC for the American market was experiencing delays and the updated target date for its completion was the third quarter of 1991. Moreover, its designated sales price of around $5,000 was no longer competitive with Hughes' new product.

A number of internal events were also unfolding at Spacenet. The American domestic sales group, which was headed by our most outspoken opponent, Joe Barna, failed to meet its sale targets for that year. Consequently, their budget was frozen, and they were prohibited from hiring new people. Furthermore, the staff of forty-five people that collaborated with NEC failed to meet its timetables or stay within its budget. In contrast, the group of twenty employees that worked with us was young, hungry, and vibrant. It started to gather momentum and increasingly gained the organization's trust. I expended a considerable amount of time and effort on 'our' group. I sought to bolster their motivation level with the help of war stories from the business world, including our deals with Ingenico and Olivetti. Moreover, I constantly reminded them of our joint product's vast potential. All of a sudden, ever more voices in Spacenet were clamoring for the NEC and Gilat products, and Glen Sacra boisterously demanded that our product be sold in both the international and American markets.

For the first time, serious legal discussions were held between Gilat and Spacenet on an international agreement, which would include marketing rights and a mutual price list. In a meeting that was called by Jerry Waylan, Joe Barna refused to support Gilat's product and thus formally entered our enemy list. Notwithstanding the objections, we began to notice the first, tell-tale signs of a penetration. Moreover, both parties agreed to order equipment from each other. We ordered auxiliary parts from Spacenet for our first systems, and they forwarded us a $200,000 order for the system. As far as we were concerned, this was grounds for a true celebration, as this was our first order since the Australian disappointment.

Nevertheless, not everything went so smoothly. Selling into Spacenet still required a huge effort on our part. In addition, Spacenet explained to us that the standardization of a product demands a huge investment in documentation, training, exhibitions, marketing material, support, seminars, and more. They estimated that the cost of launching our product would be $10 million (in fact, it came out to much more). They also wavered over how to position the product within the framework of their current product line.

That said, it was impossible to ignore the positive momentum as Gilat merited more exposure than ever before. We met with Jerry and his vice-presidents, spending tens of hours working with myriad groups within Spacenet's while attempting to remove any doubts that they still had about us. For the first time, we started to build a relationship with the sales group that was responsible for the American domestic market. The wind was shifting in our direction.

When the sun shines, or so the saying goes, it sheds its light on everyone, and we were certainly starting to feel its warmth. On January 23, 1991, at the height of the first Gulf War — when everyone in Israel was gathering into sealed rooms and donning gas masks — our fax machine started to churn out the first orders. The maiden order arrived from Thailand: $78,000 for two transmitters and five one- way receivers. Following in its footsteps were the first two orders from Spacenet for $220,000. We passed the orders from hand to hand like little kids unwrapping birthday presents, as these slips of paper constituted the very first orders for our company's products.

The fun was just beginning. On February 12, 1991, thanks to the admirable efforts of Nissan Leviathan, we signed a $500,000 contract with Olivetti for the initial system and ten two-way terminals. Before the final signing, I planned to travel with Nissan to Italy in order to hammer out the final details of the contract. However, the Scud missiles were still falling on Israel; so before taking off for Italy, I visited my parents in Savyon (an affluent village near Tel-Aviv) and tried to calm them down, particularly my mother who was on the verge of a nervous breakdown. I tried to explain to her that, "The probability that a missile will fall on you here in Savyon of all places is one in a million".

After reassuring my parents, Nissan and I flew to Italy and checked into a hotel in Milan. In the morning, Nissan woke me up (in order to save money, it was company policy to only rent one room) and handed me the telephone: "It's your mother from Savyon". Distraught, she informed me that one of the scuds had landed not too far from their house. The damage was negligible, save for the shattered widows, but I had a hard time calming her down: "You and your probabilities", she lashed out at me.

Shortly after signing the contract, we received an advance of $50,000. It was the first payment that Gilat had ever received for a product it had manufactured. With each passing day, we felt as if we were making history. Yet another order arrived that same month from GTECH, a company that provides equipment and services for lotteries throughout the world. GTECH ordered fifty terminals for $250,000. Within the span of a single month, we had received orders totaling nearly $1 million. Gilat had become a bona fide company that sells what it manufactures – and even deposits money into its bank account.

Orders also have to be filled, and we were consequently in urgent needed of staff. Simona, who had relevant experience from her service in the Unit, coordinated the war effort, and it took us several days to organize an operations department. By late February, the equipment for Thailand was ready. Since this was the first order that had ever shipped out of Gilat, none of us could resist the temptation of taking part in the momentous occasion. Everyone rushed to help Simona and Shlomi, the warehouse clerk, pack the devices into improvised carton boxes. At the end of the day, when everything was packed and ready for shipping, I smiled to Simona and said, "If there is one person in the company that I would be happy to trade jobs with today, it's Shlomi. It's a true pleasure to pack and ship Gilat's products".

Additional meetings were held at Spacenet in March 1991. As usual, the deck had been reshuffled, and we had to respond to the new status quo. For example, we heard about a new initiative to develop a cheap product with a small antenna. Our product had yet to be completed, and it was already becoming obsolete. We learned that any successful company must constantly wage a two-pronged war: against both existing products and those that only exist on paper, even if it is highly doubtful that the latter would ever mature into actual products. In addition, Spacenet's sales people informed us that they had signed an agreement with a large provider of credit-card verification services in the United States, which was also interested in purchasing our product. This was a huge potential deal involving a network of one thousand sites and revenues of $3 million. The pilot was set for June 15, 1991 and the tests were due to begin in April. In addition, we received a $500,000 order for a system to verify credit cards for fast-food restaurants.

Hughes was then offering its small dishes for, what we were told, between $5,000 and $6,000, evidently the price Chevron paid for its aforementioned system. Consequently, new customers that turned to Spacenet were demanding a lower price. For the first time, the name of one of the potential customers was mentioned: Rite-Aid. The huge drug-store chain demanded a price of $5,300 dollars for each installed, two-way site.

Meanwhile, Spacenet's merger with Contel was continuing. This process did not make our lives any easier, nor did it reduce the amount of confusion in the organization. By then, some thirty people were already working on our project at Spacenet. They were concentrating on the primary aspects of the development program: a small antenna, higher throughputs, additional frequency bands, and support for other features that the international market requires. Even as this work continued, we were confronted with some good news: Our arch enemy, Joe Barna, was leaving and was being replaced as head of the American market by John Mattingly, the former top man at Contel ASC. John supported our product, but the group he headed also represented NEC's new system. John is extremely tall and well-built, with blond hair, penetrating blue eyes, a sharp voice, and an authoritative style. To wit, he has a tendency to lecture instead of talk and commands respect. At the time, he was somewhat frustrated with his current position, which he viewed as a step down compared to his prior position. In any event, this was the man who stood between Gilat and the American market. John explained to us his take on the project, the newly-configured organization, and the manner in which the two organizations were to work together. He did not believe that NEC was capable of offering a suitable solution and thus planned on turning to Qualcomm, a large American company that specializes in cellular phones. Moreover, John was worried about Gilat's manufacturing capacity and whether we had what it took to become an established company that was built for the long haul. He presented us with the principles of his proposed plan: neither the words Gilat nor Israel would appear on the product's package. Spacenet would have exclusive marketing rights throughout the world; he expected an especially low price from us; and informed us that he wanted to control all the product's branding and advertising in the media. It was abundantly clear to us that we still had quite a way to go.

We tried to process this flood of information. It was quite evident to us that Gilat's future obviously hinged on two cardinal points: the marketing rights and the price of the product. Without marketing rights and with a low sales price, we would not be able to turn a profit, even if the product succeeded. Instead, Gilat would essentially become Spacenet's slave, and our chances of flourishing into a major corporation would be slim. Therefore, it was obvious that we had to fight over these two crucial points. Namely, it was imperative that Spacenet purchase the product from us at a price that enabled us to make a profit and survive. In addition, we wanted independent marketing territories so that we would not be absolutely dependent on their good will. That said, we knew that we weren't worth a lick without Spacenet.

Gilat's board of directors convened in early April prior to the negotiations with Spacenet. As indicated in the protocols of the meeting, we were given contradictory instructions: "…it is imperative that Gilat sign an agreement with Spacenet (as if we didn't know…). Spacenet should be given exclusivity only for North America. Other continents and markets will be discussed separately. Europe should not be included in the agreement. Spacenet must purchase at least one thousand units per year at a price of $2,500 to $3,500 per unit. It is paramount…that the new technologies that Gilat develops not be automatically included in the agreement in order to avoid being trapped by Spacenet".

These were difficult directives for us all, particularly Joshua, who had turned into a veritable trapeze artist. He tried to cater to everyone's demands without conceding any fundamental points. By dint of the wonderful set of relationships that Joshua forged with Spacenet's purchasing and engineering personnel, we managed to constantly milk them for small orders. At the time, his office looked like a war room: towering stacks of paper; marker boards densely covered with writing; and used rolls of fax paper tossed about in every corner of the room. There was barely enough free space on the desk to spread out a notebook and write something down.

Spacenet assembled four competing teams for the purpose of evaluating four distinct alternatives for its future product: NEC, Qualcomm, internal development, and Gilat. The company behaved as if it was a powerful empire, despite the fact that people who understood the market knew that it was losing tens of millions of dollars a year. Therefore, our immediate objectives were to form a strong, pro-Gilat lobby within the organization; defeat all the other options; ensure a competitive future product (beyond the first generation); and safeguard our autonomy by holding on to enough of the marketing and pricing rights, so that we would be left with ample room to maneuver and reasonable profits. We resembled a juggler trying to keep as many balls in the air as possible

Towards the end of April, Jerry Waylan came with us to Paris for a meeting with Ingenico. This gave us a great deal of "face time" with Jerry — a heretofore rare experience — as well as many brownie points. Jerry was deeply impressed with Ingenico, especially their knowledge of the technology, the potential of their market, and their marketing skills. He showered us with compliments for landing the deal with the French. Furthermore, the Ingenico account would help us down the road, as it served as decisive proof that we merited our own marketing rights.

We continued to make headway on the negotiations with Spacenet. Joshua, who presided over the campaign, made a heroic effort to construct a pricing model that would convince Spacenet to work with us. His idea was simple yet brilliant. "Spacenet", Joshua claimed, "would never manage to sell many units. Therefore, there is nothing wrong with showing them low prices for purchasing at high quantities. We will show them the figures they want at the bottom, right-hand corner of the table".

Together with Amiram, Joshua built an ingenious two-dimensional table, which we called 'Joshua's magic table'. The first dimension consisted of the pricing for present orders, from 100 to 10,000 units, while the second dimension depicted the pricing for cumulative orders of 10,000 to 20,000 units and for the prices once they surpassed the 20,000 benchmark. Joshua believed, and justifiably so, that the prices would decrease in any event. Therefore, if we managed to fetch a high price during the development phase, when the number of orders was still low, we would be able to finance the development as well as earn a nice profit. It was indeed a magical table, as everyone saw the prices that they wanted. We knew that the amount of orders from Spacenet was not going to skyrocket. Consequently, when taking into account the fact that our actual per unit cost was $1,500, a sales price of $4,000 per unit would generate a considerable profit. Conversely, Spacenet was attracted to the numbers on the right-hand side of the table, as once their sales surpassed the 20,000-unit mark, they would only have to shell out $2,500 per unit.

By virtue of the table, we managed to persuade Spacenet to go ahead with the deal. In fact, these figures endured for years to come and enabled Gilat to become a highly profitable company. It is doubtful that we would have reached these profit levels in any other fashion.

The issue of marketing rights was far more complex. Try explaining to a large and arrogant organization — part of a giant telecommunications company — why the hell they should grant any marketing rights whatsoever to a fragile and small Israeli company that is merely one of its hardware suppliers. From their vantage point, we were a "bit player". Gilat adopted a characteristically integrated strategy. The first element of our approach was to play it tough: "Our board doesn't allow us to give marketing rights". This bravado was augmented by an assortment of logical explanations: "Look at our success in Europe with Olivetti and Ingenico. It is inconceivable that our hands should be tied behind our backs after we proved our ability to market the product on our own". In addition, we reminded them that they were also selling NEC's products. "How are we to know whether you are really pushing our products?". Finally, we took advantage of all our connections within the organization. All of us exerted pressure on our allies and conveyed the following message to them, which they then forwarded onwards: "The agreement with Spacenet is very important to us. Consequently, we are willing to compromise, but only to a certain extent".

The first to blink was Jerry, the all-powerful president of Spacenet. After he returned from Paris, where he had witnessed our successes first hand, he ordered his people to "work with Gilat on this". In the American business code, this phrase expresses a willingness to make some sort of concession. That said, we had lost the battle for North America before so much as a single round was fired. Mattingly left no room for doubt, and I immediately jotted down the following valuable lesson in my notebook: "It's pointless to enter battles that you have no chance of winning. You have to choose your battles carefully". We thus retreated, but not before securing certain marketing rights for the lottery industry and the monitoring and control of gas and oil pipelines.

As a result, our major battle was over the international market, with the focus obviously being Europe. At the time, two large deals were in the making: Rite Aid in the United States and Renault, the French automotive manufacturer and distributor. Spacenet busted their tails on the Renault deal, and large groups traveled to France and met with Renault.

We got the impression that after our success with Ingenico and Olivetti, Spacenet was not going to concede Europe to us without a fight. We attempted various ploys: Our first suggestion was that both sides take turns selecting a country. In this fashion, we would fairly divide up the countries with attractive markets one by one. They smiled, but didn't take the bait. We then offered to split up the marketing rights by continent: Europe would be ours and they would get Asia and Latin America. Once again, they refused. Incidentally, this turned out for the best because it later turned out that these markets were a substantially larger opportunity for Gilat than Europe. Alternatively, Spacenet proposed a setup whereby they would initiate contact with the customers and we would then join them. We politely turned them down. Gilat was in no rush to close a deal because John Mattingly had lost interest in the European market once he was certain that the American market was firmly in his grasp. This enabled us to slowly deflect attention away from the topic of marketing rights and postpone the talks until the next round of discussions.

In the end, the two parties signed a memorandum of understanding that divided the marketing areas into four categories: The first category was 'Spacenet territory', such as the United States, in which the Virginians were given absolute exclusivity. The second was 'Gilat territory' in which we were granted absolute exclusivity. Although examples were not brought forth, to us it was clear that they had in mind countries such as Micronesia and perhaps, on a good day, Israel as well. 'Neutral territory' referred to markets that both sides were permitted to sell to. This category was an immense achievement for us, for it encompassed nearly the entire world, save for the United States. The final category was 'uncharted territory' that would be discussed in the future. We etched a big checkmark next to the topic of marketing rights and moved on to the next issue: the rights to technologies that Gilat would develop in the future.

"Every future two-way VSAT initiative", the agreement stated, "shall be brought to the attention of both parties for the purpose of conducting an estimation of its significance on the existing market...Spacenet shall then have the right to decide whether or not to allow Gilat to sell this improvement on its own, but approval shall not be unreasonably witheld. If Spacenet comes up with a new initiative, it will provide both Gilat and NEC an equal opportunity to compete over the contract. The final decision will be entirely up to Spacenet".

In other words, Gilat was prohibited from selling any future version of the system without Spacenet's approval, while Spacenet merely undertook to notify its two partners of any future development. Gilat and NEC would then battle over the right to develop the concept. We weren't exactly thrilled with this particular clause. In fact, it was the source of much heartache in years to follow, but we didn't have a choice. A skilled negotiator has to know when to give ground.

In return for all our concessions, Spacenet was generous enough to consider a commitment to purchase 5,000 units over three years for around $20 million.

Although we still didn't hear the actual words "We're going to work with you", we felt as if we were gaining ground. Moreover, they always tried to camouflage their intentions with expressions such as "Let's try reaching an agreement. If we succeed, great; if not - then no hard feelings". Nevertheless, they provided obvious hints that we were heading towards an agreement.

The first drafts of the agreements were submitted during comprehensive meetings on November 19th and 20th 1991. Advanced negotiations ensued for the purpose of hammering out mutual commitments and prices. In addition, they agreed — perhaps on account of our successes with Ingenico — to establish a joint team that would work on the Renault project. This was truly an unusual step, for until then we got the feeling that Spacenet was doing everything in its power to keep us out of the sales process with their potential customers.

Furthermore, by the end of October, several principles were hammered out and three proposals were drawn up: two inter-company purchase agreements (for Spacenet to purchase Gilat's equipment and vice versa) and an international marketing agreement. Thereafter, a non-binding memorandum of understanding concerning the two purchase agreements was signed. Nevertheless, there were still a couple of setbacks during that period. Spacenet representatives were scheduled to visit Israel, but postponed the trip. In the meantime, we were informed that Spacenet would be conducting a bid between Gilat and NEC for an affordable global product. Overall, however, the mood remained upbeat. Throughout this period, Joshua managed to discreetly extract small orders out of Spacenet — $100,000 here, a quarter of a million there. Moreover, 'our' technical group at Spacenet was constantly growing and had reached some forty engineers by late 1991. Soon, they would surpass the group that supported NEC. Spacenet was gradually getting behind the program.

The date for signing the contract was set for December 23, 1991, two days before Christmas. I flew in from Israel, and Virginia, as well as other large swathes of the United States, was wraped in snow. Although I was invited to sign the contract, I had mentally prepared myself for the nerve-wracking, last-minute negotiations that tended to arise on these sorts of occasions. However, much to my surprise, the contract was ready — due to the excellent work of Joshua and our attorney Gene Kleinhandler — and no one wanted to haggle any longer. After the signing, my surprise turned into shock upon receiving an $800,000 order for 250 units and the possibility of an additional order for around $1.2 million. That night, Joshua and I went out with Spacenet's management to celebrate. We opened a bottle of champagne and raised a toast for the continued success and growth of both companies. "You deserve it", Jerry Waylan said while looking at Joshua. "You did an exceptional job in our corridors…Now we'll see if you're as good at implementation as you are at selling…"

"You haven't seen nothing yet", I confidently replied.

I stayed in Virginia for follow-up discussions that lasted into Christmas Eve. The pace of events was dizzying. They nonchalantly handed me a detailed offer request from Rite Aid that caused my heart to skip a beat. The pharmacy chain was interested in a system that would service a whopping three thousand sites. I instantly realized that many parts of the request were written by Hughes, which inserted specifications that granted them a significant advantage over Gilat. Before returning to Israel, I managed to take part in a discussion on the ground rules for our joint endeavors in Europe.

The conference room was crammed with participants, and the key note speaker was the vice-president for international marketing and sales, who repeated his familiar speech on how GTE aspires to become a services provider with a global reach. We then clarified several unclear points with respect to the international marketing rights. Despite the fact that the agreement was signed, I left the meeting with the sense that Spacenet was still worried that the day would come when they would find us on the other side of the playing field as their competitors and that this was the reason they were so cautious with us.

I barely found a place on the flight from Virginia to New York, on route to Israel. All the domestic flights were packed with people heading home for the holidays. As soon as I got back home, I rushed over to Amiram to show him the signed contract. We were both elated and glowing with pride.

Companies invest a great deal of thought and preparation on the announcement of a new product. Spacenet indeed chose the right time for the announcement of our joint endeavor: a big communications exhibition in Washington D.C. on January 28, 1992. Within the space of a couple of days, the company issued a press release, convened a press conference, and introduced the product to the entire world. In parallel, P.R. people pushed the story to as many media outlets as possible. Spacenet invested hundreds of thousands of dollars on the product launch and the interest it engendered was enormous. Hundreds of people stopped by their booth, met with Spacenet's representatives as well as Joshua, asked questions, and took written material about the product: "A satellite terminal featuring a dish with a diameter of only about three feet, at an incredible price of $4,500…"

Obviously, Spacenet took all the credit for itself and tried to conceal Gilat's role as much as possible. Only those who read through the entire press release would have discovered (on the bottom of the third page) that a company called Gilat was involved in the development of the new product: "Spacenet worked with Gilat Communications Systems in order to develop the service…" We were not surprised that our role was understated. We didn't expect anything better. However, the world would eventually understand our part. The thoroughbreds were off and running.

The real journey had begun.

4

The Epic Battle for Rite-Aid

It is difficult to describe just how surprised I was upon entering the main lobby of Rite Aid's headquarters in Harrisburg, Pennsylvania for the first time. I asked myself, "Could this really be the entrance to such a large and powerful organization?". At the corner of the lobby stood a solitary desk of a reception clerk, who simultaneously filled the jobs of five people: receiving and dispatching packages, answering all in-coming telephone calls, and taking down visitors' personal information. The armchairs in the lobby were worn out (yet clean); the company's annual reports were spread out across a table; and the walls were adorned with pictures of the founding family and assorted awards. Clear messages of "we also make our money by saving" and "profitability runs counter to the size of the lobby" emanated throughout the building and bolstered the prevailing atmosphere of thrift.

Rarely does a single event in the annals of a company determine the course of its development and seal its fate. For Gilat, the competition over the Rite-Aid contract was just that sort of an event, as a small, anonymous Israeli company won its first multi-million dollar sale to a huge customer—among the largest chain stores in the world. The reward from Gilat's standpoint was immense: it snatched up a "prestige" customer that catapulted both its value and reputation. We subsequently worked with larger, more distinguished customers than Rite-Aid, but none of them provided us with what the American pharmacy chain did: the story, prestige, and boost that we so very much needed.

Rite-Aid's initial overture came in mid 1991. The chain defined its needs, and Gilat and Spacenet assembled a joint team to toil over an integrated product that would meet its demands. The specifications were then forwarded to the engineering departments and labs in order to continue the job, but it was obvious that it would still take quite a while to complete the joint product and deploy the entire system. In fact, when Rite-Aid informed us that they intended to reach a decision over which product to purchase (ours or Hughes) by the end of 1991, Spacenet decided to offer them a different product.

In January 1992, after the announcement of the joint product at the Washington exhibition, the product's market price plummeted from $9,000 to $4,500. Rite-Aid pounced at the opportunity and requested a new offer. They immediately understood that even if they did not ultimately buy the equipment from us, the negotiations with Gilat would strengthen their hand vis à vis our giant competitor, Hughes. Rite Aid indeed has a reputation for aggressively insisting on lowering the price of every item on its shelves and is willing to go to extremes to get a supplier to reduce the price of a toothbrush from 47 to 43 cents. Clearly, they were not going to voluntarily spend a fortune on a communications system that they could obtain for half the price.

We prepared a highly detailed proposal and sent it to their offices. Since Rite-Aid is an American customer, it was obvious that they were in Spacenet's sales territory. Therefore, although Gilat was responsible for the development and production, Spacenet was to handle the marketing.

To the credit of our adversaries at Hughes, they immediately realized how critical the Rite-Aid account would be for Gilat. Consequently, they did everything in their power to foil our plans. Hughes invested an inordinate amount of resources to study the customer and its needs, and they assembled an impressive sales team to handle the bid. Part of that team eventually came to work for us, and we compared the efforts of the two organizations. It turned out that Hughes invested much more at the initial, preparatory stages than we did. In fact, no one less than the company's president, Jack Shaw, was personally involved at every phase of the competition: from preparing the offer to running the negotiations. Moreover, Shaw made repeated efforts to foster a personal relationship with the Rite-Aid team.

One day, it suddenly dawned on me that I had unintentionally become the principal sales person of the Rite-Aid account, not only during the negotiations and sales process, but for years to follow. It all started with an unexpected call from Jerry Waylan, which was the first time that he ever took the trouble to personally call me. "The owners of the chain, Alex Grass and his son Martin, are proud Jews", Jerry informed me. "Alex serves as the national chairman of the United Jewish Association (one of the major Jewish philanthropist organizations in the United States). I recommend that you find a mutual acquaintance that can put you in touch with them, so that you can emphasize the Israeli dimension". Jerry thus taught me the importance of influencing people not only from a professional standpoint, but on the personal and emotional level as well. This lesson was so obvious and so true, especially under the given circumstances in which an Israeli company had a clear advantage over the competition. So why not take advantage of it?

Alex Grass, who was then about 65, built the chain of pharmacies with his own bare hands. From two stores in 1966, the business blossomed to 2,700 by 1992. He knew practically all the chain's employees; was aware of every problem; and was on top of every figure. Alex is a man with a serious demeanor — he lacks an ego and a sense of humor — and is sharp, tough, and occasionally cruel. Although a passionate supporter of Israel, Alex made it clear from the outset that he was a business man and that the decisive factor was his company's best interests.

His son Martin Grass is an entirely different kettle of fish. At the age of 33, he already served as the chain's president. He called all the shots at Rite-Aid and caused the company's employees to tremble with fear. Martin was trained at an early age to conduct negotiations in a firm and aggressive manner. During our meetings, I always concentrated on his gleaming eyes and cold stare that fixed in on the speaker. He is a man bereft of feelings and a walking depository of negotiating ploys.

The person in charge of the organization's computing was Joe Phillips, an older, experienced man. He tended to talk quietly and was usually quite pleasant, but when he got mad his voice intensified and his tongue sharpened. Joe was extremely sensitive to danger — in other words, he never took risks — and jealously safeguarded his position and status. In addition, he held a resolute opinion on every topic, especially those that pertained to the requirements of his communications network. As far as Gilat was concerned, Joe's most prominent feature was his deep attachment to Hughes and his fervent belief in their ability to deliver a product that would cater to the needs of his network.

The last figure that was intimately involved in our negotiations with Rite-Aid was our mystery consultant. The guide to the art of war stipulates that business people involved in a complex sales transaction should find a coach or mentor to help them plot their course. The mentor should be capable of elucidating the way in which the purchasing organization's decision makers think; its internal politics; and its formal and informal balances of power. Moreover, the mentor should be able to expound upon the exact problem that the proposed system is supposed to solve: does the customer expect the product to help the company turn a profit, or is it intended to overcome an existing obstacle, such as an old system that no longer answers the organization's needs?

We had a superb mystery consultant. He invested countless hours on this assignment and showed us all the ropes. The consultant had previously worked for at a company that had a business relationship with Rite-Aid. Therefore, he was well acquainted with the organization, and taught us both its strengths and weaknesses. The man took his job extremely seriously and made quite an effort on our behalf. Whenever we met with him, we found ourselves on the defensive and felt like school children who had come to class unprepared.

Joshua and I spoke with him for hours on the phone. In fact, during the critical stages of our negotiations with Rite-Aid, we spoke at least once a day. During these long conversations, he gave us homework and repeatedly reprimanded us for failing to induce Spacenet to react because in his estimation Spacenet's active participation was the key to our success. He had us revise the technical proposal and price offer on numerous occasions. In addition, he also skillfully conducted a substantial portion of the negotiations in our name, and on occasion did much better than we could have done on our own. Despite his vital role in our sales effort, Spacenet didn't quite understand where he had come from or what business he had attending the negotiations to begin with.

Rite-Aid was then the third largest drug-store chain in the United States, and at its zenith had even climbed to the first place. Almost all their stores were the same exact size, 6700 square feet, with a similar floor layout. All the stores sold medications, cosmetics, cleaning products, and small appliances. Rite-Aid primarily catered to lower socioeconomic classes. The chain's total sales reached

$4 billion per year, but it is worth noting that the average sale was only $4. In other words, Rite-Aid processed about one billion sales per year.

During our first meetings with Rite-Aid, immediately after submitting our proposal, we were forced to brace ourselves for a frontal attack. Their senior team assailed all of Spacenet's weak points: a new and untested product; Spacenet was yet to sell a similar system to a comparable customer; and the product's problematic response time. They noted the inexpensive price of our product as an aside, but naturally harped on the negatives.

The response time dominated these discussions. As per their specifications, the new technology was to provide for all the communications between the stores and the central database, with the exception of telephones. In other words, the transactions that occur at the point of sale: for example, processing each purchase item; inventory control, and the verification of credit cards. In addition, the product would enable the pharmacists to confirm the validity of all the customers' medical insurance and whether they are authorized to use the medication that they are requesting.

Joe Phillips, Rite-Aid's computers and communications chief, refused to budge from his requirement that every query was to receive a response within two seconds. He contended that after two seconds the pharmacist gets tired, the customer gets fed up with waiting, and the productivity of the entire pharmacy is hindered. This was no simple demand. Although the satellite reacted within a second, it required an additional second to transfer the data back to the store. Moreover, the simultaneous arrival of data from several stores further delayed the response time, and this was more than likely to be a rather frequent occurrence.

For the first time, I witnessed the differences in style and marketing between Hughes and Spacenet. Hughes first words were always, "No problem!" And their second sentence was, "We can do it and Spacenet can't…" As far as Hughes was concerned, nothing was more important than landing the deal, even if this meant taking no prisoners. In contrast, Spacenet sent Ron Krontz to the front. Ron, an engineer that was in charge of the mathematic modeling that simulated the network's performance carefully maintained his professional integrity and only provided honest and accurate assessments. In essence, there wasn't a significant difference between the solutions offered by Spacenet and Hughes, but during the negotiations it appeared as if Hughes was light years ahead of us. You had to hand it to them; they simply read the customer much better than we did.

Gilat found itself in an odd predicament. Spacenet insisted that the joint product didn't meet the customer's demands, and all our efforts to convince them to claim that it did were futile. We attempted to explain to Spacenet that these are merely temporary technical estimates. In practice, no one was going to measure the response time, and the contract would not entail penalties for failing to meet the two-second limit. However, Spacenet would not budge an inch, lost altitude, and played straight into the hands of Hughes and Joe Phillips. Similarly, we tried to explain to Rite-Aid that there was nothing wrong with a response time of 2.2 seconds, but their response was, "Maybe you have another product that does react in two seconds?"

Spurred on by Jerry Waylan's sage advice, I turned over every stone in an effort to find someone that could connect us with the Grass family. We knew that Shimon Peres was on excellent terms with them, but it seemed inappropriate to involve a man of his stature at this point in the game.

I asked Yadin Kaufmann from Athena — who was well-connected and had helped us immensely after our initial round of financing— to speak to Alex Grass on our behalf. Yadin agreed and I soon received an unexpected phone call from none other than Alex Grass: "Listen, Mr. Gat", he opened.

"Yoel", I interrupted, in an attempt to overcome the surprise and break the ice. "Mr. Gat is my father".

"Okay, Yoel. Pressure won't work here. We love Israel and contribute a lot to the country, but as far as our business is concerned, we will only do what's in the best interests of our company. We won't buy from an anonymous Israeli company unless we are certain that the purchase will benefit us".

"Alex", I told him, upon recovering from the shock, "we are talking about GTE, and not us. We're merely their hardware vendor. Please, set an appointment with us so that we can all get acquainted and discuss the topic".

The meeting was set for March 25, 1992. Rite-Aid's representatives were Alex Grass, his son Martin, Joe Phillips, and Nick Putz, the communications manager that worked under Joe. Our contingent consisted of Jerry Waylan, John Mattingly, Ray

Marks, Spacenet's vice president of marketing, and myself. We came prepared. We studied the system's needs, prepared models of the proposed architecture, set parameters for the solution, constructed a price offer, and did everything else that was needed. Jerry also made an appreciable effort to understand the nuances of the deal. In essence, this was the first time that Jerry had studied our joint product. Spacenet's engineers even provided us with lengthy updates on the system's performance during the two and a half hour drive from Virginia to Pennsylvania.

Along the way, we stopped for lunch at a Chinese restaurant. As is customary, we had fortune cookies for dessert and my fortune was, "Remember, only he who dares wins…" Incredibly, this was also the slogan of our unit in the army. We laughed and felt optimistic. We were ready to dare, believed that fate was on our side, and psyched ourselves up for the crucial meeting.

Upon arriving to Harrisburg, we were left out to dry in Rite-Aid's Spartan lobby for an hour and a half. It was bad enough to treat me this way, as it was my first meeting with a potential customer of this scale — and if truth be told, I would have waited for another two weeks if that's what it took — but how could they dare leave Jerry Waylan, the legendary president of a division at the great GTE, in the lobby for so long? Jerry replied that, "Chain-store owners treat suppliers like trash. This is their way of letting you know your exact place in their pecking order".

The cold treatment also continued when we were finally invited to enter the conference room, which was incidentally among the least impressive rooms in the building. The Rite-Aid team entered the room in a rather frigid manner, as they didn't even bother with the customary hand shakes and pleasantries that usually grace any initial acquaintance in the business world. As soon as we took our seats around the large table, Martin went on the offensive: "Your price is really exorbitant for a product without any other customers and that is inferior to the competition's products…"

"From our standpoint", Alex chimed in, "meeting our requirements is critical. Do you meet the two-second response time?"

We were caught completely off-guard. I didn't anticipate such an opening. I wanted to stem the tide and turn to them in a more personal tone. Something along the lines of, "Good afternoon Martin and Alex. This is Jerry Waylan, the president of Spacenet, and I'm Yoel Gat. Remember, we spoke on the phone…" But at that very moment, I was gasping for air.

Fortunately, Jerry took the initiative, and proved why he is considered Spacenet's top sales person. "Hello Alex, hello Martin. This deal is very important to us, and we'll make every effort to earn the contract and become a vendor that you'll be proud of work with. We'll discuss the price later, but for now please allow me to introduce you to our organization and the people sitting before you…".

At this juncture, John Mattingly assumed the lead and embarked on a riveting speech on Spacenet: the organization, its customers, work methods, and advantages. Thereafter, I ran slides and described the product and our offer. We indeed managed to captivate their attention, as they took an interest, asked questions, and made comments. Everyone took an active part in the conversation. I felt as if we had overcome the terrible start and regained our bearings. The best part of the meeting was the discussion of the system's maintenance, for in this area we had a clear advantage over Hughes. Whereas Hughes' left the maintenance to sub-contractors, our maintenance would be provided by Spacenet's own employees. Jerry and John elucidated every point in an organized manner until it was absolutely clear that we had conveyed the message in its entirety.

A business meeting is akin to a battle. All the plans quickly unravel, and the side that is best prepared has a big advantage insofar as controlling the direction and content of the discussion are concerned. Throughout the proceedings, Alex and Martin passed notes to each other. Naturally, I didn't know what they were corresponding about, but to me it seemed like a good sign. Joe attempted to intervene and Martin vulgarly silenced him. We elicited satisfied laughs from a slide featuring a Rite-Aid advertisement and from the name that we chose for the proffered satellite: "the retail satellite".

As the meeting drew to a close, Martin told us that they planned on making a decision by May 5 and completing the deployment of the system by late 1992. I shook my head in agreement, even though I wasn't quite sure how we would accelerate our pace of production from its current rate of ten devices per month to 2,700 units by year's end. After handing us a copious list of technical issues to attend to, they asked us to cut $2 to $3 million (a 15% discount) off our asking price.

The end of the meeting, three and a half hours later, was exceedingly more pleasant than the awful opening. Alex warmly shook everyone's hands and parted ways with a comment aimed directly at me: "If possible, we would be happy to do business with an Israeli company".

On the way back to Spacenet, we set work rules for the immediate future, and we all agreed to look for ways to cut costs to meet Rite-Aid's demands. I also asked Jerry to see to it that the Spacenet people visit Rite-Aid on a regular basis; continued to work with them on the technical levels; and meet with their technical people. Finally, Jerry also unexpectedly expressed a willingness to come to Israel in the near future in order to get a first-hand look at Gilat's operations. I considered this gesture a considerable achievement.

I returned to Israel, assembled the entire staff— all twenty-five of us — and recounted the war stories. I wanted them to feel like partners, even on the personal level. I gave detailed descriptions of Alex, Martin, our mystery consultant, Joe, and Nick; reported on the discussions; and emphasized which points would have to be tended to. Above all, I tried to convey to them what it meant to land a customer like Rite-Aid, even if I didn't quite grasp its potential significance myself.

We had less than a month and a half to meet their demands and complete the proposal. Before I returned to Israel, Jerry, Mattingly, and I agreed to hold conference calls in order to keep track of the progress and update each other regarding the upcoming steps. However, I quickly realized that their gushing enthusiasm had petered out somewhere along the road from Pennsylvania to Virginia. The conference calls were suspended and eventually cancelled. Jerry stopped returning my calls, and Joshua was unable to get hold of Mattingly. Those Spacenet employees who couldn't avoid us claimed that everything was under control: "Sure, we're busy preparing offers, talking to Rite-Aid, and everything is fine". At the time, I still didn't understand those were American business euphemisms for "leave me be" and that, in practice, they didn't so much as move a finger. Although we were progressing with the development and pushing deals on the international market, we gradually fell out of touch with Rite-Aid.

And then Rite-Aid lowered the boom on us. On May 6,

1992 well before the official notice, we were informed over the phone that Jack Shaw, the president of Hughes, and Martin Grass shook hands on a deal. This sort of information always tends to wander about in the corridors and reaches you before the actual announcement. In any event, we appeared to be out of the picture. Rite-Aid had met its self-imposed deadline of early May. The Spacenet people were outraged and received a detailed explanation from Joe Phillips, who preferred the competition to begin with: "Hughes sells their products in large quantities, controls 70% of the market, and lowered the price. There are no technical problems with their products; they have many prestigous customers; and were in touch with us the entire time. How did you think you could land the deal without having done even a small portion of these things?"

I felt as if we had really blown it this time and that perhaps this was the end of the line. We had let a huge opportunity slip away and had a hard time coming to grips with the news. After the initial wave of regret came the stage for drawing conclusions: From hereon, we can't leave the ball in Spacenet's court. They were the ones who had dropped the ball by not even bothering to forge a relationship with the customer. Is this the way a serious company is supposed to behave with an important customer?

Amiram, Joshua, and I went into the room and got our mystery consultant on the line. "What did you expect?" he reprimanded us. "I warned you all along that nothing is happening at Spacenet, while the enemies were constantly lying in wait and staking out the prey…"

"Please", I interrupted him, "let's save the reprimands and morals for later and see what we could do to get back in the picture. Give us some ideas".

Two days later, a war room was established at Gilat. We attempted to contact a wide range of people who may be able to touch base with Martin or Alex, in order to see if we could get back into the running and, if so, what would it take for Gilat and Spacenet to land the deal. Among those we turned to were Henry Taub (the founder of Automatic Data Processing), Amnon Neubach, Yossi Tzachnover, Harvey Krueger, a senior official at Lehman Brothers, who was known for his involvement in the Israeli business community, Yitzchak Shamir, the serving prime minister, and Shimon Peres. They were all listed as people who could help the cause.

Amiram coined a new mantra that he spread throughout the ranks of Gilat: "In order to win the battle, we must be better than the competition in every line item and not just overall". He presided over a technical group that was charged with the resolving the product's real and perceived (primarily the two-second cap) technical problems. Correspondingly, Joshua led an in-depth review of our precise costs in order to determine how much we could lower the price, for we knew that we could tempt Rite-Aid with an attractive offer.

However, we sensed that Spacenet had resigned itself to defeat. It wasn't easy getting them back on the saddle. "What do you expect?" people at Gilat scoffed. "They are used to losing to Hughes". A reverse process began to take hold of me. I decided to fight for the Rite-Aid account as if our future depended on it. Rite-Aid consumed my every waking breath, even though I didn't really believe that there was a chance that we could win. No one had done Hughes any favors and they had indeed earned the customer entirely on merit.

My notebook from that period — in which I meticulously documented all of Gilat's history — deals with but one topic: Rite-Aid. I felt that this was the deal that would either make or break Gilat. The mystery consultant, Amiram, Joshua, and I discussed this issue every day. We coaxed each other into going that extra mile. "You can always do one more thing on this matter", I asserted. In the days to follow, we manned the phones and spared no effort to convince Rite-Aid to renew the dialogue with us, but to no avail.

One night, the telephone in my house started ringing at two in the morning. Barely conscious, I picked up the phone and heard the voice of Micha Angel, a member of Gilat's board of directors, who then passed me on to Harvey Krueger, a well-known and well-connected business man, who served in a senior position at a large investment bank. Harvey is a proud Jew and a known contributor to the State of Israel, who gives not only his money, but primarily his time and good will. The conversation that ensued was undoubtedly one of the worst moments in my life. "We don't know each other", he said, "but I am well aware of the huge effort that you are making on this matter: firing away on all cylinders and using all the cannons at your disposal. I spoke with

Alex and it's a lost cause. Reconcile yourself with this, turn a new leaf, and move on. Don't waste your connections with the Jewish community. You'll be needing them quite a bit in the future. I ask of you and recommend in no uncertain terms that you drop it!"

Needless to say, I couldn't fall back asleep after that. The combination of the conversation with Krueger and our inability to light a fire under Spacenet left me in a state of depression. The next morning, I had a long talk with Joshua and Amiram. Towards the end of our discussion, I first perceived the pessimistic tone in their voices: "Perhaps it's a lost cause. We'll try to find another customer…"

But I wasn't ready to back down quite yet. In my view, the Rite-Aid account was a life or death issue. My gut instinct told me that Gilat's future was riding on this deal. Few are the times when one is forced to make a decision in which all appears to be lost, but nonetheless has a strong sense in the righteousness of his way and the importance of the topic. We were steadily running out of options and failed to generate any momentum, but I refused to throw in the towel. The business world was aware of the heroic battle that was being waged over Rite-Aid, and the loser would have a hard time coping with defeat, especially if we were the ones who came up empty-handed.

That evening I went to my father. He heard me out, offered his support, and sent me to his friend Bondi Dror, a close acquaintance of Shimon Peres. I went to Bondi and asked him for a personal favor: to ask Peres to turn to Alex and persuade him to meet with us again, if only to explain why we had lost. I wanted to stick my foot into the crack in the door and push it open. Bondi spoke with Peres, and Peres, in all his greatness, agreed to see what he could do, despite the fact that he was in the throes of an arduous election campaign. He asked for a document summarizing the situation and received it within two hours. Peres then immediately turned to Alex who couldn't turn him down.

The meeting was set for May 28.

Spacenet didn't believe that Rite-Aid would grant us another chance. According to accepted business convention, once a company has selected a supplier, it immediately cuts off all lines of communication with the other competitors. Therefore, Spacenet was surprised by the new development.

Gilat and Spacenet buckled down for the decisive meeting.

As is often the case, the struggle united the ranks. Everyone tried to contribute, each in their own field. Amiram and his development group improved the product's technical performance twofold. Joshua came up with the idea that Gilat would install a substantial portion of the sites on its own at a much lower price than Spacenet's, on the condition that the savings would be passed on to Rite-Aid. John Mattingly also contributed to the effort by doing his best to cut costs as well. Yoav Leibovitch, Gilat's new vice-president of finance , who had just joined our staff and brought with him extensive experience in the field of mergers and acquisitions, prepared new proposals with Spacenet's finance people. Finally, Jerry Waylan kept a close eye on developments.

We devised innovative solutions for the problematic two-second response time and prepared new price offers, lists of installations, dates, commitments, and much more. I felt like a student defending his thesis. Although all the cards appeared to be stacked against us, we sought to use the meeting as a springboard for getting back into the race.

The meeting began at 2:00pm, with the same cast of characters that had attended the first meeting. However, this time the reception was much more congenial. The meeting began on time and was held in Rite-Aid's more pleasant conference room.

As usual, Martin cut straight to the chase: "You got the meeting you wanted, so what's up?"

"We have come with new technical and price offers", Jerry responded: "A better product at a significantly lower price".

"Now this is something that we are always willing to listen to", said Martin.

The introductions concluded, the bell sounded, and the first round was underway. A technical discussion ensued, which naturally commenced with the issue of response time. We informed them that our product was well within the two-second limit. In fact, they were astonished to learn that it's throughput was twice as fast as our previous model and featured many other new innovations as well. Furthermore, we were willing to throw in a connection to six devices in each store at no additional charge.

Nevertheless, Joe Phillips was as hostile as ever: "Are you sure that you understand what is demanded of you?" Before anything else, he asked to see a demonstration and managed to sour the atmosphere. The first round ended with Gilat behind in the count.

I took down a blow-by-blow account of the meeting in my large notebook. Martin realized what I was up to and was curious as to what I was jotting down the entire time. This is indeed a legitimate question: why do I take down every word? Is it a desire to preserve the events for history sake, or is it simply a way of releasing tension? Apparently, the second answer is more accurate. I was extremely nervous and felt as if the entire fate of our company was riding on this meeting and these people. The Rite-Aid representatives left the room for consultations and returned half an hour later with technical questions, all of which we answered to their satisfaction. Gilat took the second round.

It was already 4:30pm when the third round got under way. The discussion once again focused on the two-second cap, which was no longer a problem. With the help of a slide show that was prepared by a joint team of engineers from Spacenet and Gilat, I explained our methods for approaching the satellite and how we would stay within the two-second limit. Another hour passed and we took round three.

The fourth round was devoted to installation and maintenance. We discussed the timetables, costs, and contractual clauses that comprised the entire issue of maintenance. Along the way, demands totaling some $500,000 were thrown into the equation, which we didn't quite know how to finance. Nevertheless, the fourth round also went to Gilat.

Pricing dominated the fifth round. "We are convinced from a technical standpoint", Martin said. "Now let's deal with the price. We are prepared to sign a contract next week…" I nearly fell over and wrote down in my notebook that, "All we wanted was to get back in the picture". A lengthy discussion ensued on the costs of installation, maintenance, and shipping. They demanded that we finish installing the systems in all 2,700 stores within six months. Obviously, there was no way that we could have possibly met that time table, but we didn't so much as blink an eye. Thereafter, the discussion turned to linking the payments to the consumer price index when, out of the blue, Jerry delivered a ferocious left hook: "If we offer a $500,000 discount, while including all the upgrades we talked about today, can we close the deal?"

Martin immediately responded with an authoritative voice "No".

"How much will it take?" Jerry asked.

"A good enough offer so that we won't resume negotiations with the competition".

"Well, how much?"

"We'll look into it right now".

They left the room for another hour of consultations.

Upon returning, Martin demanded a further discount of $4.5 million. Jerry's face turned white and Martin amiably turned to him and said, "Don't worry; we have all night to work on it".

"I don't know if there's any point to it", Jerry replied.

"Think it over".

We went out for a coffee break, and my brain didn't stop churning. "I have an idea for how we can slash $1.6 million off the maintenance expense", I told Jerry. "Gilat will assume the risk of repairs and provide you with a ceiling that guarantees that Spacenet's expenditures do not exceed the amount that is stipulated in the current business plan".

Jerry accepted my offer, while I wondered what they were going to say about all this in Israel. We made a couple of calls and discovered that we can save another $1 million on the satellite cost. In all, we managed to hack off $2.5 million, which still left us $2 million short.

Jerry returned to Martin and told him, "$3 million. I don't see how we can do it for less".

"Not enough", Martin answered. "Go home and come back with a better offer".

It was two in the morning, and we had already been in the building for twelve hours. The deal was nearly in our hands, and we left with mixed feelings. We tried to get some sleep on the drive back to Virginia.

The next day, Spacenet and Gilat continued to crunch numbers with a vengeance. Everyone was interested in bagging the deal and sought to cut costs, but we could not consent to a situation in which we would lose money. All of us tried to come up with as many creative ideas as possible in order to whittle away at the price tag. Gilat found itself in a rather tricky situation: We still did not know how much the product would actually cost us to manufacture and thus how much we stood to profit from Rite-Aid's counter offer. To date, we had manufactured less than a hundred units, so that at this phase any estimate had to be taken with a grain of salt.

It was indeed a mad dash to slash costs. I entered Jerry's office and cheerfully informed him that we had managed to come up with another half a million. Correspondingly, Spacenet had cut another $1.25 million, which left us with combined savings of $3.75 million. Jerry called Martin in my presence: "We've reached $3.75 million", Jerry proclaimed, "and we can't budge another inch".

"$4.25 million", Martin demanded.

"Sorry, I can't do it".

"Give him what he wants", I whispered into Jerry's ear. "It's a shame to lose the deal. I'll cover part of it".

Jerry covered the earpiece and provided me with a poignant and valuable lesson for the rest of my life: "In order to close a deal you have to hit the breaks at some point. Otherwise, it will never end".

An extended silence ensued, and I felt as if I was about to burst.

"The deal is yours", Martin said.

I couldn't believe my own ears. Martin's voice suddenly disappeared, and it took us fifteen minutes to contact him again. "Jerry", he whispered, "I have Jack Shaw on the other line…"

I nearly fainted.

"Just kidding", Martin said. "The deal is yours. Go celebrate. You've got a lot of hard work ahead of you".

I left the room in a sprint. Joshua and John Mattingly were standing outside, the door. "We won the deal", I shouted, struggling to hold back the joyous roar that was about to burst out of my mouth. The news resonated throughout the corridors. There was great joy in Spacenet that day. In the final analysis, we had all wanted the deal. I could only imagine the grave faces at Hughes that same day, as they were accustomed to beating Spacenet and sweeping up all the customers. This time, however, the pendulum had shifted, and it was a sign of more to come.

Joshua smiled, slapped me on the shoulder, and returned to his office. A few minutes later, he was already completely immersed in another deal.

We immediately called the offices in Israel and heard the screams of joy from across the sea. The significance of this deal as far as Gilat was concerned was immense. Besides the fact that we had acquired a prominent customer, a reputation, and what not, there was also quite a bit of money involved. The deal was worth $10 million to Gilat, which was a tremendous sum for what was still a start-up company with only twenty-five employees. No less important than the money, we proved our fighting spirit. We didn't give up, even when all appeared to be lost. We did not shame the Gilat spirit.

That night, Joshua and I went out to celebrate at a modest restaurant, not far from our hotel in McLean. We raised a toast, and for the most part just smiled at one another. The one sentence that best summarized the great battle was, "Whoa, we've really become a serious company now!"

The celebrations ended and the problems began. Spacenet conceded on practically every clause in the contract in order to get it signed as quickly as possible, and Rite-Aid fully exploited this by inserting all sorts of small clauses that were not in our best interests. The first site was installed immediately. Following some minor difficulties in the lab, the prototype simulated the application in a highly satisfactory manner. However, the first five units that were installed in the field were an absolute catastrophe. The system crashed every hour, and the engineers at the site didn't find a moment's rest. In addition, we had an engineer stationed at Rite-Aid's operation center twenty-four hours a day, where he vigorously repaired malfunctions. At first, Rite-Aid was understanding and let us work out the kinks, but after a couple of days, when the rate of crashes decreased to "only" one per day, they began to lose their patience and the pressure that we were under intensified.

Notwithstanding the problems at the initial five sites, we started installing the first hundred systems in accordance with the timetables, but the situation steadily deteriorated. Amiram paid a visit to one of the stores that had already been hooked up. He bought a tooth brush and 'innocently' asked the cashier how she confirms credit cards.

"By the satellite", she answered.

"And how does it work?" he insisted.

The cashier sighed and lethargically motioned her hand upwards: "Ever since they put that stuff on the roof..."

We decided to enter crisis mode. Spacenet appointed Chatterjee, a young and robust Indian engineer — who was later promoted to chief engineer of Spacenet's engineering and development division — to head the repair effort. He worked closely with the customer and made sure that we were attuned with their expectations. Amiram assumed command at Gilat, and both groups held daily discussions on the problems and proposed solutions. So long as sites were being added to the network, the traffic increased and the software was thus coping with situations that we had never tested before. In quite a few instances, we revealed glitches that paralyzed the system and caused it to crash time and again. Rite-Aid's frustrated pharmacists incessantly complained that they were unable to complete a sale. For the first time, the customer expressed veiled threats that they were considering whether to call it all off and return to Hughes.

As the pressure mounted, I learnt an important lesson on crisis management. Our initial handling of the crisis was a failure. We lacked the necessary business experience to deal with the situation properly and committed every mistake in the book. Any organization has to think long and hard before declaring a crisis; for once the decision is made, the entire organization is consumed by the crisis. Upon entering crisis mode, many things have to happen at once: You have to appoint a senior official in the organization to serve as the crisis manager. The crisis manager commits her or himself to solving the problems twenty-four hours a day. The entire organization directly reports to the crisis manager, who is authorized to give an order to any other employee, and everyone must respond to his demands instantaneously. In essence, the crisis manager is the one calling all the shots and turns into the organization's president until the end of the crisis.

The first step that a crisis manager must take is to conduct a comprehensive analysis of the situation, which includes timetables for tending to the problem and coming up with primary solutions. This assessment must be realistic and take into account unexpected problems that are bound to surface in abundance. Thereafter, the manager must turn to the customers and attempt to adapt their expectations to reality, while keeping commitments to a minimum. That said, the crisis manager cannot tell them the entire truth, for this is liable to cause them to panic and cancel the project. The sales people must also take part in the pacification efforts in order to attain the maximum amount of time for tending to the problem. This is a critical element because eventually the results will come to light.

The crisis manager's ability to preserve the company's integrity in the customer's eyes is crucial. If the customers lose their faith in the vencor's ability, they will obviously call the whole thing off. As a rule, the crisis manager must be open and honest with the customer whenever possible; otherwise the company's trustworthiness will plummet. In fact, managing the expectations of the customer is the primary component of any crisis. Your senior management must strengthen its ties with the customer's senior executives and allay their fears in a manner that goes beyond the mere technical issues involved.

The better the relations at the senior levels, the more time the technical ranks will have for dealing with the problems. During the Rite-Aid crisis, I frequently crawled on my knees to their management in order to buy more time for our people in the field. When relations are poor at the top, the patience of the customer's technical staff is limited. It is thus imperative that the customer's technical employees are cognizant of the fact that their superiors support the vendor.

The crisis team must convene on a daily basis. Representatives of the senior management, marketing and sales staff, and all the relevant technical groups are to take part in the meetings, which are to be presided over by the crisis manager. The participants review what took place the day before and what is planned for the day ahead. Everyone can voice their opinion, but the crisis manager has the final say. If the company president decides to intervene, he or she must then assume the mantle of crisis manager and put all other matters aside. However, the president can only fill this role if he or she is an expert on the technical aspects of the product.

Discussions must be held with the customer's senior managers twice or three times a week, and they must be provided with full documentation of your efforts to solve the crisis, including the tests that are being conducted. It is incumbent upon the crisis manager to immediately notify the customer of even the slightest improvements as soon as they are attained. Handling a crisis primarily consists of handling people. Almost every technical problem can be solved, but this must be accomplished at a pace and in a manner that will persuade the customers that the vendor is capable of identifying and solving all problems.

When a network with a new technology is deployed, the

problems are inevitably bigger. In our particular case, Rite-Aid simultaneously deployed new equipment at the cash registers and at the points of sale. Glitches were also revealed with this equipment, which forced us to upload software on a daily basis via the satellite system. The upload did not always work and constituted an especially challenging problem.

The managements of Spacenet and Gilat stood behind the project, and both companies were heavily involved in solving the crisis. At Gilat, it was our top priority, or as Joshua dubbed it "the only priority". The joint effort bore fruit. In the midst of the crisis, we devised a system that allowed us to simulate the conditions in the laboratory before we even installed the updated software or component in the field. Consequently, we were able to foresee the problems and solve them before they even arose in the field. The problems were steadily solved, and over one hundred sites were up and running by the end of the year, which more or less satisfied Rite-Aid's desires even though it was a far cry from the 2700 sites that were supposed to be installed by then.

Towards the end of 1992, Gilat received a $5.8 million order from Spacenet. In contrast, our sales for all of 1991 totaled $1.7 million. We increasingly began to focus our efforts on other customers, and felt that Gilat was ready to go public. The meteoric rise has begun.

The Rite-Aid deal was indeed the turning point in Gilat's short history. From an anonymous Israeli company trying to break into a new field, we became a global factor in our industry, with a market share of 15%. After overcoming some daunting growing pains, we had a reference customer that enabled us to sweep up additional accounts. By dint of Gilat's — not Spacenet's — efforts, Hughes was forced onto the defensive. The days in which they beat out Spacenet every time were over.

Many factors played into our hands during the battle over Rite-Aid. Our so-called 'miracles' were actually a combination of the following mere-mortal factors: creative solutions to technical problems; utilization of text-book and occasionally unconventional methods for lowering prices, which we also put to good use in future deals; the close and fertile cooperation with Spacenet; and the hands-on involvement of both organizations' senior managements, which in Gilat's case was absolute.

We also drew many lessons from the Rite-Aid episode. First and foremost was that Spacenet could not be relied upon. We had to be intimately involved in every deal and manage the entire process: examine, push, propose, and think. We also learned that we could not afford to wait for orders to come in the mail. Another conclusion that we reached was that new products are deployed with blood and fire; there are no short cuts. It is impossible to simulate the real world in the laboratory. Therefore, one of the major differences between companies that "could have" and those that "have done it" is the ability and willingness to work in the field: to lay down under the car, get sullied with grease, and repair glitches on the fly, regardless of their size or frequency.

In order to get over the hump and become a successful company the first, large sale is pivotal. The entire organization must focus on the target, refuse to give in, and use every means at its disposal. This is the only way to ascend from a start-up to a full-fledged company with large customers that predicate their business on your company's technologies.

This is exactly what we became after landing the Rite-Aid account.

5

The Darlings of Wall Street

Flying from London to New York during Gilat's IPO (Initial Public Offering) in March 1993, I leaned back in my seat aboard the sonic Concord airliner. I detached from all the turmoil around me — with the help of a tape of Ethnix, an exciting Israeli rock band — closed my eyes, and began to think. I tried to picture Israeli companies that are worth $100 million. Tempo, a beverage company that was established in 1954, six years after the founding of the State of Israel, was the first example that came to mind. This company, which dominated Israel's soft-drink industry and, as of the early 1980s, beer markets, was a huge empire — at least by Israeli standards — with thousands of employees, multiple factories and production lines, and a large fleet of trucks. Its market value was $118 million, just above Gilat's anticipated value after the IPO. Despite the fact that our company was only in existence for six years and could still assemble its entire staff in our building's medium-sized conference room, Gilat was practically on par with Tempo. In business terms, we had skyrocketed overnight and surpassed Israeli companies that needed tens of years to consolidate their status.

Each one of Gilat's five founders was worth $7 million on paper. This substantial sum did not turn us into different people, nor did we abandon "the tunnel". My friend Micha Angel once smiled at me and remarked that after company founders make their fortune, they usually buy a Porsche and get divorced. However, we didn't follow this track. I have already stated my belief that the primary goal of entrepreneurs is not to hit it big. If it happens, then all the better, but more than anything else Gilat's founders wanted to succeed as a company and then take Gilat on to the next steps: to conquer another mountain; land another customer;

82 • Yoel Gat

capture another market; and forge our way into first place.

Companies that have proved themselves have a license to print money. They take a note, write the words 'stock certificate of our company' on it, and sell it. At first, the stock is only sold to professional investors or venture capital funds, but when a company goes public — namely, sells its shares on the stock exchange — anyone can purchase a stock certificate. In order to entice people and institutions to invest in your company, you have to release detailed information to the public on the firm's performance and exhibit the wherewithal to market and sell your 'product' — namely your stock. Like any other product that hits the market, you have to persuade potential customers to buy your stock.

A company is interested in offering its shares for several reasons. Firstly, it wants to raise cash, and the stock constitutes a tradable currency. Secondly, it can use the shares to reward its employees in the form of options. Lastly, it seeks the recognition and credibility that any company merits upon becoming a pubic company.

An IPO is an ingenious financial process. If it succeeds, everyone profits: by the first day of trading, the investors who bought shares realize profits of 10% to 30%; the company not only raises capital, but creates a liquid market for its stocks; and the investment bank that coordinates the public offering reels in a hefty fee. Nevertheless, a company will only initiate an offering if it has what it needs to sell, whom to sell to, and knows how to market its goods. If all these factors are not in place, the offering is likely to fail and the company won't accomplish any of the goals that it has set for itself.

The main element of any IPO (like any fund raise) is **the story**. Accordingly, Gilat's IPO was made possible thanks to the Rite-Aid deal, as we suddenly had a story. A company's war chest is comprised of information on its technology, marketing outlets, products, and potential. The company is only ready to go public when these components combine to form a credible yet fascinating story.

When we decided to go public in early 1993, Gilat indeed possessed a powerful story: a company with a unique technology in the field of small earth stations for satellite communications; few competitors (Hughes was the only major threat that stood in our path); our prices were the lowest on the market; Gilat had three products — one-way and two-way satellite systems, and rural telephony products (a satellite-based technology for connecting public telephones in remote areas that cannot be reached in any other way); products that were being marketed by large, reputable distributors (Spacenet, GTECH, and Comsat for its telephony products); major principal customers including corporations such as Rite-Aid, British Telecom (BT), Alcatel (the French telecom giant), and Bosch (a major German automotive technology company); and orders for the next year that were twice as high as its sales during the year of the IPO. Furthermore, we boasted two vital components that would enhance the reputation of any company in the eyes of potential investors: manifold systems that we were already selling; and interesting and multi-faceted applications for our technology. What more can a company looking to convince investors that its prospects are excellent possibly ask for?

Before the IPO, we hired a new creative manager, Ian Tick, who was charged with designing Gilat's corporate identity, advertising, exhibitions, and media. Ian prepared what he referred to as a "new corporate identity". First of all, he changed Gilat's logo as well as its name, from Gilat Communication Systems to Gilat Satellite Networks. We had a hard time accepting the change, but after several failed attempts at persuasion we eventually gave up, as we came to the realization that the new name was a much more accurate description of what the company actually did. Ian got us to think about the way we marketed ourselves in a much more serious fashion. A company that is going public requires a respectable corporate identity, which entails all the elements that comprise its image: corporate stationary; a business card; the logo on its products; fonts; and a uniform format for presentations. Ian even designed a logo for our maintenance trucks, which would distribute and service our products all over the world. Gilat still didn't own a single truck, so that when we saw Ian's picture of a squadron of trucks sporting the prominent new logo, we couldn't help but smile. The IPO "book", after all, referred to a company worth $100 million and not a mere $10 million.

Gilat had a story, a logo, and a corporate identity book. Now all we needed were professionals to get the IPO off the ground: that one-of-a-kind breed known as investment bankers.

Investment bankers consist of a number of sub-species: There are the bankers that are responsible for the customer's relations with the bank, and we had a working relationship with several of these 'customer reps'. Next in line are the various analysts, experts with broad insight into their particular areas of interest. Gilat also had decent connections with some analysts, who were affiliated with the aforementioned investment banks and would write reviews of Gilat. During the IPO process, the analysts to survey Gilat were from neither the wireless nor the satellite fields, as analysts that covered these fields barely existed in those days. Instead, we were profiled by analysts that covered emerging markets and Israel. This was a disadvantage because analysts have tremendous influence over the IPO process. Investors rely on their advice with all that concerns the market situation and rely on their assessments of companies that are going public. At any given moment, there are quite a few companies that are going public. Therefore, it is imperative that you persuade analysts to invest their time and energy on your company.

Of course, you also have to contend with the executives of the various investment banks. A company going public only gets a glimpse of these hotshots when they are trying to sell you their services. Once they land the customer, they disappear into the lavish offices perched atop Manhattan's skyscrapers. Most of these executives are extremely intelligent and graduated from the prestigious business schools at Harvard, MIT, Stanford, and Yale. They all enjoy hefty salaries and are thus expected to bring in big revenues. Almost all of them are endowed with exceptional personal skills. Much of their time is devoted to creating a sense of "value" for companies that they believe to possess promising potential. With this in mind, they attempt to forge close relationships with these sorts of companies' decision makers, so that the latter will feel "uncomfortable" about not awarding the bankers a juicy portion of the proceeds from the IPO.

A single investment bank is more than capable of underwriting an IPO on its own, especially if it's a hot offering. Nonetheless, a company that goes public is interested in as many underwriters as possible in order to ensure, above all, that several analysts will cover the company after the IPO. As part of the underwriting deal, the investment bank commits to "covering" the company with in-house analysts who possess the skills to present a trustworthy and captivating picture of the company and it's markets. It is important for companies to choose investment banks with good analysts and guarantee that the analysts they want would indeed be covering the company after the IPO. However, the investment bank is not always prepared to guarantee a specific analyst so it is up to management to convince the top analysts to write reports concerning their company.

An additional and no less important reason for working with several banks is that they provide insurance. If the lead banker fails to land enough investors, there is always the possibility that the other bankers would come through. Although the process is dominated by the lead banker, the others get a share of the cut even when their involvement is relatively minor. At the end of the day, bankers collect millions of dollars in fees from successful IPOs.

The process of choosing banks to underwrite your IPO is rather complicated and usually involves much deliberation. Beyond the credentials of each of the candidates, the number of bankers is normally indicative of the amount of money that the company wants to raise. In our particular case, I gave responsibility for the selection process to Yoav Leibovitch, our CFO. Yoav did an excellent job, evaluating the candidate firms according to their analysts, prices, and the extent to which they were willing to support us.

Gilat fell in love with a small, quality bank named Furman Selz. We already had a long working relationship with them, and their executives had tracked our progress since 1991. The key player was Brian Friedman, the head of Furman Selz's investment banking department, who became one of my better friends on Wall Street. Smart and savvy, Brian was the type of guy who had seen it all. He examined everything in a methodical manner, and his estimates of both the business and financial aspects were always predicated on past experience. He appeared to be the ideal person from whom I would have liked to receive the check at the end of the process… His partner was Joel Maryles, a proud Jew and a hard-working man. Joel accompanied us throughout the arduous process and provided us with a great deal of assistance. Furman Selz was the first bank to submit an offer to underwrite the IPO, which we then brought before Gilat's board of directors.

Notwithstanding our preference for Furman Selz, Discount Investment (one of our partners, after investing in our first round of financing in 1990) had a long-standing relationship with another investment bank, Lehman Brothers. The very same Harvey Krueger — who had advised me to drop the Rite-Aid deal — was in charge of their Israeli 'franchise,' which at the time was the most active bank in Israel in the field of IPOs. Lehman Brothers sold themselves as the only leading investment bank that maintained a full-time office in Israel, which was indeed true, and had Alex Sena, a capable analyst, on its staff. Lehman was much bigger than Furman Selz and claimed to be a more qualified organization that cared more about Israel. Incidentally, both assertions in our minds, then, were less than accurate.

When two teams pound away at each other, a third one inevitably ends up walking away with the prize, and we ultimately went with Oppenheimer, a mid-size bank with extensive experience in technology IPOs for companies of our size. Oppenheimer's key players — the investor banker Stanley Stern and the aggressive, Israeli analyst Lior Bergman — did everything in their power to land the deal. During the countless meetings with Oppenheimer that preceded our decision, they marketed themselves as an organization with greater focus and commitment than the other candidates. They also featured an intelligent analyst that would assume an active role in much of the sales process. Moreover, their industrious and assertive president, Nat Gantcher, exerted pressure on anything that moved. In a compromise that was characteristic of Gilat's board of directors, we chose Oppenheimer as the lead banker and Lehman and Furman Selz as the secondary bankers.

All three bankers subsequently paid visits to Gilat's offices in order to see what we were actually offering. We prepared a vast array of presentations for their visit on every conceivable topic: technology, products, markets, financial reports, manufacturing, and quality. Each of the underwriters sent at least one banker and one analyst, all of whom asked a ton of questions, some of which were right on target.

We were extremely concerned about their encounter with our building on Barzel Street and its humble surroundings in Tel-Aviv's Ramat Hachayal neighborhood. A company that purports to reach the stars and wants to issue stocks to the tune of $100 million is expected to project an impressive aura and work out of a dignified residence. I am certain that our offices were unlike anything that they had ever witnessed before.

The group arrived in late January 1993. They wandered about the building and inspected our administrative and R&D floors. Our visitors also met with most of the company's personnel, which was not a particularly difficult feat considering the fact that we had less than sixty employees at the time. We took them up to the roof, on top of the fourth floor, to see the large antenna that we had mounted — we only had the budget for one — and some fifteen small antennas. The scene on the roof was somewhat surrealistic. Dignified members of the Wall Street community — professionals beyond reproach donning designer suits and ties — were laying their eyes on the adjacent properties: a huge watermelon market; heaps of garbage; cars haphazardly parked in make-shift spots; unpaved roads; and streams of sewage flowing alongside the old sidewalks. It looked more like Bombay than a modern industrial park in Tel-Aviv.

Fortunately, they ignored the panoramic backdrop and concentrated on the passion and power in the corridors of Gilat. Ray Marks, a senior vice president at Spacenet, was "coincidentally" in town — we had naturally planned it all weeks in advance —and made a tremendous impression on the bankers. Colorful, out-going, and full of humor, Ray answered all their questions, which came at him from all angles: about Spacenet, the market, the technology, and Gilat's standing. My heart skipped a beat towards the end of the meeting when one of the underwriters asked Ray what most worried him about Gilat. Naturally, Ray kept his composure and provided them with an honest answer: "I am definitely worried about their manufacturing capacity. We'll bring them orders for tens of thousands of terminals, and where are they going to manufacture it — on the fifth floor?" he asked with an innocent smile, as the entire room burst into laughter.

The IPO got underway and we entered the tunnel. For the next two and a half months, practically all we dealt with was the IPO. From the moment we decided to go public until we were a public company took all of 72 days. The entire process usually takes much longer, but we broke yet another record for an Israeli company on Wall Street (and more was yet to come).

The first step of any public offering is the preparation of a prospectus or an offering memorandum. This is no ordinary step, as the fate of the entire IPO is riding on this one document. Consequently, companies spend a fortune preparing a worthy prospectus, as the tens of pages cost hundreds of thousands of dollars and can occasionally even run into the millions of dollars.

Incidentally, it is surprising that such an expensive and

time-consuming document merits such sparse attention from most investors (who are the reason the prospectus is put together to begin with). Most investors pore over the first and perhaps even the second page, but merely skim through the rest, glancing at the pictures and headlines on the front and back cover in order to get a feel for the company; little wonder this document is frequently referred to as a "red herring". The decision over whether to actually invest in the company will be made later on, during the one-on-one personal meetings over the course of the road show. The seasoned bankers even told us that the slew of companies that are in the process of going public at any given moment prevents investors from reading everything and they tend to concentrate on the summary page and the handful of colorful pictures. Nevertheless, we discovered that there were quite a few investors who read through the entire prospectus, cover to cover, and we had to learn how to deal with them.

By its very nature, the IPO prospectus is a document rife with contrasts. On the one hand, it is a legal document that illustrates the status of the company and underscores the risks that it faces in cold and exacting legalese. On the other hand, the prospectus is the issuing company's exclusive marketing document, for the law prohibits both the company and its bankers from providing an investor with any other document.

All the groups that are involved in the public offering participate in the formulation of the prospectus: the company, the bankers underwriting the IPO, the company's accountants, and a string of lawyers representing both the company and the banks. The prospectus is indeed a 'mass production,' as no less than thirty people are simultaneously present in the conference room during the drafting sessions. Incidentally, all the lawyers and accountants fetch a handsome sum for their efforts. The entire writing process usually entails three or four rounds, each of which last for several days. After each round, numerous drafts and comments are disseminated among the participants. Once the agreements are hammered out and the final text is ready, time and thought must then be invested on designing these four glossy pages on the company and its products that are permitted by law.

We learned that the opening page is the most important part of the entire prospectus. On the opening page, we presented Gilat as a company that designs, develops, manufacturers, markets, sells, and supports satellite communication products that operate via small dishes. We outlined the advantages that we had over the traditional, ground-based networks of phone lines: an inexpensive price, high flexibility, and a system that enables the customers to monitor and control the entire network. Moreover, our new product was more reliable and less expensive than the competition's networks. All these factors promised to expand our market share and increase the amount of potential customers. We noted that the company intends on selling two million shares over the course of the IPO at a price of between $9 and $11 per share, so that after the issue there would be about eight million existing shares of Gilat. Therefore, we assumed that the company's value would reach between $72 and $90 million.

We weren't exactly shy in all that concerned our descriptions about the major customers — Rite-Aid and the English companies BT and Mercury — that we had managed to acquire in the short period of time since we had launched our product onto the market. Nor were we tight-lipped with respect to the important strategic relations that we had nurtured with companies such as Spacenet, GTECH, and Comsat, who sold our products as an integral part of their systems. We proudly highlighted the fact that we sold $5.6 million worth of products and had reaped profits of $500,000 in 1992. Moreover, our backlog for deliveries in 1993 (the prospectus was only assembled at the beginning of that year) already stood at $12.5 million.

A no less important part of the prospectus dealt with the fundamental risk factors that an investment in Gilat entailed. At this stage, the lawyers set the tone, while the executives usually argue with them over every period and comma in an effort to downplay the risks that appear on the prospectus. The warnings in prospectuses are indeed a hard pill to swallow considering how much time and money is invested in the booklet. However, we maintained our composure. "Please, write whatever you see fit", we told the lawyers who helped prepare our prospectus, "and we'll help you write some more".

The cautious lawyers did not omit so much as one item off their long list of dangers: Gilat lacks a history of past operations *vis à vis* its plans for expansion, and it is thus unclear whether the company will meet its obligations; a high degree of dependence on Spacenet and other "key relationships"; its dependence on a small number of "key products", which necessitates the development of new products; its problematic location in Israel; and so on and so on… We did not argue or rule out a single item, nor did the list have an impact on the eventual success of the stock offering.

Obviously, not everything went smoothly. In fact, we encountered our first problem during the earliest stage possible, the preparation of the prospectus, when it came to our attention that the bankers intended on talking with our customers and striking alliances. We were not worried about Spacenet's opinion, for it was in their best interest to assist us. Hughes attacked us wherever possible and presented us as an Israeli company that no one has ever heard of. Spacenet thus knew that if we would become a public company, it would enhance our credibility as well as their own. We weren't worried about GTECH or Comsat either, as our relations with them at that juncture were excellent. Our main concern was over what Rite-Aid would have to say about us. The growing pains that had accompanied the roll out of our system in the drug-store chain were not over yet and had even intensified during the drafting of the prospectus. One ill-timed telephone conversation between a banker and un-briefed Rite-Aid employee could have sent the entire IPO down the drain. With butterflies fluttering in my stomach, I called Martin Grass, Rite-Aid's president, and explained the delicate situation. Martin immediately calmed me down: "Don't worry Yoel. I understand the situation you're in. It's going to be alright". True to his word, Rite-Aid did not let us down, as Martin sang our praises to the bankers. We got by Rite-Aid in one piece.

The next problem arose two days prior to the submission of the prospectus to the United States Security Exchange Commission (SEC). One of the bank's wily lawyers delved into our agreements with GTECH and Spacenet and claimed that there was a contradiction between the two contracts: Whereas Spacenet had exclusive marketing rights in the United States, GTECH received international marketing rights in the lottery industry, which also included the United States. She insisted that this apparent contradiction would have to be rectified before proceeding any further and refused to budge an inch. Consequently, we were forced to crawl on our knees to Spacenet and ask them to change the agreement. Our timing was far from perfect. Joshua took it upon himself to persuade John Mattingly to revise the wording. However, the night before Joshua dropped in on him, Rite-Aid had pestered Mattingly about technical problems. Joshua, who had merely stopped by to ask for a small favor, received the cold-shower treatment. Only after a nasty exchange of words and lengthy discussions with Spacenet's lawyers did Mattingly finally agree to revise the relevant clause that gave Spacenet exclusive rights to the American market. Another miracle along the way to the offering…

However, we weren't out of the woods yet, as the biggest obstacles usually turn up where you least expect them. One of the most difficult problems that we were forced to contend with was the options that we had distributed to Gilat's employees three months earlier. Many companies reward their employees by allowing them to take part in their success, and one of the best ways to do this is by distributing options. An option is basically the right to purchase stock in the company at a set price. Options are usually distributed during a company's early stages, when its market value is low. The recipients can usually exercise their options for a period of up to ten years at the price that was set when the option was first issued. Upon exercising their options, the recipients purchase the stock at the pre-determined price. If the company's stock has significantly appreciated since the distribution, the employees can exercise their options and sell them at the market price for a considerable gain.

In December 1992, before we embarked on the IPO, we decided to distribute 500,000 options to many of our employees at a price of 33¢ per share. However, by March 1993, at the height of the IPO process, we were seeking between $9 and $11 for those same shares. Consequently, if the IPO were to succeed, the employees stood to make a killing off their options. Incidentally, the recipients didn't understand this until after the public issue, when the stock was being traded at a price that was abundantly higher than the cost of exercising the option. Only then did they realize that they were holding onto an asset that was worth forty times more than what they would have to pay in order to exercise their right. In fact, some of our employees held options that were worth hundreds of thousands of dollars. At the time, the very notion of distributing stock options was not all that common. Very few pubic companies granted options, and most of the employees didn't even know what they meant. The options craze of high-tech employees was still a long-way off. In any event, by dint of these options, we gained the loyalty of these employees for many years to come.

Even back then, the SEC was well aware of and very sensitive about the entire subject of cheap stock that companies distribute to various employees, stakeholders, and friends. In many instances, they require companies that go public to account for such bonuses as expenditure. If we had been forced to mark off the options as an expense, then instead of showing a modest profit of $500,000, our balance sheets at the end of 1992 would have pointed to a loss of millions of dollars and not one banker would have been willing to touch us with a ten-foot pole.

As soon as the SEC hinted that our options were a cause for concern, we understood that the fate of the IPO rested entirely on the way this issue would play itself out. When the troubling news reached us in the US, I was sick with the flu and Yoav entered my hotel room looking as if he had seen a ghost. We spent hours articulating the reasons for the sudden increase in the stock's value from 33¢ in December to $11 in March: the high level of risk in the beginning of 1993; the problems with Rite-Aid only took a turn for the best in early 1993; the new orders that came in; the very announcement of the IPO appreciably added to the stock's value due to its anticipated tradability; a new agreement that we signed with GTECH; the substantial rise in the potential of the rural telephony market during that period; and much, much more. As per the advice of our attorneys, we hired a firm called Giza to prepare an in-depth report on why the value that we had set for the stock in late December was a realistic estimation of its fair market value at the time. Giza put together an impressive report, and the SEC was content.

Simultaneous to the mad dash after the IPO, we continued to contend with major problems at Rite-Aid. We had already installed 250 sites by the beginning of 1993, and the number of mishaps was growing in proportion to the size of the network. The network crashed every few hours, and engineers from Gilat and Spacenet spent days and nights at Rite-Aids's IT center in an effort to get the system up and running. For every glitch that was repaired, a new one immediately popped up. As a result, we were constantly on the phone with the people handling the IPO as well as those sweating over and complaining about the Rite-Aid network (for example, Martin Grass).

After completing the prospectus and handling all the problems that had surfaced along the way —with flying colors, if

I may say— all that remained before becoming a public company was one small step: to sell the stock. The sales trip, which investment bankers refer to as a 'road show', entails two intensive weeks of flights, long drives, meals, speeches, hotels, and dozens of individual and group meetings with investors. The entire purpose of this grueling effort is to rouse interest in the company and attract orders before the slated public issue. Yoav and I were Gilat's primary representatives, while Amiram and Joshua joined us at certain stops along the way.

The night before I departed for the road show, I took a walk with my eldest son Yonatan, who was about eleven at the time, through the streets of Shikun Dan, our neighborhood in Tel-Aviv. We held hands as I told him that I would be away for over two weeks.

"Why is it so important?" he asked, and I explained to him.

"And why is it so important to you?" he insisted.

His question stopped me in my tracks. I answered that "I want the company to be secure, with a lot of money, so there won't be any fear that it will ever close down".

"But why is it important to **you**, dad?" he asked again. I understood that he completely distinguished between the benefit of the company, which I so intimately identified with, and my personal happiness.

"And will you work less afterwards?" he continued to make things difficult on me.

"We'll have more money, and we'll be able to do whatever we want", I tried to explain to him again. "Unfortunately, I don't think that I will be able to work any less".

Yonatan tightened his grip of my hand. "Then it's not worth it to me, Dad. Don't go. Stay with me!"

I felt all the air leaving my body, as if it were a big balloon, and all my energy instantly evaporated. The immense price of success had suddenly become so evident. However, I obviously couldn't pull myself away from Gilat. The gun was already brandished, and we were off to battle yet again.

I have already mentioned that I am an inveterate writer and that I essentially became Gilat's official historian. Every event, every change, every accomplishment, and every setback — everything is meticulously documented in the 53 large notebooks that I filled during my tenure at Gilat, to include the grueling road show:

Mar 8, 1993: El-Al's overnight flight from Israel's Ben-Gurion Airport to New York. At 1:00am, four members of the Gilat team — Yoav, Ian, Gene, and myself — take up four of the five middle seats in row 26 of the tourist-class cabin and nod off into an oft-interrupted sleep. After landing, we assemble into the hotel room, go over the presentation, and decide that we have to buy a color Macintosh for the presentations.

Mar 9: We rush over to Oppenheimer's offices and give our first presentation. Absolutely dreadful! We are tense, unfamiliar with the slides, unorganized, and utter a great deal of nonsense. It is among the worst presentations I have ever given. While eating sandwiches, we try to draw conclusions from the abysmal showing. We change several of the slides and revise the order of the entire presentation so that our strong points are already emphasized in the opening frame. Following an update from Israel on problems in Germany, we gallop straight to the offices of Furman Selz, one of our co- underwriters. We give a presentation to their sales people — the ones charged with actually selling our stock — which goes over very well. Brian Friedman, the Investment Banking executive, comes over and shakes my hand and tells me that, "The quality goes through…" Nonetheless, we attempt to cut the presentation down to twenty minutes in order to save time for questions.

It is already late afternoon when we proceed to Lehman Brothers. An announcement is made on the building's PA system: "The presentation of Gilat Satellite Networks will begin in two minutes in room G2…" Thirty people are waiting in the small room, and one of their analysts opens the meeting with a five minute introduction. He conveys most of my key points, which leaves me puzzled and confused. The presentation is mediocre, but their sales people's questions are on target and the forum is engaging.

At 6:45pm, we go out to dinner with the bankers. I hold a short conversation with one of Lehman's analysts about his two-year model for Gilat, which sounds as if he is taking us to the moon and beyond; if only he were to succeed. The bankers invite us to the Broadway show Miss Saigon. By the end of the opening scene, I am fast asleep and wake up in panic when a huge helicopter lands on stage. I have no idea where I am or what is happening.

Mar 10: I have a difficult time getting out of bed, after only four and a half hours of sleep. It usually takes me until about 11:00 in the morning to get up to speed. I always say that until then you may get my body, but not my soul. Forty minutes after getting out of bed, I am already at a meeting with a sharp investor, who annoys me with questions on Rite-Aid and Comsat. I try to stay on top of the presentation and comprehend the questions in order to accurately address the point that the investors perceive to be problematic. We are competing with five other companies that are going public at the same time, as all of us are going to be turning to more-or-less the same investors for their time and money. Therefore, it is imperative that we remain on top of our game at all times.

We then head off for a meeting with JRD, a large New York-based fund, which has ties with Israel and had invested in Israeli companies. Its representative is an inordinately thin woman (who looks like an x-ray negative). While most of the other meetings concentrate on technical issues, this time the questions are mostly concerned with marketing. We are pleased with the presentation, and it appearss as if her fund is going to order shares.

It suddenly dawns upon me that I am going to have to repeat this presentation at least another fifty times over the next two weeks. How am I ever going to cope with fourteen more days of this?

The next appointment is with BEA Associates, a huge fund that was established shortly before our offering. BEA is represented by, among others, Adi Raviv — the former executive of Lehman Brothers' offices in Israel — his boss, and other analysts. The meeting lasts an hour and a half and concentrates on our advantages over Hughes. At the end of the conversation, they cordially shake our hands and remark, "Another impressive Israeli success story…"

We get in another three meetings. The first presentation with Morgan Stanley leaves a bad taste in our mouths. It is the first time we faced a hostile investor. Their guy had even visited our offices in Israel, but he is highly skeptical and doesn't have any faith in Spacenet whatsoever. One of the two remaining meetings is with a tough investor from Chicago. We receive a comprehensive briefing from his sales woman about his areas of interest, which really helps us emphasize the right points during the meeting.

After the final appointment, we fly to Washington D.C.

and arrive in the nation's capital at 1:00am . I fall asleep as soon as my head hits the pillow and get up at 7:00am for an intensive day at Comsat, our rural telephony partners.

Mar 12: Early next morning, we drive to the offices of Legg Mason in Baltimore. They have an incredible view from the 45th floor, but I sit with my back to the window so as not to be distracted. Apparently my strategy worked, as I give my best performance to date. The questions are pertinent and we get the feeling that they are going to buy.

After an hour and a half drive from Baltimore, we arrive in Philadelphia and immediately step into a fancy restaurant for a lunch meeting. The three investors are ignorant, but the French cuisine is superb. Unfortunately, the salad dressing is of greater interest to them than Gilat's story. It is difficult to describe how frustrating it is to talk to people who are looking down at their plates. You feel like a court jester and, to add insult to injury, it makes your stomach growl as well. That night we return to New York in our limousine for two late meetings.

Mar 13: Saturday in New York. At long last, I get to wake up at a quarter to ten. Over two inches of snow have fallen during the night, and the city is draped in white. I call home and share my feelings with my wife Simona: "I'm cold, sad, tense, and lonely…" Simona offers to join me at once. I thank her but politely refuse. Right after the conversation with her, I call up Stanley Stern, the banker in charge of our IPO at Oppenheimer. Apparently on account of my grumpy mood, I am hesitant about sharing my feelings with him and lodge a series of complaints instead: "We did whatever you wanted. We appointed you the lead banker and agreed to your prices. And in return, you send children to the meetings and don't even find the time to give me a call. It appears as if you guys are already working on the next customer, in the hopes that the expenses on our deal will be minimal…You're holding back information on stock orders that arrived after the meetings; you're not helping us with the questions from the SEC…It will be unfortunate if we have to tell other companies what we think of you…"

Mar 14: Another snowy day in New York. After a meeting with Stanley and Oppenheimer's lawyers, we fly to San Diego. The flight is delayed due to heavy snow at JFK Airport, and we arrive late at night.

Mar 15: The first meeting is held at six in the morning with a laid-back guy in a T-Shirt, who represents the Pacific Fund. He is quite familiar with the technology and asks relevant questions. At 7:30am, we have another appointment with a small, local investment fund. We deliver a half-hour, formal presentation to a hard-nosed investor who asks us two simple questions. From there, we hustle over to a meeting with Jeff from Nicholas Applegate, one of the largest funds in the United States. He takes us to a restaurant downstairs and orders some breakfast for himself. I take him through the presentation sheets, while he is chewing on some bacon and eggs.

We take off for Los Angeles at 11:30am. Upon landing, a limousine brings us to the luxurious Checkers Hotel, where investors are already waiting for us. In the afternoon, we meet up with the folks from Pick, a large fund with an affinity for investing in Israeli companies. It's our best meeting yet. They ask about our personal backgrounds, Gilat's corporate culture, and our personal outlooks.

The senior member of the group (who is seated next to a friend of Yadin's from his days at Harvard) fires away at us: "I know you guys. Once you raise the money, you'll stop putting pressure on customers to pay up…"

I look the guy straight in the eye — one of which was blue and the other was green — and respond: "That's not true. We supported the company for three years without raising any capital. We understand the value of money".

At 6:00pm, we again board a plane on route to San Francisco. That night, I go out with my brother Arnon for dinner, and we talk until one in the morning. I tell him how the IPO is going, and he offers me the sound advice of a big brother.

Mar 16: After tossing and turning in bed all night long, we convene for a meeting with twenty-five invited guests, among them ten investors who are gracious enough to accept our invitation for breakfast at the exquisite Park Hyatt Hotel. As usual, I have difficulties getting my engine running in the morning. The waiter serves eggs benedict and everyone digs in, while I stand near the slide projector and deliver a speech. The presentation is fair, but during the ensuing question and answer session we are faced with the first question throughout the entire road show that we didn't foresee and thus lacked an answer for: "If the market is worth $300 million a year and you claim to control 26% of it, then why do your orders only amount to $17 million?" The answer that I eventually come up with is that we did not include orders that had yet to come to the company into our calculations. Another noteworthy question follows on its heels: "Hughes has much more R&D resources than Gilat does. Is it not conceivable that in another six months the bankers will call the investors and tell them that the company is not meeting its forecasts?" The San Franciscans also ask about the Iridium project — telephones that operate with the help of satellites — and a bevy of financial questions, including queries on the Israeli tax code. The presentation is nothing to write home about, but obviously not every performance can bring down the house.

Following another meeting with an investor that is really inspired by our vision, we meet with Oscar Castro from G.T. Capital Management, a fund that specializes in technology companies. I enter the room and start setting up, but Castro surprises me right off the bat. He flicks his wrist and declares: "No need for a presentation. I just want to ask questions…" He already knows everything about us, and the prospectus in his hand is riddled with yellow highlights. Castro then bombards us with questions on every possible topic: our future, risk factors, geography, and product line. He is particularly impressed with the deal that we recently signed in Argentina. From there, we scamper to the airport to catch a plane for Minneapolis. We land in the evening and head straight to bed.

Mar 17: In the morning, we attend two meetings with representatives of large funds. From there we head off to Denver and arrive way behind schedule. Lunch was called for noon, but we got there after 1:00pm. One of the investors was fed up and left, but the rest have stayed. I give an impressive performance to a group of technology investors. They ask an array of questions on future trends — the size of satellite dishes, the price of equipment and services, throughputs, etc. At night, we fly back to New York.

Mar 18: Six meetings, some of them outright violent, as I have to contend with outbursts like the one heaved at me by Jonathan Hart from Kaufman Bros.: "Why are you teaming up with Spacenet? Everyone knows they suck…" However, by this point of the road show we have already hit our stride and nothing could stop us. We easily fend off these assaults and head on to our next destination.

A luncheon is planned at the Waldorf Astoria Hotel for some seventy-five guests, forty of whom represent some of the largest and wealthiest institutions in the country — serious money. The event generates a brisk demand, as many people show up uninvited. Spruced up in a suit and tie, I give quite a show. Our lead banker's representative starts things off with a brief introduction on Gilat: "Another Israeli success story…" The waiters enter with the first course, and everyone munches away while keeping their eyes on the speaker. I speak for thirty-five minutes and field questions. Almost everyone that was present at the luncheon orders some of our stock. As usual, we grab a cold, quick bite and run straight to the Oppenheimer offices. Our bankers inform us that we have already received orders for 3.6 million shares, while all we planned on selling was 2.3 million.

Mar 19: Seven meetings and lunch in Boston, including an appointment with the investment fund giants Fidelity and Wellington. By then, the orders have reached the 4.2 million mark. Later that day, we face another round of questioning from the SEC, but at this point their questions seem like a stroll in the park. It appears as if the entire process is going smoothly. "An amazing story", the investors keep saying.

From Boston we rush to make our flight home for a weekend in Israel and manage to get to the plane at the very last minute. Although our suitcases didn't quite make it, the main thing is to spend a couple of days at home with our families.

Mar 22: A presentation at the Dan Tel-Aviv (one of Israel's most renowned hotels) for all the local investors. The forum is hostile: "Why is the price so high? Why aren't you setting aside more shares for Israelis?" Overall, though, the presentation was fine. Yadin is satisfied and my father is impressed.

Mar 23: We touch down in London and head straight for lunch with fifteen investors. I already have the presentation down and am confident in myself, so that the presentation goes over well, and the questions are simple as well. We have two more meetings in 'The City' (London's financial district) before hopping back on a plane — this time to Stockholm. On the way to the airport, I manage to squeeze in a long telephone conversation with another American investor. Yoav, Nissan Leviathan (Gilat's sales person in Europe), and I share a room in the hotel; they snore and I lie awake thinking…

Mar 24: The morning starts with a stroll around the hotel, followed by several calls to investors in Milan and Copenhagen, before heading off for a luncheon with fifteen people. The presentation is so good that none of them have any questions. Before nightfall, we take off for Paris, where Yoav and Nissan drag me out to a show at the Lido (a famous nightclub). The orders continue to pour in, but we are worried about the fact that the SEC had yet to get back to us with a final answer.

Mar 25: The final luncheon of our road show is in the City of Lights. We invited twelve people and twenty show up. Among those in attendance was the president of the European Telecommunications Satellite Organization (Eutelsat), whose very presence makes an impression on the rest of the investors. The attendees respond to the presentation with insightful questions. After my final answer, I mention that this meeting marks the last leg of our wonderful IPO run. The guests stand up and honor us with a warm round of applause. What a great feeling.

From charming Paris, I head off to London, where I board the Concord for New York. I am forced to take the Concord because I have to be in the United States that very night in order to address the final concerns of the SEC. Before taking off, I give Yoav a ring. Yoav is already in New York for a meeting slated for setting the final pricing of the IPO. I wanted to talk with him, but am somewhat annoyed to find that he does not have time for me: "We're in the middle of discussions", Yoav said. "You just cut off Nat Gantcher, Oppenheimer's CEO". I immediately call Joshua in Israel. In the background, I hear the conversation between our board of directors and Nat and Stanley, who were in Israel: "No one is sure how you pulled it off, but everyone wants shares. As we speak, the demand is for 12 million shares and it's constantly rising. It's becoming a red hot issue. Europe is asking for another 2 million shares". The original offer was $9 to $11. Nat recommends that we raise the price to $12 per share. Following a brief consultation, we agree to the new price.

After hearing the good news, I boarded the Concord, which was an experience in its own right. I felt as if I were flying in a fighter jet. The ceiling was so low that one has to bend down in the aisles, and the chairs were luxurious yet narrow. The pilot constantly explained what was going on. There was no movie; and the service was quick and efficient. The cabin reeked of fuel, which contrasted sharply with the excellent wines and champagne that were served throughout the flight.

The jet took off like a missile; the flight speed was twice as fast as an ordinary jetliner; and the objects on the ground also seemed to move faster than usual. The noise of the engines was almost deafening. Within thirty minutes, we reached an altitude of 30,000 feet and commenced the acceleration into mach speed, which left me clinging to my seat. We had reached an altitude of 57,000 feet and a speed of mach two, when I experienced a thrilling phenomenon for the first time: the plane had caught up to the sunset, and we were going back in time. In fact, we arrived at our destination an hour before the departure time.

Before I knew it, we had traversed the Atlantic and began the descent. I felt as if the plane was attempting a crash landing as the pilot slammed on the breaks. Three hours and eighteen minutes from London to New York. As soon as I disembarked from the plane, I heard my name being called on the PA system: "Yoel Gat, a message is waiting for you after customs". I rushed through passport control and customs and received the following notice: "Get to Oppenheimer, ASAP".

I immediately called Yoav from JFK. He informed me that there were problems with the SEC. The chief reviewer had entered the picture and had a heaping pile of reservations about the IPO. Most ominously, the problem could not be solved within a day or two. I felt the euphoria give way to depression. "But there is also good news", Yoav continued. "The orders are going through the roof. We have already received orders for over 20 million shares for an issue of only 2.3 million. We've got a sizzling IPO!"

I rushed over to Oppenheimer on a helicopter. This may all sound glamorous — a helicopter shuttling you from the airport and landing next to one of Manhattan's skyscrapers — but I had not joined the ranks of high society overnight. Given the conditions that we were working under, this was simply the most efficient means for saving time. Moreover, the helicopter was part of the package: all Concord passengers were entitled to a helicopter ride to their final destination free of extra charge. In any event, I got to Oppenheimer at 7:30pm and was immediately pulled into the discussions with the lawyers and my colleagues from Israel. After the talks, I met with Tom, the head of capital markets at

Oppenheimer and thus in charge of our IPO as well. Tom, who we dubbed as the 'system engineer', gave me the run down of the situation and explained how they were going to allocate the shares. Two days earlier, the demand for shares from American financial institutions stood at 6.5 million, but by that night the orders had already reached 13 million. In addition, European institutions and private investors had ordered 4 million shares a piece. Especially surprising was the nearly endless demand from Israel, for at the time we were hardly a household name in our own country.

The proportion of orders to issues was obviously gigantic. However, despite the escalating demand, the offering company does not increase the supply of its shares. Tom estimated that by the end of the first day of trading the stock would be traded at between $14 and $15. When an offer heats up like ours, Tom explained to me, investors understand that there is a shortage. Consequently, they ratchet up their orders in the hopes of getting the amount of shares that they really want. We had ten times the number of orders than the number of shares that we planned on issuing. Therefore, as far as the investors were concerned, an allotment of over 10% of the actual order that was placed would be considered a success.

On the first day of trading, a large portion of shares usually changes hands between investors trying to make a quick buck. Consequently, in order to increase the demand, bankers allot shares to those they believe will continue to hold onto their shares. In our case, the bankers took advantage of an option that the company grants the underwriters which enabled them to eventually sell 15% more than the amount of shares that the company had originally planned on issuing. This option is referred to as a 'greenshoe,' in honor of the first company that executed such a transaction in the history of Wall Street. Once all the shares were sold, the bankers immediately entered the market as buyers in order to bolster the value of the stock. The logic behind the greenshoe option is that stocks occasionally "slip" out of the underwriters' hands. In other words, the share price goes up significantly and becomes too expensive for them to continue buying it. Therefore, the greenshoe essentially constitutes a generous bonus that the bankers receive from the issuing company.

Tom showed me the allocation table, and I noticed that giant firms, like Fidelity & Wellington, received about a quarter of their requests, whereas other investors received considerably less.

Accordingly, few shares were allocated to private customers or Israel. Tom was convinced that the problems with the SEC would be solved. He scoffed at that obstacle, but he wasn't the one who would have to face the SEC and convince them to allow us to go ahead with the issue.

By the scheduled day of the IPO, Friday, March 26, 1993, we left Oppenheimer and headed downtown to the Millennium Hotel. For $250 a night, I received an incredible view of lower Manhattan.

Mar 26: The day of the IPO, and the problems with the SEC had yet to be resolved. I woke up this morning with the sense that I had to mentally prepare myself for the possibility that the offering would be delayed and that I would have to remain in New York for the weekend. By 9:00am, I was at Oppenheimer's offices, where we anxiously waited for the SEC to inform us of their decision. The underwriter's lawyer, David Lefkowitz, tried to calm me down, and I bet him dinner that the issue would not take place that day. We whiled away the time making phone calls to the SEC.

At 10:15 we received a call from our lawyer: "We are effective!" The SEC approved our offering. Screams of joy echoed throughout the office, and the IPO was underway. All the parties signed on the underwriting agreement, and we ran to the trading room at Wall Street to witness the incredible spectacle: our stocks were being traded on the NASDAQ and the name 'Gilat' was flickering on the screens.

The trading began at 10:32, and Gilat opened at $13.25. Within minutes, our price rose to $15. Just like the movies, the room is full of screens and masses of tense people are constantly shouting. All the sales people came to shake our hands with looks of admiration etched across their faces. The young woman who was assigned to explain to us what was going on also gave us an adoring smile, and the heads of the investment banks called to offer their congratulations. It was as if we were in a dream. It is difficult to describe the immensity of the moment.

And suddenly, with one fell swoop, it was all over. The stock concluded its first day on the market at $14.58. I left the floor even before the end of trading and was surrounded by a strange sense of emptiness. At long last — after three weeks of chasing investors across three continents; countless questions, both good and bad; myriad hotels, which I could no longer remember where they were or what they looked like; sleep deprivation; and presentations that I had long since memorized — the mad dash was over and an equally strange sense of silence prevailed. For the first time in months, I didn't have something to do that very minute.

I opened the top button of my shirt, undid my tie, and left the Exchange. My feet led me outside, and I aimlessly wandered the streets of Manhattan for hours, just to feel the freedom and immerse myself in the sense of victory that was awash with exhaustion. I knew that by tomorrow I would already be contending with new challenges, but I didn't want to think about these things just yet. Several hours later, I went to the airport and boarded the overnight flight to Israel.

When I arrived at Gilat's offices for the first time after the IPO, I was barely able to pass through the hallway, which was congested with bouquets and flower pots. One of the bouquets was larger than the rest, and I went over to read the card:

Dear Yoel,

For us all, this is enough. Our wish for you, though, is that you will continue to conquer new heights.

From the entire company stuff

It would be impossible to conclude without a few words on the party that the bankers threw several weeks later for everyone involved in the IPO. We asked to be pardoned, but they insisted and I got to spend a couple of hours with everyone that contributed to the great success. I was among the last to leave the fancy restaurant in central Manhattan. As I made my way for the door, the head waiter came up to me and asked: "Excuse me, but who is going to pay for all this?"

It turned out that none of the hosts had bothered to handle the bill.

"How much is it?" I asked.

"Seven thousand dollars".

My face turned colors, but I took out my credit card and paid up. Not everyone issues a company for over $100 million.

6

Growing Pains

We barely had a chance to bask in the glory of a company worth over $100 million,
when we were swept back into the daily grind. Once again, we were forced to contend with the never-ending problems of our major customer, Rite-Aid, as the system would suddenly freeze up and crash. Naturally, we received more angry calls with every passing day.

On May 4 1993, Rite-Aid initiated an urgent conference call with Spacenet and Gilat. Rite-Aid's participants were Martin Grass, Joe Phillips, and Nick Putz; while Spacenet was represented by Howard Svigals , who had replaced Jerry Waylan as president, John Mattingly, and Amiram and myself — who happened to be at Spacenet's offices — represented Gilat.

"How long will it take you guys to solve the problem?" Martin opened. "If you tell me that we have to wait another three months, I want out of the deal now!"

We didn't anticipate this sort of an opening, and the fun was just beginning. "We started installing the system in August", Joe Phillips continued. "It's already May, and it still doesn't work…We can't run our applications…, the response time is way too high… Do you have enough resources to get the system under control? Do you guys really understand your own system?"

By this point, all the Spacenet and Gilat representatives were in a state of panic. Howard was the first to recover from the shock. Bald and heavy, beads of sweat shimmered on his head as he attempted to formulate an answer. "There are no fundamental problems with the product itself", Howard stammered, "only software problems. We have other customers with thousands of sites that execute hundreds of transactions per minute…"

Before long, all of us were tripping over our tongues in a feeble attempt to reassure the Rite-Aid team that everything was going to be fine. I observed the Spacenet people and realized that they were not convinced that they could actually solve the problem. The relationship between the Gilat and Spacenet people were extremely tense. Although we were on the same side, they tried to blame us for the mess. Dark thoughts of newspaper headlines informing the business world that Rite-Aid has replaced us with Hughes kept racing through my mind. If my prophecy fulfilled itself, the collapse at Rite-Aid would be mere child's play compared to the collapse of our stock.

Martin's tone turned violent: "You haven't convinced us that you have any idea of what's going on. (He's right, I thought to myself.) -We'll think this through and get back to you in a few hours". Before the teleconference was adjourned, he asked that I — only me — call him right away.

My legs were trembling as I left the room and picked up the phone. I thanked him for the recommendations that he gave the bankers before the IPO and reaffirmed our commitment to the project. For his part, however, Martin did not let up: "Can they fix it?"

"Yes", I answered, "but they need time".

"They better succeed. I am well aware of the fact that your equipment works fine and that the problems are with their software, but you guys are their partners. If the problems persist, we'll be forced to terminate the contract. You had better get yourselves deeply involved in the project and start personally managing it. Your lives depend on Spacenet!"

As I reentered the room, the large group of Spacenet people, who were anxiously waiting for my return, stared at me with glances that expressed a mixture of hope and hostility. They had still not gotten over the shellshock. I gave them a rundown of my conversation with Martin and explained to them that time was running out. Everyone in the room agreed with me, and we decided to immediately appoint a crisis manager. Their choice was Joe Chisholm, an experienced operations engineer. Until further notice, the entire organization would report to Joe, and all the reports on Rite-Aid would be sent directly to him. Chisholm appointed an engineer to head the test lab and established a work plan and guidelines, which included the preparation of a report on every single crash. As well, Joe presided over a daily meeting that we also joined. Moreover, everyone agreed to a new division of responsibilities in all that concerned communications with Rite-Aid: Chisholm would speak with Joe Phillips and I would keep in touch with Martin.

I got back to Martin and described the work procedures that had been set up. Moreover, I asked to hold a daily teleconference with the Rite-Aid people. He instantly agreed and asked to personally receive a daily report on the situation. After our conversation, Martin got back to Howard and let him know that the continuation of the project was going to cost Spacenet a lot of money. Spacenet's new president nearly had a heart attack (I would have, too), but calmed down once he understood that it was only a matter of money. Shelling out cash is a far easier pill to swallow than losing your flagship customer. At least, this terrible day had ended on a slightly more optimistic note.

The talking stopped and we got down to business. Both Spacenet and Gilat were focused on handling this challenge, as solving the Rite-Aid problems became the primary objective of both organizations.

As if the problems with our own product were not enough, we soon discovered that Rite-Aid had replaced all their cash registers with new equipment, none of which had been examined by our engineers. In addition, new versions of software were being loaded on to the cash register on a daily basis, and each version had its own difficulties interfacing with our equipment. Despite the objective hardships involved in introducing two new systems at once, we were naturally blamed for everything.

We set up another lab at Spacenet with a hundred terminals. Rite-Aid sent us the new cash registers, and we conducted thorough tests. We reinforced the Spacenet groups with our own software engineers. The entire team toiled together on a revolutionary software version, which consisted of major changes and many new elements that were introduced by both Gilat and Spacenet's engineers. June 15th was the target date for installing the program. Under normal circumstances, no engineer in his or her right mind would upload such an extensive software package in one fell swoop, but we had no choice. This was a do-or-die situation, and we called it 'life or death version'. Everyone understood that our necks were on the line.

In order to bolster the war effort, all our top development people served long tours of duty at the Spacenet labs and at Rite-Aid, including Gidi, Erez, a product manager that had recently joined us, Danny and Osher, our key software engineers, and Arik, who arrived with his wife and baby daughter, born only weeks earlier. The entire team lodged in the nearby Holiday Inn for eight weeks.

I am convinced that the game plan we adopted is the only way to complete the development of a new product. A complex technological product — encompassing hundreds, if not thousands, of man years on the development of hardware and software — is bound to have its fair share of these sort of crashes. You have no choice but to contend with all the initial problems on the run.

On June 10th, we held another teleconference with Rite-Aid. The atmosphere this time around was considerably calmer, as three days had passed without so much as a single crash. Amiram presided over the discussion and asserted that, "The objective is to stabilize the system so that there are no crashes at all, or the number of crashes is negligible. It is only natural to go through a series of crashes after fine tuning an extremely large number of parameters in a system as complex as yours. However, if the tuning succeeds, it will not only stabilize the system, but improve its performance as well". Amiram also decided to send system engineers to Rite-Aid.

Rite-Aid concluded the meeting requesting to meet our senior staff. Consequently, Joshua, Amiram, and I made plans to be at their offices even before the engineers arrived.

Despite the tens of millions of dollars that entered Gilat's coffers after the IPO, we rode to the meeting at Rite-Aid in a junk car that only Joshua would buy. Naturally, the car broke down along the way, and we were in serious danger of not making it on time. Just the thought of having to swallow our pride and explain to them exactly why we were late sent shivers up my spine. We gave a call to Rudi, who was in charge of logistics at our office in the United States, and he drove two and a half hours, both ways and in his own car, in order to take us to Harrisburg, Pennsylvania.

Notwithstanding the delay, we got there on time and the meeting was fine. On the way over, we tried to think of how we would contend with their claims and demands. Joshua facetiously offered an original excuse: "But Martin, we're also Jews…". Fortunately, we did not have to resort to this. We convinced them that there was a direct connection between the glitches and their new cash registers, and showed them the results we received from the lab tests. Moreover, we mapped out our game plan for future versions, timetables included.

Although we knew that it would take another six months to finish the job, we were forced to commit to a four-month deadline. If we had cited the more realistic figure, they probably would have thrown us out the window.

"I am coming to Israel in October", Martin wrapped up the discussion. 'Let's hope that by then all the problems will be behind us".

"Maybe not exactly behind us, but close…", I cautiously summed up our end of the equation. We shook hands and parted ways on a positive note.

Naturally, the deadlines were pushed off a bit. The first version, which was scheduled for June 15, was installed on the 1st of July. An additional, larger version that was supposed to be released on July 15 was delayed until August 15. What we coined 'the mother of all versions' was slated for October 15. Martin came to Israel beforehand and comported himself in a dignified manner, despite the fact that there were still occasional crashes. He visited our offices, heard lectures, took in the sites, and was impressed. Moreover, he left us with a pleasant parting gift: "We'll start paying you again next month".

Avraham Ziv Tal, the legendary Israeli sales person, who was pushing distance learning systems at the time, invited me to a meeting with John Caldwell, the director of training and distance learning at the Ford Motors Company on August 10.

"The Japanese are eating us for lunch", John confided. "Our only hope is training and remote learning". He then embarked on a long discourse about his grand plan to save the empire: six interactive training channels for the dealers of Ford vehicles, which (in contrast to Israel) also serve as the garages that repair the cars. With a gleam in his eyes and emphatic hand gestures, John mapped out his vision: "Our mechanics will have access to multimedia channels. By merely pressing on a terminal with their grease-stained fingers, the mechanics could order a file that will guide them through the steps for repairing the gears of, say, the

1987 Escort that was dropped off at their garage". Today, in the era of the internet, this seems rather obvious, but in 1993 it was indeed a visionary concept.

As John avidly continued explaining his dream, I attempted to assess the customer's seriousness: Who are the decision makers at Ford? Do they have the budget for a project of this magnitude? What criteria will they use to select a supplier? What are the weaknesses that the system is supposed to overcome? And what is Ford expecting to gain from the construction and operation of this sort of network?

John then asked us to drop the prices to the ground — $4,000 for each installed dish and another $100 per month in service fees — but these were numbers we could certainly live with. He informed us that he had also turned to Hughes. In the same breath, John admitted that he "detests working with Spacenet". Why? For the same reasons that we had heard from others: "They never pick up the phone; never respond to your requests; and give the impression that they couldn't give a damn about anything".

Thereafter, I met with the IT project manager, Bob Everhart, a highly respected figure at Ford, and John Marshall, his communication assistant. For the first time, I discerned the tensions that existed between the training and communications groups over the control of the distance learning system. Everhart told me that Ford had good relations with Hughes, despite the fact that the latter was a subsidiary of Ford's arch rival, General Motors. As an aside, he hinted to me that he was aware of the problems Rite-Aid was having with our product. "How on God's Earth", I asked myself, "does he already know about that?"

John Caldwell set the timetables for the rest of the process. We would receive the Request For Proposal in October and our proposal would have to be submitted by December. Ford would then make a decision by the first quarter of 1994. "Except for moving into my house", John added, "Hughes is doing everything to land the project. You'd better get yourselves under control. If you have a chance, it's that Ford would prefer not to give business to our direct competition and not to be dependent on them in such a sensitive field as communications".

From Ford, we rushed over to Spacenet for a preliminary discussion on whether to submit a proposal. We were already somewhat familiar with how the market worked and knew that in these circumstances the company that wins the project is the one that cultivates the best relationships with the customer's decision makers and trend setters. Although Hughes had a considerable head start on us, we believed that Ford would ultimately prefer to avoid buying the system from the subsidiary of their arch rival. We goaded Spacenet into entering the race, and they appointed an experienced sales person to head a small team — too small for our taste — to start preparing the proposal.

On December 2, a decisive meeting was held at Spacenet on whether to submit a bid. Preparing an offer for a project of this magnitude — we're talking about a contract worth over 50 million dollars— would demand a huge financial investment. Moreover, quite a few staff members would have to put aside their ordinary responsibilities and plunge into the project. Therefore, we had to decide if the whole venture was worthwhile in the first place. I made all the arrangements for the meeting and set the agenda. A multitude of people assembled in the conference room and heard me explain why we should submit a bid, even though there was a large gap between Ford's expectations — John Caldwell's vision — and what the system was actually capable of doing. I outlined the main obligations we would have to take upon ourselves if we were to win the contract as well as our primary advantages and our most glaring drawback: we had no experience in the automotive industry. As usual, the Spacenet people took a negative approach. "It's a waste of time", they said. "Hughes drafted the bid themselves months ago in line with their own specifications".

Just as the discussion was beginning to heat up, the acting president, Howard Svigals, burst into the room. "We just received a telephone call from Rite-Aid, and there was another crash", he informed us, unable to conceal the agony on his face. The discussion screeched to a halt. Instead of discussing the Ford proposal, we started talking about Rite-Aid. I tried to get them back on track, but by that point Ford was the last thing on their minds.

In any event, Spacenet ultimately decided to go ahead with the Ford bid. Once again, we assumed the lead and asked Spacenet to place a technical writer, engineer, sales person, lawyer, cost accountant, and software manager at our disposal. This may sound like a sizable team, but it was actually undermanned considering the fact that the deal was worth over 50 million dollars. We took a mental accounting of the primary advantages that we had over

Hughes — price, the leverage of the GTE name compared to Hughes and GM, and our creativity in installation, integration, and services — and got cracking. We sent people to Ford dealers in order to learn their work procedures. Thereafter, we prepared precise descriptions of a typical site and the procedure of installing the entire system. In addition, we put together a list of the required material and a price table. I personally wrote the executive summary (another writing experience…), and flew in six people from Israel to help draft the proposal, which would be submitted in Spacenet's name.

By that point, we were fed up with our partners at Spacenet. Besides Ford, there were several other large projects on the table, but Spacenet acted as if none of this mattered to them. While Gilat made every effort, including lowering prices, to reel in every potential customer that came our way Spacenet remained ambivalent at best.

We expended a vast amount of energy on the Ford proposal. Although the quality of a proposal doesn't guarantee a contract – it is a good stage to dance on. The more comprehensive and attuned it is to the customer's requirements, the better the bidder's chances are. Our proposal certainly met the above-mentioned criteria. It filled seven thick volumes (if you placed them one atop the other, they were over three feet tall) and contained in-depth information on everything Ford had to know about Spacenet, our products, our customers, the key people in the organization, the proposed product, operation and maintenance, pricing, and more. Although the document was written in Spacenet's name, it was entirely the fruit of our own labor and we took great pride in it. In fact, the document would serve as the basis for all the proposals that Gilat submitted to potential customers in the years to come.

After receiving the offer, Bob Everhart led a team of Ford representatives down to Virginia for a meeting at Spacenet. The Ford people were impressed by the proposal and held a preliminary meeting with us on technical issues: the size of the antenna; our methods for accelerating the transfer of information; and the cost of the satellite transmission. A long discussion ensued on the installation process, including how long it would take us to deploy the entire network. At the end of the meeting, they showered us with praise for our serious approach and detailed proposal. The Ford reps also told us that they might pay a visit to Israel in the near future.

As usual, a bit of praise from a well-placed VIP never hurts and we started to search for personal contacts that might improve our chances of winning the bid. We got in touch with Richard Rich, the former "near" president of Ford and Mr. Manning, the president of a division at Ford. Moreover, we were assisted by senior officials at AIPAC (the pro-Israel lobby in Washington) and frequently consulted with Amnon Neubach, Israel's economic attaché in the United States, who was quite helpful.

Everything else appeared to be going smoothly so we concentrated our efforts on the Ford bid. However, just when we thought the coast was clear, we were hit by another powerful earthquake in the form of a scathing letter from Rite-Aid's Martin Grass: "We are fed up with being your guinea pigs. If the problems are not solved by April, then we're going to call the whole thing off!"

The letter appeared out of the blue. The entire network was already installed, and we were unaware of any unusual mishaps. Had we again reached the point in which we were oblivious to what was going on at Rite-Aid? A brief investigation revealed that they had loaded a bundle of new applications onto the system, and the crashes returned with a vengeance.

"Why didn't you tell us what's going on?" Amiram lashed out at Spacenet.

"We thought we could handle it ourselves", was their answer.

Yet again, we immediately entered crisis mode: Test labs were reopened, and development teams consisting of system engineers from Gilat, Spacenet, and Rite-Aid swung into action. We conducted version tests and controls, reinstituted the daily meetings and overload tests, and attempted to navigate our way through the customer's expectations. Martin lost his patience and called Spacenet parent GTE President every day. In turn, the latter would then attack Howard, who went through quite a difficult period. Lastly, Amiram and I vowed that we would put an end to this mess once and for all.

After a long dry spell in which we failed to land any new customers, we closed two major deals in early 1994. The National Stock Exchange of India purchased thousands of VSAT's in order to enable its brokers to transfer data and trade shares via satellite.

We reeled in the account thanks to an integrated operation that was orchestrated by Amiram and Yoav. The two ferried legions of men from Spacenet and Gilat to India and ultimately defeated the principal competition, none other than AT&T. The second bit of good news came from Mexico, where we bagged a large chain of electronic equipment shops thanks to the efforts of Phil, Gilat's first American employee.

As a result of the success, there was a strong feeling in the air that the company was on the verge of an imminent breakthrough. Gilat was adding five new employees per month. At this pace, the building on Barzel Street would not suffice for long. We were already a big company that provided medical and fringe benefits to our employees. Notwithstanding the staff increases and perks, there were complaints of burnout and Gilat experienced some employee turnover. In other words, we were going through all the usual problems of a maturing organization.

Gilat even had an in-house newspaper, which was called *Ha'tzahabon shel Yaron* (Yaron's Tabloid). The paper was the initiative of two engineers — Yaron Sofer, the product manager of the two-way product, and Nitay Argov, the quality control unit manager. Through their cynical writing style, Yaron and Nitay let off the steam that would accumulate due to their frustration with Spacenet, customers, management, and themselves. Despite the criticism that was aimed at us, the management, we helped them get the paper out to print. I didn't get in the way, and Amiram even occasionally wrote articles under a pen name. To follow is an excerpt from an article on our affair with Ford, which is indicative of the paper's spirit:

The Giant Gilat Cooperates with Midget Ford

In an impressive reception held in Jerusalem…Ford celebrated the receipt of Gilat's proposal. "We didn't believe that a company like Gilat would agree to give us a proposal!" admitted John Marshall, Ford's elated representative.

Gilat's representatives ambivalently informed us that they do not understand the reason behind the great joy: "This is not the first time that we agreed to offer a system to an American customer. Au contraire! Gilat has plenty of experience collaborating with American companies. We provide the muscles and they provide the Jewish brains", explained Mr. Alper, a member of Gilat's negotiating team.

The paper was a part of the Gilat environment for many years. We all looked forward to the next edition and knew how to digest its humor, even if it was occasionally too sharp for my own taste.

After submitting the offer to Ford, we patiently waited for the results of the bid. We naturally availed ourselves of contacts with connections with the Ford management and hoped that lady luck would smile down on us. On the face of things, our proposal was superior to Hughes in terms of the price and the product. The only advantage that Hughes had was their ties with the decision makers at Ford. However, they were indeed way ahead of us in this area and thus won the account. It turned out that two factors, both of which were connected to Spacenet, spoiled our chances: the problems with Rite-Aid and GTE's decision to sell Spacenet.

Nevertheless, we decided not to give in and considered an assortment of possible courses of action. One option was to write a letter to Evetrhart's supervisor at Ford. Another thought that crossed our minds was to pass on the information to the Detroit Free Press. The fact that Ford stood to buy communications equipment from its main competitor was quite a scoop. Such a transaction would not only endanger its communications operations, but could create information security problems as well. I conferred with Manning, a senior official at Ford, and he asked for a couple of days to scout out the terrain.

Manning got back to me and reported that it was a lost cause. Although our proposal was superb, the primary factor that turned the scales against us was the doubts surrounding Spacenet's future. Furthermore, the Ford team asserted that Hughes had an abundance of experience in the field and were convinced that they could do the job. Given Spacenet's uncertain future, they were simply afraid of taking a chance. I asked Manning to see if Ford's management would agree to hold another meeting with us on the subject, and I hinted that we would consider lowering the price even more. However, Manning explained that Ford doesn't haggle over money. "Once a decision is made at Ford", he said, "it's final".

Manning had made it clear that it was a done deal, and I was forced to throw in the towel. I was flat-out disappointed. We had made a colossal effort only to fall short because GTE decided to sell Spacenet the month before. We were better than Hughes on every line item and did a marvelous job. Our chances were excellent, but Hughes had manned the ramparts long before us. They had excellent intelligence, were in touch with the customer all the time, and forged strong relationships with many people at Ford; Spacenet didn't bother to do any of these things. Hughes was more expensive and their product was inferior, yet they were the ones that walked away with the prize. It was an invaluable lesson for the future. Fortunately, the defeat barely affected our standing on Wall Street. The stock dipped a bit on the day of the announcement, but quickly rebounded to its previous level.

At the time of the epic battle over Ford, a struggle was also being waged over the supermarket chain Winn-Dixie. Our competitor was Scientific Atlanta and their capable president Alan Freece, who eventually became a senior executive at Gilat. The company specialized in the supermarket niche and didn't even bother competing over bids in other fields. Heretofore, Scientific Atlanta had raked in all the contracts in this particular industry, but that was before Gilat appeared on the scene.

Winn-Dixie skillfully exploited the competition between the two rivals. As usual, Joshua commanded the battlefront while Spacenet went AWOL. In order to win the account, we were forced to concede to both the chain and Spacenet on nearly every issue. Gilat signed a letter of bondage with Winn-Dixie whereby they received the central hub unit free of charge, which constituted a savings of about $1 million. We also shelled out 280,000 dollars on development and purchased equipment from Spacenet for tasks that were entirely their responsibility; they should have paid for this equipment out of their own pockets. Moreover, we lent Spacenet many units, paid their commissions, and more.

Notwithstanding the humiliating expenditures and compromises, as far as Gilat was concerned the deal was excellent from both a financial standpoint and in terms of the momentum it generated for us in the American market. However, the entire episode also underscored just how problematic our relations with

Spacenet had become.

We first heard that GE (General Electric) stood to acquire Spacenet from GTE from an analyst on Wall Street in April 1994. Given our background as ex-military intelligence officers, we were disappointed in ourselves for failing to pick up on these developments earlier. Apparently, our connections with the upper level management of the Wall Street investment firms were not quite as intimate as we had supposed.

Upon hearing the news, I called John Connely, the CEO of GE Americom, which was a subsidiary of General Electric that dealt in satellite communications. After introducing myself and Gilat, and I asked to meet with him before the deal was closed in order to provide him with an in-depth look at Spacenet's VSAT business. I was aware of the fact that John had received reports that painted Spacenet's VSAT business as an unprofitable product line, while singing the praises of its treasure trove of satellites that were supposed to link up with GE's satellites. Consequently, it was incumbent upon me to defend our product to our new strategic partners.

Connely made a wonderful first impression. He explained the sales process to me and admitted that they were wary of entering the VSAT market: "We are watching numbers (financial metrics) like hawks", he said. Finally, he said that he would certainly be happy to meet me in person. It took me a while to understand the style at GE. They have perfect manners and say all the right things, but a couple of hours later they are liable to behave like wounded animals protecting their youngsters...

It was depressing to pass through the corridors of Spacenet in the days before the sale. I remembered how impressed I was the first time I was at their complex, especially with the hustle and bustle in the corridors which evinced the power of a large and creative company that was thrusting forward. However, this time around, it was a completely different story. This was the first time I had personally witnessed a phenomenon that I would later become quite familiar with. I dubbed this period in a company's life "the decline of the Roman Empire". Spacenet's employees were well aware of the fact that the company was going to be sold. On one hand, it was business as usual; on the other hand, though, everyone did as they pleased: Most of the staff were hunting for new jobs and looking out for their own interests. The sales people tried to cut self-serving deals and rake in some more commissions before the collapse. Accordingly, telephone and entertainment expenses skyrocketed, and there was no supervision over budgets. Everyone went out for dinner on the company's expense in order to bemoan their fate. The house is burning and they are all playing violins...

On May 18, five representatives from Gilat met with the executives of GE Americom at their headquarter in New Jersey. We prepared a presentation titled "Are VSAT's an Interesting Opportunity?" which sought to answer several key questions: Is this indeed an interesting market opportunity? Where did Spacenet go wrong? How can Spacenet be run more efficiently? The executives were treated to an in-depth survey of Gilat, our customers, the VSAT market, our accomplishments, and potential customer base, which by our count comprised over 100,000 sites. We also analyzed Spacenet's strengths and weaknesses based on our experience as their partner. Furthermore, we presented them with a mutually beneficial proposal. A joint partnership in the development of Spacenet's VSAT technologies. Alternatively, we offered to buy the VSAT business from GE Americom together with another partner.

The presentation went over rather well, as the GE Americom people took an interest and asked many questions. In addition, we conveyed all the points on our agenda in a coherent manner. That said - it took us a while to understand what a mistake we had made, a mistake that would have a profound impact on our relationship with GE for years to come. Instead of telling them that the Spacenet purchase is a complicated and dangerous endeavor and that the only chance for them to turn the company around was by cooperating with Gilat, we praised GE on their foresight and trumpeted Spacenet's potential. We told them that all they had to do was to tidy up the ship, run it more aggressively, and fire up Spacenet's troops; then the profits would start rolling in. Although we tried to give the impression that we were unperturbed by the change in ownership, it was difficult to conceal our true feelings, for Gilat's very fate hung in the balance. At the drop of a hat, GE could have decided to shut down Spacenet and cut its ties with us.

We were basically caught in a Catch-22. If we had told

GE that they could expect setbacks along the way and would have to spend a great deal of time, energy, and money in order to turn things around, their expectations would have been lower and their patience considerably higher. However, this approach was also liable to scare them off and thus unintentionally make closing down the VSAT business a real option. We chose the easy way and ratcheted up their expectations. Consequently, we were forced to contend with the high standards we had helped create for many long years.

In any event, we advised them to convey a reassuring message of 'business as usual' to the concerned customers, employees, potential customers, and investors. Together we prepared a game plan for handling the customers. Both sides agreed on who would call whom and what to say. We also recommended holding a conference for Spacenet's customers, primarily in order to reaffirm the message that Spacenet was planning to honor all its commitments. Of course, we had a wide range of ideas on how to right the ship and attract big customers. Finally, drawing on lessons from the past, we asked them to grant us a more prominent role in marketing the joint product. In turn, the GE executives introduced us to Gino Picasso, their candidate for the position of Spacenet's president. Gino, a young and energetic Peruvian, said all the right things and most importantly had considerable experience in the field of business development.

GE has a particularly aggressive corporate culture. The parent company's strategy is that all GE operating companies have to be in first or no less than second place in any market they are involved in and aim to be the lowest cost producer in their business fields. In addition, GE runs a lean and mean organization: their executives possess technological depth and superior survival skills; and the corporation knows how to take advantage of its reputation and enormous financing capacity. Their basic premise is that strategy is not a long-term plan, but an evolutionary process that is a requisite for competing in a world of constant change.

Following the initial meeting, we entered a series of negotiations with GE for the purpose of hammering out an agreement between the two organizations. The talks focused on the product lines, market rights, and transfer pricing. We were contending with a classic problem: how can two distinct units, Gilat and Spacenet, compete against Hughes, a single organization that did it all? Within two years, the price of Spacenet's product fell from \$4,000 to \$2,400, but GE and Gilat agreed to conduct separate negotiations for every large deal. We also discussed the possibility of cutting down the size of the antenna. Finally, we presented GE with a list of our own candidates for Spacenet's new president, but quickly realized that there was no chance they would give any of them serious consideration.

Connely called on June 30 and informed me that the contract for the purchase of Spacenet would be signed that afternoon and that an announcement would be released to the press right after the ceremony. He asked to meet with us within a week for the purpose of reaching an agreement. I invited him to Israel and sweetened the invitation with a slew of enticements: meetings with international customers; a luxurious cocktail party with the country's elite; and a grand tour of Israel for him and his wife. The icing on the cake, which we offered to every customer or important guest, was a helicopter ride over the country. Connely couldn't resist and agreed to come.

In the meantime, 'the decline of the Roman Empire' at Spacenet had hit new records: The GE people were already parading through the corridors of Spacenet's complex in McLean, VA as conquerors. The seventh floor, which housed the senior executives and was always the complex's most extravagant wing, looked like a city in ruins. Everyone was trying to extract the maximum from the existing situation, before the anticipated dissolution in September.

Since GE was unfamiliar with Spacenet's staff, Joshua — who knew every employee in the company — forwarded them a list of names, each of which was accompanied by a grade: A- contributes, efficient, an exemplary employee; B- contributes to some extent, is somewhat efficient, a decent employee; and a C- negative employee, doesn't contribute, his or her departure would enhance productivity.

I also learned how big American corporations fire their staff. Upon arriving at their offices in the morning, some employees find boxes in their rooms or cubicals. "Why is there a box in my office?" they ask.

"Because you're going to be moving to another wing of the building next week", a manager replies.

Others ask, "Why didn't I get a box?" the others ask.

"Don't know. We didn't receive any instructions regarding your situation".

There are also the heart-wrenching scenes of subordinates being called into their supervisor's office, where they are handed their walking papers. Meanwhile, the teary-eyed ex-employees discover that while with the boss, someone already took the liberty of packing their belongings into a cardboard box. Before they can so much as regain their bearings, a security guard escorts them out the building, without so much as being able to enter their computers one last time or part ways with their friends at work.

These traumatic scenes made quite an impression on me. When Gilat was later forced to initiate a painful, yet necessary, downsizing process, I did everything in my power to let go of the employees in a more compassionate manner to avoid trampling on their dignity as human beings.

In the midst of all the mess in Spacenet, we decided that the time had come to deal with a long list of topics that were likely to impact Gilat's performance and progress over the next few years: How do we become the market leader? How do we increase our market potential? How do we continue to ensure our high level of quality? How do we prevent our corporate culture from eroding as a result of our continuous growth?

It was incumbent upon us to reorganize our sales operations. Moreover, we reevaluated our problematic level of dependency on other companies and the way we supported our customers. Finally, we had to overcome our characteristically Israeli, arrogant attitude towards customers. For example, by the water cooler, some of the engineering staff members would refer to our customers as "those monkeys".

Conversely, we also made note of all our positive attributes: fulfilling the mission no matter what; a potent capacity for development; wonderful human relations; a voracious appetite for success; our staff's understanding of how crucial it was to preserve our status as the price leader; and Gilat's overall competitiveness and willingness to fight over market share with a 'knife between the teeth' attitude.

During the first months of 1994, a new topic was placed on our agenda that had nothing to do with a new bid or some frenzied competition. Gilat's operations were dispersed among three buildings on Barzel Street. For the first time, we began to openly discuss what would subsequently come to be known as *"Beit Gilat* (Gilat House)". It was no secret that not all of us were thrilled with our offices on Barzel Street. Both the location and the work conditions left much to be desired. Moreover, we were humiliated at having to maneuver past pot holes, broken curbs, and the countless garages and grimy workshops that lined the crowded street, especially with important customers and dignified guests in the back seat. I am certain that any VIP that had previously been to Hughes' or Spacenet's luxurious complex cringed upon taking in the sites that Barzel Street had to offer.

As a result, we began to seriously examine the possibility of constructing a new facility and received several interesting offers. One of the properties was located in Kiryat Aryeh — an industrial park in Petach Tikva (a large town near Tel Aviv) — adjacent to a factory that produced cooking oil, *Aitz HaZayit* (the Olive Tree). The questions we faced were both philosophical and practical: On the one hand, does a high-tech company need to own its own building? And does the fact that we have money justify an investment in real estate? On the other hand, there were the difficulties of constructing infrastructures in leased buildings. Like all our competitors, in order to conduct essential testing we required a veritable forest of antennas on the roof, some of which were quite large. How could we be sure that our landlords would continue to let us turn their roofs into a gallery of assorted satellite dishes and huge antennas.

Similar to all Gilat's executive meetings, manifold opinions were bandied on every conceivable issue regarding the potential lot in Petach Tikva. Amiram, skeptical and cautious as ever, recognized the need for infrastructures, but questioned whether a building was a sound investment decision. The next morning, Amiram even drove from his home in Ramat-Gan (another large town bordering Tel-Aviv) to Kiryat Aryeh to see whether he was willing to make the commute on a daily basis. Yoav was amused by the idea and came up with yet another gem: "At least the value of the company will have a floor — the value of the building". I was somewhat amused myself, but more enthusiastic than the others. Accordingly, I raised a few marketing arguments in defense of the purchase: "We'll construct a building that fits our needs with large antennas, special infrastructure for quality control, and test ovens…Imagine the route visitors will take through the building. It will make quite an impression on them and help us close deals".

Simona was the most vehement objector. She had a somewhat better take than the rest of us on the implications of such a step. She foresaw many of the problems that would accompany the move, including the cultural problems. "In the end, we'll have no choice but to place some of the employees in windowless offices and in open spaces", she claimed. "These factors will cause a lot of damage to the company's culture and moral". Another reason against the purchase of the property in Kiryat Aryeh was the oil manufacturer next door. A factory that processes oil isn't exactly the most sterile or orderly place in the world. What's the point of replacing the sewage of Barzel Street with the smell of burnt oil and the smokestacks of Kiryat Aryeh?

We debated the issue for months and all arguments, both for and against, seemed to make sense. It is also worth noting that Gilat's board of directors opposed the purchase on the following grounds: "It's not considered acceptable for high-tech companies to construct buildings". We were indeed among the first high-tech companies in Israel to even raise the issue. In the end, we received an ultimatum from the owner of the plot to either take it or leave it, and we decided to take it. As fate would have it, a couple days after signing the purchase contract, the oil factory closed down. Spurred on by what we referred to as 'beginners luck,' we rolled up our sleeves and turned our attention to planning the new facility. Among its many attractions, the building included the following: a spacious 'antenna farm' on the roof; easy access to massive amounts of cables that were laid down for the purpose of connecting the engineers' offices and the labs to the roof; demonstration rooms; central equipment rooms; R&D labs; training rooms; and more. In sum, it was a facility that was tailor made for our needs — the dream of every high-tech entrepreneur…

Meanwhile back at Spacenet, we were surprised and overjoyed to hear that GE took us up on our offer to appoint Joshua as the vice president of marketing at Spacenet. We held an emotional farewell ceremony in his honor at our offices in McLean, and I delivered the keynote address:

"A mythological founder; the only one among the founding

group that had any experience in high tech; the man who became the organization's central ideologue; One morning, Joshua got up, took his family, and set out for the United States. He explained to me that the vice president of marketing at Gilat has nothing to do in Israel…

We all know Joshua. He is hesitant, rough around the edges, aggressive, and at times a bit violent. It's not easy to work with him, but he is one of the company's main assets. He would never take 'no' for an answer; a man of principles, who works twenty hours a day and thinks about Gilat during the remaining four; he is dedicated and robust. Joshua is a living embodiment of the cultural power and *modus operandi* of the Gilat management team: he knows every last person at Spacenet, and there is no one better at getting decisions passed in the corridors or landing orders in the restroom…

You, Joshua, were an integral part of Gilat's success so far. A large share of the orders arrived by virtue of your efforts. Even if we occasionally had our differences, Gilat, its customers, employees, and shareholders, as well as your fellow founders, highly appreciate your work. You not only had an impact on Gilat, but on the entire industry. Now go leave your mark on GE as well".

After parting ways with Joshua, we began to prepare for John Connely's visit to Israel. Even before the visit, we started to sense that John was going to be tough. He made his position crystal clear over the course of a long telephone conversation: "We are not interested in co-owning Spacenet with you. The company will earn 25 million dollars in another five years and will be worth 250 million dollars".

I was obviously disappointed by his decision. We had envisioned a true partnership with GE with closer ties, a semi-united team with mutual exclusivity, and collaboration on the international market. However, Connely left no room for doubts; to paraphrase his position: "GE is the boss, and you will listen to what we have to say. Don't forget that we are the multinational company and you are merely Gilat, a small company from Israel". Connely also informed me that GE was not interested in investing in Gilat and that Gino was appointed president of Spacenet.

Notwithstanding the disappointing conversation, Connely's week-long visit in Israel was a huge success. To this day, his wife tells me that of all the places that she has been to, Israel was the most beautiful and memorable. We gave them the red-carpet treatment: meetings with the ministers of finance and communications and six of Gilat's largest customers, who flew in from abroad especially for the occasion; arranged a special cocktail party in his honor at the Tel-Aviv Hilton to which all the country's dignitaries were invited; organized a visit to Jerusalem and the tunnels beneath the Wailing Wall; and scheduled a captivating helicopter tour of Israel, which culminated with a landing on the Masada (a desert fortress where Jewish rebels made a heroic last stand against the Roman army). It was evident from the final meeting with Gilat's employees that Connely was truly moved by the entire trip: "There will no longer be Spacenet and Gilat", he said; "there will be Tel-Aviv and McLean. Gilat, its culture and way of thinking, will ultimately leave its mark on GE".

My response was no less emotional: "You have revived the spark in our eyes. When I see the determination and the desire for victory in your eyes, alongside GE's aggressive culture, I cannot help but call upon all of us 'to set out to battle and slash our enemies'…"

I was not surprised by Connely's reaction, for he was neither the first nor the last to part ways with us in such an exalted state. These visits were always a success. Understanding Israel's riveting history — which most of our guests, including the non-Israeli Jews, were not familiar with. Add to that the helicopter ride and landing on Masada amidst the thrilling, biblical vista and it always leaves a huge impression on every guest. Atop the fortress, a tour guide recounts the events that transpired on that very site over 2,000 years ago and explains its special significance to us Israelis to this day and age — "Masada shall never fall again".

While they were still under the spell of by the desert and the bravery of Masada's defenders, we would take our guests to Gilat, where they encountered a different sort of passion — one of creativity, faith in the righteousness of our path, and a winning cultural and technological powerhouse. All this, alongside meetings with the country's most power figures (who almost always took part in these events) resulted in every one of our visitors to depart Israel on an emotional high. Moreover, our relationship with them were always ratcheted up a notch, as we took advantage of the opportunity to befriend our guests and their spouses. Many of these friendships have endured well after the business ties have ended, for it is a known fact that people don't give money to strangers and prefer to do business with people they like.

We felt that Gilat was on the verge of a significant breakthrough. This optimism was expressed in the 1994 annual report in which I outlined the objectives for the year to follow. On account of its four sides, we dubbed the plan the "Diamond Mission":

1. To become the lowest cost producer of quality products.
2. To become the market leader by expanding our product line.
3. To increase the number of strategic partners.
4. To build new distribution and marketing channels and develop mass applications.

"Gilat counts among its assets the wining spirit and strong commitment of its employees", I wrote to the shareholders. "This spirit — along with the company's financial base, its aggressiveness, and its creative utilization of opportunities — should enable Gilat to achieve its mission". The annual report also showcased the optimistic figures from the past year: a 60% increase in revenues compared to 1993; in 1994, Gilat accounted for a quarter of the total small antenna units that were sold throughout the entire world; we sold rural satellite-based telephony products in China and Russia that provided telephone services to remote areas. "This year has brought a sense of maturity to Gilat", I wrote in the report's conclusion. "It has been a very encouraging year for consolidating our present position in the industry, expanding into new areas and ventures, and widening our customer base and installed base".

Without any advanced notice, Gilat's positive momentum was bolstered by Simon Bull of COMSYS, a leading market-research company in England. Simon, who is considered an authority on the VSAT market, put together a comprehensive market survey. He contacted every customer who purchased a VSAT system and secured all the pertinent details of each transaction: the product that was purchased, how many units, the level of customer satisfaction, and more. It was difficult to wipe the proud grins off our faces as we read Simon's report: "The major challenge to Hughes over the past two years has come from an unlikely source — the combination of GTE

Spacenet and Gilat. Gilat was a tiny Israel-based company which introduced a highly functional yet cheap one-way data broadcasting system… The company had big plans for an interactive product and was constantly talking about its relationship with GTE Spacenet — an understandable attitude from a company as small as Gilat. GTE Spacenet on the other hand, whilst never denying the fact, never really appeared comfortable talking about its joint-venture with Gilat. In 1992, the two companies announced the Skystar Advantage. A new, low cost, highly functional interactive VSAT terminal based on a new satellite access scheme which was intended to sell for approximately $4,500 (compared to a market price of $9,000). Hughes reacted strongly and the first major contract which was fought over, Rite-Aid, was bloody and very cheap. For the first time a user obtained a price per site per month of less than $200. Since than Hughes and the GTE/Gilat combination have been locked in battles for major contracts. Some of which Hughes won…and some of which Gilat took. In each case the issue has finally come down to price per site per month which has been driven further and further down".

Simon then explained how "Gilat's system sold well internationally", such as India's National Stock Exchange, in China, Germany, Texas lottery network, Argentina, and Poland. He also noted how odd it was that the reaction of everyone in the international market — both customers and competitors alike — with whom he discussed the product was always the same: *'You mean Gilat's product?'* It appears that the connection to Spacenet has gotten lost somewhere along the way…"

In addition, Simon Bull reiterated how important it was for Gilat to sell its product via a strategic partner. There is practically no other choice for small Israeli companies but to work this way, even though it threatens to leave the unheralded company in the dark, without meriting the international recognition it deserves. However, this is not the case with Gilat, Simon noted. Even though the partner attempted to push the Israeli company to the margin, the customers know that the product belongs to engineers with broken English accents dressed in T-sirts and not to the grandiose and spruced up business people in suits from Spacenet.

"From the status of non-player in 1989", Simon concluded, "Gilat has become a central factor in this market due to its desire to work with other companies, develop its products, capture new markets, and offer new applications. GE is a big and powerful company that does not enter markets unless it intends to capture them. This, in turn, is likely to propel Gilat to the status of market leader".

This was the first time that anyone, ourselves included, had ever raised the possibility that we would vault to the top slot. The fact that the man behind the forecast was one of the leading experts in the field was a real boost to our egos, especially considering the fact that we were only in existence for all of six years. As the ancient Hebrew proverb puts it, "May you be extolled by the mouth of the stranger, and not your own".

Towards the end of the year, discussions were held on the strategic targets for 1995. These talks marked the first time that there was a substantial gap between our own expectations and those of our investors and the satellite industry's analysts. For example, we were suspicious of GE, and it was unclear how we would reach the sales levels and profit margins that we had set for 1995.

In fact, we were not the only ones nursing doubts. We invited the middle level managers to take part in the discussions and were astonished by the intensity of their complaints: a high degree of employee burnout; quick and unregulated growth; and the emergence of of red tape – bureaucracy – within the company (Gilat had 136 employees by late 1994). They also accused us of recruiting senior people from outside the organization instead of promoting from within and of being out of touch with the needs of the employees: "You are spending all your time at GE, on Wall Street, and with potential customers like Peugeot, and not with us", they lashed out at me.

"What can I do?" I answered. "I'm your foreign minister. I have to invest my time setting the backdrop, maintaining our strategic alliances, and bringing in new business".

Our middle level managers were asking for tools and pointed to the contradiction between the external success and internal exhaustion. They complained that they didn't have enough time for forward planning and wanted me to devote more of my time "inwards". In other words, they felt that I should be spending more time in the corridors speaking with the staff. We tried to respond to their complaints and, above all, made a personal note of all the issues that were raised.

As we suspected, the honeymoon with GE came to an abrupt halt. We soon found their aggressiveness and heavy-handedness were creating problems. The business model between GE and Gilat was rather simple. We built the hardware and sold them units at a profit, while they added the software, marketed and sold the product — an immense effort in its own right — and provided the customers with end-to-end services. However, they claimed that the service bottom line was in the red and that they were losing money because we were turning a profit. When two companies sell a joint product, there is inevitably going to be an ongoing struggle over the profits, as both sides soon become dissatisfied with the profit-sharing agreement. So long as the financial statements remain behind closed doors and each party is unaware of the other's profit margins, there is a reasonable chance that everyone will remain content. However, Gilat was already a public company that was legally obligated to publish financial reports. The troubles began once our numbers made their way to our partner's corridors. For example, when Spacenet's sales people discovered that they were purchasing our equipment at a considerable cost and that they were not being awarded commisions because all the profits remained at Gilat, they obviously started to voice their frustration. We explained to them that our profit margins from sales to Spacenet were rather modest, that we nevertheless allocated 40% of our manufacturing capacity to meeting their orders, and that nearly all our profits stemmed from other markets. However, our concerted efforts at persuasion were greeted with skeptical smiles, for they were quite familiar with our financial statements.

When relations start to get testy, this usually has an adverse affect on many different areas. All of a sudden, GE was less than thrilled about the fact that Joshua was serving as a vice president at Spacenet and wanted him to step down. Moreover, they prevented us from participating in meetings with customers, despite all our earlier agreements to the contrary. We got the feeling that they wanted to isolate us from the market and ensure that all the sales went exclusively through them. When the first discussions were held on extending the agreement between Gilat and Spacenet for three more years, they forwarded us a draft that we dubbed "a slavery agreement". To make matters worse, their sales of the joint product lagged behind our expectations. Nevertheless, they had the nerve to lash out at us on nearly every possible issue. I called up Connely in an attempt to clear the air between the two organizations. I had hoped that our good personal rapport would make a difference, but he told me to work things out with Gino at Spacenet. Needless to say, our relationship with GE and Spacenet was deteriorating at a rapid pace.

Gilat held a regular teleconference every quarter with our primary investors and the analysts that covered our industry for the investment banks. In all, about forty people would take part. During these meetings, we would survey the last quarter's financial results and discuss the central topics on the company's agenda. At the present meeting, most of the tough questions centered around our relationship with GE. As is my custom, I stressed the more positive aspects: "…Our products are the only ones that they are marketing, and they have completely stopped selling other products. The negotiations with them are complicated and entail numerous technical, marketing, and quantitative factors".

In addition, we held the first discussion on the possibility of executing a secondary offering on Wall Street. The first time around we went with Oppenheimer as our lead banker and Furman Selz and Lehman Brothers as the secondary banker, but since then things had changed. The leading investment bank on Wall Street, Goldman Sachs, was looking to get a foothold in the Israeli market. From our standpoint, this was a wonderful opportunity to work with a top investment bank, which could very well have been our ticket to the major leagues.

Our current investment bankers were furious at us; and Oppenheimer spearheaded the attack: "They won't invest even a quarter of the attention that you will get from us", Stanley Stern warned us. "You're a drop in the ocean as far as they're concerned. You won't manage to turn on their machine. Your offering is too small for them. With us, you'll always be the king". In any event, the spirited bankers at Goldman Sachs were pushing us to complete the negotiations with GE, build the story — which is the critical ingredient in any offering — and formulate our plans for the upcoming battle.

However, hammering out an agreement with GE was no walk in the park. They reopened clauses that were presumably closed, increasingly tried to wring more concessions out of us, and slapped on a full-court press. After three months of negotiations, we were about to explode. At an emergency meeting, Gilat's senior management unanimously decided not to give in to their pressure. We were all adamant: "We won't manage to recover from a one-sided agreement", Amiram said.

Yoav added that, "It is preferable to incur the damage now instead of down the road. Later on, we'll be even more dependent on them".

Joshua, who probably had the best vantage point of all from his lofty perch as the vice president of marketing at Spacenet, took the most radical position: "I live and breathe the air in their corridors and pick up on how much they hate us. I would be hard pressed to say that a concession on our part would improve the air. It will only invite more pressure".

Several days later, I received a call from Nissan, our legendary sales person in Europe. "I have some good news and I have some bad news", he said. "The good news is that we landed Peugeot Citroën's chain of car distributors in Europe". This was indeed a major development, as the deal consisted of 4,300 sites and was thus the largest network ever sold in Europe. "And now for the bad news", Nissan continued. "There are rumors that Spacenet is developing an independent product for 1997".

We were still wavering over whether to execute another offering. The decision ultimately rested on the fateful question of whether we should disconnect from GE. In other words, could Gilat scrap its long-standing strategy of working with a large American partner and compete on its own? In the end, we decided to go ahead with the offering. We had to free ourselves from the dependence on Spacenet and reposition our story. Therefore, the primary objective this time around was not to raise capital, but to boost the company's profile and pull ourselves to the next stage.

As our previous bankers warned us, the 40 million dollars offering was appreciably less than what Goldman Sachs was accustomed to. Goldman assigned an analyst from the defense field, who was not really appropriate for our product, to handle our account. That said, Goldman Sachs possesses undeniable advantages: the quality of its people; the fact that they are considered the leaders on Wall Street; and their excellent connections with all the Fortune 500 companies in the United States. Nevertheless, they also have a few disadvantages that cannot be overlooked. So far as we were concerned, their cardinal fault, unlike our traditional allies on Wall Street, is that they refuse to commit themselves to small offerings. In other words, it was unclear if they would go out on a limb for us at the moment of truth. However, we were unable to resist their allure and went ahead with the offering with Goldman Sachs as our lead bankers.

Meanwhile, the relationship with GE was about to go up in smoke. As the game clock wound down, Amiram and Yoav rushed off to close a deal with our partner, as both sides felt that there was no other choice. Following hostile negotiations that were concluded with reckless abandon, the respective parties quickly hammered out an agreement, which could best be classified as a classic *hudnah* (Arabic for an extended ceasefire): GE undertook to purchase a specific number of units from Gilat over the next two years, whereas Gilat caved in on the price, the most important topic of all. We agreed to sell them the product at a price that was considerably less than what we had previously viewed as our absolute minimum. The marketing issues were intentionally left unresolved, and each side interpreted these clauses as it saw fit. The agreement was less than ideal, but we were left with little alternative but to settle with GE before the offering.

7

On the Verge of Taking Off

During the second half of 1995, some two and a half years after the IPO, we executed our secondary offering. For better or worse, the changes that transpired during the intervening years forced us to modify the emphasis of the story. Whereas the 1995 edition stressed the company's marketing efforts, the current prospectus underscored our technological leadership. The new prospectus drew a clear line between the developments of the VSAT market in the 1980s — the pre-Gilat era — and the 1990s, when Gilat played a central and pivotal role in the industry. Moreover, the 1995 prospectus set its sights on the new millennium in an effort to predict the products and markets of the future.

There was yet another significant difference: this time around we were not only selling potential, but achievements as well. We invested the money raised during the IPO wisely and had a solid product. Therefore, the prospectus did not focus on GE or Spacenet, but on the products themselves: one-way and two-way systems, and satellite telephony for remote areas. Nevertheless, we did make note of all our strategic partnerships and obviously detailed Gilat's financial accomplishments: an increase in sales from $5.6 million in 1992, before the IPO, to $27 million in 1994; a huge upsurge in earnings from $500,000 in 1992 to $6 million in 1994; and over the same period, the number of VSATs that we sold vaulted from 1,300 terminals to 6,620. The prospectus also sought to explain the reasons behind our optimistic forecast for continued growth at an annual rate of 30% to 50%: the expanding market; Gilat's rising market share; GE as a better partner than GTE; and that Gilat had new products which were only just beginning to bear fruit. We ended the prospectus with a page of pictures called "Gilat around the World", that mapped out the global reach of our networks.

But something was missing from the second prospectus; we were less focused. It lacked the exciting story that characterized its predecessor. Perhaps this is the reason why the first prospectus managed to get its point across in only forty pages, while the second edition required ninety. If truth be told, the offering itself was much more difficult. Not only did we present a technological vision that necessitated long, technical explanations, but the story was burdened with unspoken doubts, the most glaring of which concerned the future of our relationship with Spacenet. The overall message simply was not as catchy as that of the first offering: Instead of an innovative product that was being sold by powerful partners, we depicted a technological leader that offered an array of products across various, far-reaching markets. The original prospectus projected a powerful vision of an innovative technology that would reshape network communications; by the second, Gilat was a technology product store.

The 'road show' also proved to be more laborious the second time around. Our timing was poor, as two rivals, Iridium and Globalstar, correspondingly launched satellite systems that offered telephone services. The investors thus repeatedly asked us to explain what set us apart from the two upstarts. "A satellite is a satellite", the investors insisted, "so in what respects are you better than the competition?" In addition, the fact that the sales presentation consisted of many slides — nearly twice the amount of the IPO's presentation — only added to our troubles.

To make matters worse, it turned out that those who had warned us against working with Goldman Sachs were right. They are a superb investment bank and a large, well-oiled machine, but to our regret they are built for much larger offerings. Our stock value dropped by about 15% over the course of the road show. While we had hoped to issue the stock at a price of $40 per share, it eventually closed at $25, two dollars less than its closing price on the eve of the offering. Naturally we had a litany of complaints concerning our underwriters. Their commitment level throughout the entire process was lacking, as they didn't invest enough time on our offering. The bottom line is that they failed to generate enough momentum to spark a hot offering. Although we raised an additional $40 million, this was not the objective of the offering. We had hoped that the secondary offering would provide us with some positive exposure and catapult us to the next stage. Despite all the difficulties, the objective was ultimately attained, albeit at a lower level than expected.

In sum, the secondary offering could be characterized as yet another one of our growing pains.

At the time of the offering, we also prepared for TELECOM 95, an international tradeshow in Geneva. This sort of show is a test for every self-respecting company that aspires to take over the global leadership in its field, especially in the telecommunication sector. The exhibition, which is held every five years in the Swiss canton, is the premier event of the telecommunications world. It is spread out over fairgrounds that are about the size of a small suburb and features seven huge pavilions, each of which houses hundreds of booths. Hundreds of thousands of visitors flock to the show from all over the world. As a result, the exhibition is the central thoroughfare and a popular meeting place for everyone in the industry. Moreover, it constitutes a barometer for the entire industry, so that if you are not present — and in a major way — you don't exist. It is little wonder, then, that every company invests between $100,000 and $25,000,000 on the exhibit.

There are manifold reasons for exhibiting at the show: exposing the company and its products to many thousands of visitors; checking out the competition; pinning down strategic and potential partners; conducting a technological survey of the current state of the art; entertaining major customers and meeting with decision makers; participating in the daily cocktail parties; gleaning information from the network of contacts between competing firms; attending lectures; gaining an understanding of various political and technological points of view; and identifying the major trends in the fields for planning and strategic thinking.

We were not among the largest exhibitors at the tradeshow, but we prepared for the event with all the passion and ingenuity that had characterized Gilat since its inception. The key to a successful booth is rather simple: facilitating the visitors' transition from the pavilion floor to the presentation itself. However, in this sort of exhibition, the name of the game is knowing where to expend your energy and when to hold back. Not every visitor entering your booth is a potential customer. Therefore, it is critical to have a system in place that identifies the value potential of all the visitors so that you get an indication of how much of an effort to exert on each person.

With this in mind, we devised special forms to assess the potential of each visitor: People that were deemed to understand the technology and represented organizations with budgets that could potentially close a deal within a year were classified as "VIPs". Visitors that understood the technology to some extent and whose interest might eventually develop into a future contract were dubbed "Players", while those who neither understand our products nor were thinking in the direction of a project were classified as "Students", and we tried to 'boot' them out of the booth as quickly as possible.

For the most part, anyone who drops by a booth usually merits the attention of the exhibitors. During peak hours, however, an enormous number of people enter the booth. Regardless of how many exhibitors are manning the stations, many of the visitors are forced to wait their turn and some get fed up and leave. Therefore, it is incumbent upon the booth manager to ensure that all the VIPs are immediately embraced; that the "Players" aren't neglected and jump ship; and that "Students" don't waste the exhibitors' valuable time.

We thus formulated a structured battle plan, which Simona, our dedicated booth manager, implemented in the field. By means of communication devices that were fastened to the ear and mouth, she kept in constant contact with the three roaming exhibitors who constantly patrolled the booth. At any given moment, Simona had to know exactly who was in the booth and see to it that the most important visitors were given top priority. The three roamers, each of whom manned one of the booths axes, were charged with identifying potential VIPs and Players, quickly evaluating their backgrounds, and guiding them to one of the company's representatives (there were five to ten Gilat reps in the booth at all times). The roamers also served as the 'bad guys' who were charged with 'booting out' the students during peak hours. Just in case, there were one or two clerks, usually locals, whose job was to talk to meddlesome students who refused to make do with a glossy information sheet.

All the exhibitors adhered to the decisions of the booth manager. If Simona arrived with a guest, the exhibitor would immediately disengage up from the person they were talking to and receive the new visitor, and Simona would then cordially take the 'rejected' visitor to another rep — usually a lower-ranking official in the company hierarchy. There were also junior staff members in the booth who served as the distinguished VIPs' personal hosts, escorting the valued guests from one product to the next.

We also established clear guidelines for handing out material: VIPs could take whatever they wanted, including special books that we wrote about the industry (not necessarily about Gilat), which were published every four years. Uniform information kits were prepared for the Players, while the students had to suffice with a colorful page with basic information on the company and its products. The printed material was an expensive commodity, and we did not want to waste it on visitors who were clearly not going to be doing any business with us.

Ha'tzahabon shel Yaron (Gilat's company paper) devoted an entire issue to the exhibition. As usual, it managed to crack up the entire company with its unique take on the hysteria surrounding the visitor rankings:

> Right before going to print, the editorial board learned that, upon landing in Tel-Aviv, the select team from the Geneva Exhibition sighted four VIPs, eight Players, and a taxi driver among the crowd of people waiting in the arrivals terminal at Ben-Gurion Airport…

Throughout the ten days of the exhibit, we would get to the booth at 9:30 AM and close at around 6:00 PM. Every day, hundreds of people passed through our booth, including our key customers and partners. Our primary objective was to make sure that the VIPs merited the requisite attention and received all the information they wanted. Therefore, we ran the booth like an outright military command center. Every night, we poured over the completed forms and took down all the pertinent information — such as "the red-head with the trembling hand that was interested in telephony for Indonesia" — and plotted out our strategy for the day ahead. Although our evening staff sessions lasted deep into the night, we even found the time for an occasional dinner or cocktail…

We invested $500,000 on the exhibition, which was a far cry from the top 'big spenders'. However our efficient game plan and execution yielded a solid return on our investment. Every day, at least ten VIPs, twenty to thirty Players, and hundreds of students stopped by our booth.

Gilat's booth ran like a Swiss clock, as each one of our twenty regular staff members knew exactly what was expected of him (or her). Order and discipline were maintained at all times: The use of the conference rooms was pre-determined by the booth manager. Our representatives refrained from schmoozing among themselves, only indulged in a cup of coffee during breaks, dressed appropriately, and treated the guests with respect. We also designated time for our people to visit other booths for the purpose of gathering information and carrying out other assignments on the company's behalf.

As far as I was concerned, the exhibition was a smashing success. I met all our major customers, got an idea of what was going on in our market, and identified competitors and trends. Moreover, I had the opportunity to talk to the people who passed through our booth and get a feel for their perspectives and needs, particularly what they expected out of our products. I relished the smell of fire in the trenches…Gilat received substantial international exposure, particularly in the satellite market, and formed relationships with approximately a hundred VIPs and several hundred players. In fact, these connections eventually matured into over $100 million in sales.

The most memorable moment of the exhibition was the visit from Israel's minister of communications, Rabbi Raphael Pinchasi of *Shas* (a Sephardic, Ultra-Orthodox religious political party). Following his visit, Rabbi Pinchasi took me to the booth of MCI, then an American communications giant, now part of Verizon. Compared to Gilat's 120 square meters, MCI''s booth was spread out over 3,000 square meters. Their booth gave me an idea of what I wanted Gilat's exhibition to look like when we became a giant corporation. A red-headed booth manager — a real spark plug — greeted us and immediately escorted us to a senior vice president, who received us in one of seven luxurious conference rooms. A brigade of young MCI representatives in spiffy uniform wandered about the pavilion floor. Their job was to entice people into the booth for a promotional film that was screened every half hour. After every film, a lottery was held and the winner —usually not a random choice — received valuable prizes. Next to each product was a product manager, who explained the merchandise with the help of an amplification system and a presentation. I counted over

150 MCI employees in the booth, tens of whom exclusively dealt with identifying VIPs. At any given moment, there were no less than thousands of guests in their booth, so that over the course of the exhibition hundreds of thousands of people must have stopped by. There was a distinct feeling of power in the air: 'We're MCI and we're conquering the world.'

The exhibition was Gilat's headline event towards the end of 1995. Shortly after, Amiram and I put together the annual stockholders report: "This year was the fifth consecutive record year for Gilat. Sales grew by 55% over 1994 and net income grew by 40%. Gilat's share of the interactive VSAT market increased from 15% to 32%...
Gilat — together with its alliance partners GE Spacenet and GTECH — holds a dominant position in Europe, with more than a 40% interactive VSAT market share, including two of the largest networks in Europe: the PSA Peugeot Citroën dealerships with 4,300 sites, and the UK Lottery, with approximately 2,000 sites...
In October 1995, we completed a second public offering and raised approximately $40 million for the company.
In 1995 Gilat firmly established itself as a key player in the VSAT industry. We are closing the gap with the competition by leveraging on our core strengths of low-cost manufacturing, high-quality products and strategic alliances. As the world of telecommunications evolves before our eyes, we are confident that our technological edge, resources and spirit will enable Gilat to become a cornerstone of our industry".

Above all, the report articulated our feeling that Gilat was primed for another major breakthrough. Some of the deals we closed were practically delivered to our door step on a silver platter, and our new products were selling nicely. The company's image was outstanding, as we emitted an aura of innovation, quality, and operational excellence. Things were going our way.
Despite the feeling of victory, we were surprised to find that the annual strategic meeting, at which targets were set for 1996, was slightly different than its predecessors. Upon examining the sales and profit targets for 1996, we felt as if a towering obstacle had been thrust in our path. In other words, even if we were to have exerted a backbreaking, all-out effort, the targets were simply

unattainable. Moreover, a hint of exhaustion, my own included, had seeped into the meeting for the first time. Although it was undoubtedly a successful year, our joy amounted to five minutes of pure satisfaction presenting the annual results. That fleeting moment would be followed by weeks of enervating thought over the central, nagging questions: How could we ensure that Gilat would continue to grow in the coming year? What measures should the company take in the immediate future? What was going to be the 'next big thing' and how could we guarantee that Gilat would be the one to introduce it to the market? And what could we do to avoid falling into a rut? From a personal standpoint, all this planning was followed by months away from the family in unfamiliar airports and desolate hotels, consumed by worries about the future of the company that I was heading and the hundreds of employees that I was responsible for.

"Seven years ago, I established a company with four other partners", I thought to myself, "and all of a sudden the world is taking us seriously. Hughes no longer considers us a fly-by-night operation scampering between its formidable legs. They are taking us seriously, fighting us at every point along the way, and refusing to concede so much as a single deal. Do I have the strength for another year of this? Will Gilat's fighting spirit and determination simply vanish one day? Will we know how to cope with a changing market? And will we manage to fend off hungry upstarts that are willing to plow their way through those same tunnels that we took so much pride in crossing only several years earlier?"

For the first time, we seriously considered the possibility of selling the company. There was no shortage of offers, as large companies such as Comsat, Samsung, and Lockheed Martin showed an interest in us. Several weeks before the strategic meeting, we met with the executive in charge of defense and space at Lockheed Martin. We sat there for an entire day and discussed possible avenues for collaboration. Before parting ways with a handshake and tons of future plans, he cast the following offer our way: "Maybe I'll buy you guys up and be done with it…" We could have closed the deal in a flash, but we didn't want it badly enough. Presumably, GE would also consider buying the company, and we thought we could attract IBM as well. Gilat was hot merchandise, and we were sure that someone would surely put bags of money on the table. Perhaps the time was ripe, as the one-way market was maxing out and new competitors were entering the two-way market. There was a strong likelihood that one of these up-and-coming companies would adopt our model and launch a successful, inexpensive product.

Fortunately, the sense of exhaustion did not penetrate the ranks of our employees, partners, or customers. The troops continued to encounter the same Gilat spirit: determination, innovation, and creativity. We shook off the ennui, rowed out of the doldrums and returned to our former selves. As usual, we formulated an offensive strategy, which entailed new products, telephony for the two-way product, and an emphasis on the development of 'futuristic' internet products (at this stage, the internet was still an unproven network sandbox, much less the World Wide Web).

Nevertheless, I ask to be relieved of my duties of the daily management of the company and transferred some of my responsibilities to Amiram. I was appointed the chairman of the board and Amiram was appointed president and COO. After years of feverish work, I felt that I had to liberate myself from the daunting sense of being a prisoner of my success. The shaky relationship with GE had significantly contributed to my exhaustion. The agreement that we had signed with them did not solve the problems it was designed to do, and relations continued to deteriorate at a steady pace. GE may have signed on the dotted line, but their intentions always seemed to be in question. Every discussion with GE ended with an argument, and every deal was fraught with grueling negotiations; on more than one occasion I felt as if I was trapped in the Grand Bazaar of Istanbul.

Notwithstanding the heavy burden, there were also moments of immense satisfaction. For example, the construction of *Beit Gilat*, the company's new office complex, had reached final stages. Simona, the 'architect' of Gilat's new home, was also charged with planning the new 'living arrangements.' On April 1, 1996, several weeks before leaving Barzel Street for *Beit Gilat*, we convened a preparatory meeting on all that concerned the move. Some $10 million were invested on our new headquarters, and we wanted to convey the significance of the move to the staff. "You will be spending the majority of your waking hours there", I told them. "Please take care of your home…"

For me, the most memorable moment of that meeting was the chapter that I read to all the employees from C. Northcote

Parkinson's *Parkinson's Law* on the effect that a new headquarters has on an organization:

…(W)e might turn with relief to an institution clothed from the outset with convenience and dignity. The outer door, in bronze and glass, is placed centrally in a symmetrical façade. Polished shoes glide quietly over shinning rubber to the glittering and silent elevator. The overpoweringly cultured receptionist will murmur with carmine lips into an ice-blue receiver. She will wave you into a chromium armchair, consoling you with a dazzling smile for any slight but inevitable delay. Looking up from a glossy magazine, you will observe how the wide corridors radiate toward departments A, B, and C. From behind closed doors will come the subdued noise of ordered activity. A minute later and you are ankle deep in the director's carpet, plodding sturdily toward his distant, tidy desk. Hypnotized by the chief's unwavering stare, cowed by the Matisse hung upon his wall, you will feel that you have found real efficiency at last.

In point of fact you will have discovered nothing of the kind. It is now known that a perfection of planned layout is achieved only by institutions on the point of collapse. This apparently paradoxical conclusion is based upon a wealth of archaeological and historical research, with the more esoteric details of which we need not concern ourselves. In general principle, however, the method pursued has been to select and date the buildings which appear to have been perfectly designed for their purpose. A study and comparison of these has tended to prove that perfection of planning is a symptom of decay. During a period of exciting discovery or progress there is no time to plan the perfect headquarters. The time for that comes later, when all the important work has been done. Perfection, we know, is finality; and finality is death…"

All the founders were truly terrified by the move from the flowing sewage and dilapidated sidewalks of Barzel Street to the state-of-the-art facility (what Parkinson would have referred to as the 'perfect headquarters') in Petach Tikva. "Profitability is inversely proportional to the size of the lobby…", we told the employees at every opportunity. Furthermore, we hammered home our firm desire to perpetuate Gilat's fighting spirit, energy, passion, faith, and pride.

A most impressive house warming party was held a couple of months later. Gino Picasso, Spacenet's president, arrived with an entourage of executives and gave a moving speech. Bob Lessin, who was in charge of investment banking and investments at Smith Barney, declared that he was proud of the company and its development, but that he would only sell its stock once the company bought a private jet (a mistake that we fortunately never made). In addition, Dan Meridor, Israel's finance minister, graced the occasion with a short toast in our honor. The event concluded with a special performance by Yehuda Poliker, one of Israel's most respected and inspirational performing artists. The concert was held in a thorn field next to the building, which was manicured especially for the performance. All the employees erupted into unbridled dancing as Poliker did his thing. There was a true sense of joy and enterprise in the air — a sense that we were changing the world. We had made it to the big leagues.

The annual report for 1996 was submitted to the shareholders at the end of the year. Like its predecessors, the 1996 report was optimistic and festive: *"Gilat prospered during 1996,* our sixth consecutive year of growth. Our momentum was fueled by the move to our new facility, in Petach Tikva, which has enabled us to expand the production lines and upgrade the quality of our R&D operations. Our market in interactive VSATs...has grown dramatically from 15% in 1994 to 25% in 1995, all the way up to 37% in 1996".

"Will this trend continue? We would like to quote Comsys, a well-known research company devoted to the VSAT industry: 'Gilat's achievements over the past few years have been extremely impressive. It has managed to take a new VSAT technology into an established market and carve out a considerable market share.'

"The market is the message, and we are listening hard".

COMSYS's Simon Bull opined that 1996 was the first year that Hughes was finally ousted from its seat as market leader and we didn't foresee any obstacles that could stop or even curb the product's momentum. These were indeed strong words that warmed many a heart at Gilat. What did we do to deserve such praise? How did we get through the years of growing pains, a difficult phase that many Israeli companies have failed to survive?

A company that aspires to become a successful international company faces many challenges. Consequently, it must possess the following attributes in order to overcome the obstacles that are thrust in its path: an extraordinary research and development capability, which is manifest in the form of reliable products that are constantly being improved; and, the ability and desire to sell and market its wares. There is no better feeling than the satisfaction of a successful sales person who represents a leading company with quality products during an upbeat period. Sales people are the front line of the war effort. They work alone in the trenches, holed up in third-rate hotels in exotic countries, building strong relationships with powerful and demanding customers. These relations are the lifeblood of the sales process.

We learned that companies lose deals when they fail to identify key players on time. Relations with the customer's decision makers must be strong. Moreover, the management has to be aware of the company's own most glaring weaknesses. For example, we knew that our customers perceived purchasing equipment from an unknown Israeli company to be a risk. Lastly, deals are won by focusing the entire organization's attention on the target, working with the customer at all relevant levels, and positioning yourself as a leading company. In other words, companies attain their goals by investing a great deal of time and effort focusing on the customer, making him feel personally that your success is only achieved by his success.

We had a ruthless competitor in the form of Hughes. We referred to them as the "evil empire", for they reminded us off the empire in Star Wars that went out of its way to defeat a tiny band of rebels. Hughes was a company with over $1 billion in annual sales. It grew by 20% to 30% per year, had an army of over 3,000 employees, and was the subsidiary of a humongous organization (General Motors). Hughes builds and operates satellites and was in its hay day the largest supplier of satellite television services in the American consumer market. Moreover, Hughes boasted a full line of quality products and an inexhaustible arsenal of weapons. Its aggressive marketing operations consisted of scores of offices and subsidiaries throughout the world. Hughes' corporate culture demanded that its people not lose so much as a single deal. Moreover, they were well aware of their power and skillfully exploited their advantages. Every time we competed with them over a deal, for example, their opening line was always, "Why take a risk on that tiny, anonymous company from Israel?"

Over time, we learned their weaknesses and deftly took

advantage of them. Above all, they had difficulties positioning an inexpensive product. This was the crack in their armor on which we concentrated our efforts. Despite the fact that our backs were to the wall, we waged an aggressive campaign against Hughes and attempted to under-price them at every turn. We focused on the VSAT market in which we boasted a superior range of products, a complete product line, reliability, and a lower price. Our entire company would hone in on the target at hand and wage heroic battles to capture the high ground. Gilat endeavored to forge a competitive advantage, or what I referred to as "a gun in a battle of knives". By dint of all these attributes, we managed to defeat Hughes on a regular basis.

That said, market share is attained by winning the right deals; namely the large, strategic contracts that resonate throughout the entire industry. Gilat was very successful in this field, as we found the way to reel in a large share, perhaps even most, of the key deals. As a result, we slowly but surely burnished our reputation as the skilled under dog until we became the hot name in the industry.

Gilat placed a great deal of importance on its corporate culture and thus constantly endeavored to improve and cultivate its cultural prowess. We developed wonderful human relations networks and fostered an atmosphere that encouraged people to think on their own and express their opinions freely. An open door policy existed at all levels of the organization, which allowed us to build consensus. Our dynamic culture was also responsible for the faith in the 'righteousness of our path' and the dedication of our employees, who carried out their missions with 'a-knife-between-the-teeth' mentality. Practically all our employees were devoted, passionate, assiduous, and robust. Gilat's staff was indeed the secret behind our success.

Above all, Gilat had a gift for unwavering focus. We dealt exclusively in the VSAT market, developed only a limited number of product lines, and worked with a few large customers. These factors constituted a powerful vector. Whenever the situation called for it, we used the vector as a laser beam that drew all the organization's energy on a pinpointed target.

This is how you win.

8

Winds of War

1996 was an excellent year. We experienced growth in all key areas. Sales were way up, we developed new markets in new countries, improved our products, and toiled over new developments. It was the company's fifth consecutive year of growth and our workforce expanded as well. The telephony products, which were independent of Spacenet, also sold well. A young generation of strong product managers and development groups emerged from the ranks and began to make a name for themselves. Our reputation was outstanding, as the "Gilat" brand was increasingly identified with dependable equipment that does not break down and as a company that supports and takes responsibility for its products.

The best possible proof of our success came several weeks before Israel's 48th anniversary. One morning, I received a surprising telephone call from the Ministry of Industry and Trade. Every Independence Day, during the official ceremony of state, twelve torches are lit by prominent members of Israeli society. "You have been chosen to light a torch", the official informed me, "by virtue of Gilat's contribution to Israel's industry and the recognition that your Israeli company merits throughout the high-tech world".

"I am flattered by the selection and it is a great honor", I instinctively replied, "but please choose somebody else. It really doesn't suit me".

"Before you say no", the official insisted, "consult with people. Speak with your father. He'll tell you what it means to light a torch on the Day of Independence of the State of Israel".

In the end, I was persuaded to take part and the ceremony was both impressive and moving. I felt that I was not only representing Gilat, but the country's entire high-tech sector, which had then begun to gather momentum. Gilat's own ascent was no less than stirring, as there was only one area that where we appeared to be slipping behind: our relationship with GE and Spacenet.

As usual, the problem was a matter of dollars and cents, as every dollar that we earned came at their expense and vice versa. Our relationship was akin to a couple in the same bed with each side pulling the blanket in its own direction. Same bed, different dreams. GE felt that they were losing a ton of money on our VSATs, while we were turning a profit on every deal with them. Their hostile attitude toward Gilat percolated down to all levels of their organization, beginning with the executives, who took the rap for the sub-par balance sheets, and down through the sales people, who felt that the bonus money they deserved for reeling in fresh accounts was not reaching their pockets.

GE decided that enough was enough and demanded that we revise the terms of the agreement. Ironically, the first signs of outward hostility surfaced during one of Gilat's highpoints: the dedication of *Beit Gilat* (our new complex) in July 1996. GE and Spacenet sent representatives to our celebration, and their emissaries also took part in the series of periodical meetings that ensued. Four senior executives participated in the talks:

- Gino Picasso, Spacenet's young, charismatic, Peruvian president. I liked Gino. He was smart, energetic, charming and full of new ideas. It was unfortunate that we were on different colliding paths.
- Michael Augostoneli, an international sales manager that Gino recruited. He too was young and aggressive, and had a strong financial background, all of which suited GE's culture.
- Alan Freece, a legendary figure in the industry, who Gino brought on board to help him stabilize the organization. We also held Alan in high regard, and he later joined Gilat.
- The last representative was Joe Chisholm. Joe was the crisis manager during the Rite-Aid imbroglio and went on to become Spacenet's all-powerful vice president of engineering and operations.

Gino, who presided over the discussions, informed us of the new strategy that was being devised for Spacenet. More specifically, the new strategy was predicated on an in-depth study of Spacenet that was carried out by Booz Allen Hamilton, a leading strategic consultancy that charges hefty fees for its services.

From our standpoint, the meeting got off to a terrible start, as Gino opened his lengthy speech with an assessment of the joint product:

"The VSAT equipment's annual sales totals don't reach $1 billion. To this may be added related products, such as distance learning services and executive speeches to employees via satellite networks, which probably increase the sales volume to maybe $3 billion, but it's still a small market. The primary direction that we are striving towards is applications that would operate on the basis of our networks. The most compelling example is the ATM market in India that has expanded at a rapid pace. If we can charge a few cents on each ATM withdrawal, the profits will be enormous. This is the only way that Spacenet can meet GE's standards and increase its interest in this business. Only this sort of venture will convince the GE team to make a substantial investment in our company that will catapult us to the next level".

Gino wrapped up his speech, which he was evidently quite pleased with, and took a long look at our faces in order to gauge our reactions. Needless to say, his speech had a profound impact on us, but it was hardly the response that he had in mind. After his very first sentence, I was certain he had lost his mind. I peaked over towards Amiram; and from the look on his face, I knew that we were of one mind. We instantly realized that GE and Gilat were on a collision course. It was still unclear as to when the two locomotives would meet, but they were already moving down the track toward one another at break-neck speed.

After regaining our bearings, we attempted to bring the discussion back down to earth and present Gilat's second generation product to the Spacenet reps. From a technological standpoint, the new product was a significant step up from the existing product. Moreover, the fact that the equipment was slated to cost less than its predecessor underscored the fact that we were the lowest cost producer in the market. We also informed them that we had already begun to sell the product and that it had been well-received by the customers. However, it was obvious that the Spacenet people couldn't care less about our innovations, as they immediately shifted the discussion back to their pipe dreams. They opened with a long, rambling discussion on their third generation 'multimedia product'

— a magic catch phrase that at the time meant practically anything to anyone. According to their grandiose plans, the product would connect to the internet and video consoles and transfer information at overwhelming rates via a small antenna with a diameter of 45 centimeters; and all this at an extremely affordable price.

Gino claimed that GE had allocated $30 million to the new product development. Futhermore, GE indicated that if they met the designated development and sales targets, another $50 million would be forthcoming. "The dream is huge, and Spacenet will play a central role in its realization", Gino continued, "We plan on being the banker of the internet, ensuring that the majority of on-line financial transactions will be executed via GE platforms".

The Spacenet team rushed back to the United States, while we attempted to get over the shock and digest Gino's grand designs. Their plan, to our mind, was so unrealistic that we initially thought that they were merely letting us in on their fantasies again, as Spacenet had a tendency (way before the GE days) to toss around wild ideas that had no chance of ever coming to fruition. However, toward the end of the year, we began to receive reliable information from our sources at Spacenet that they were indeed developing the product, which they codenamed the "TurboSat". It was a revolutionary product with a small antennas and incredible throughput, which was slated to do everything except fry the customer's eggs in the morning. Needless to say, the TurboSat was the wildest dream of every entrepreneur, and the first units were scheduled to come off the production line as early as July 1997.

In light of these developments, we immediately inquired as to our legal status with Spacenet. We were especially interested in whether the fact that they were withholding information from us regarding the development of their new product constituted a violation of the contractual clause obligating them to disclose any new idea to us before they began development efforts. Our legal advisors' answer was unequivocal: Spacenet was in breach of our agreement. However, they also warned us that we would be best advised to provide Spacenet with advance notice of the new products that Gilat was developing before hitting the war path.

By the beginning of 1997, we understood that the state of war had advanced past the mere theoretical stage. Spacenet already began to act as if they were no longer dependent on Gilat's products and that the heroic TurboSat would ultimately enable them to carry out every deal and meet every requirement. Consequently, we began to seriously consider the ramifications of these developments. Some of our people claimed that Spacenet would never manage to get such a product off the ground and that we should therefore base our strategy on their inevitable failure. Alternatively, Amiram and I, who represented the 'conservative approach,' contended that there was no choice but to assume that they would succeed, even if they released the product much later and at a much higher development cost. I couldn't believe that an organization like GE, with its sky-high ego and unlimited resources, would enter a project of this magnitude and fail to go to market.

Three possible scenarios were raised during our discussions. The first, which ran counter to the Gilat fighting spirit, was to resign ourselves to the direction Spacnet was taking and agree to build and sell their TurboSat in the agreed shared framework. The implications of this course of action were obvious: our profit levels would plummet. Moreover, our resignation to the TurboSat and Spacenet's independence would constitute a huge concession to GE, which in the future would subsequently encourage them to squeeze us with all their might. In other words, Gilat would suffer a major setback.

The second scenario was to develop a rival product to TurboSat, establish ties with another service provider in the United States, and compete against Spacenet as equals. The radicals amongst us were not beyond adopting a third, devious course of action: sabotage. The intent was obviously not to plant a bomb in Spacenet's development center, but to employ completely legal, creative measures that would send Spacenet reeling. One step we considered was to purchase Diablo, a small development company in California that Spacenet contracted to develop some of its hardware. We obviously dismissed the third option, but I was astonished by the breadth of the ideas and degree of ingenuity in Gilat that was revealed at those meetings; they were indicative of the amount of thought invested in contending with our soon-to-be-erstwhile partners.

In any event, it became evident that Spacenet would soon try to sell their new product, even if it only existed on paper. From the moment the market heard that a new product was on the way, no one would touch the existing product — our product — for everyone would eagerly await the arrival of the mighty TurboSat.

The situation thus appeared to be rather bleak. Even if the TurboSat was a paper tiger, the fact that GE stood behind it was likely to have a disastrous effect on our sales, the value of Gilat's stock and the attitude of our other strategic alliances, for the market would immediately understand that we had lost our primary strategic alliances — Spacenet and GE.

Despite the looming crisis, we continued to behave as if everything was in order, business as usual. Our sales people continued to push our products and our support staff continued to serve our customers. Naturally, we exerted more of an effort on selling our telephony products, which we were not dependent on Spacenet. Gilat continued to radiate an aura of confidence that the cream always rises to the top.

Spacenet and Gilat agreed to hold the next periodic round of meetings on neutral territory: GE's offices in London. The agenda was rather ordinary and revealed the tensions building up beneath the surface. Both sides were scheduled to provide updates regarding their new products and Spacenet would also report on their acquisition of the VSAT business of a company called Tridom. Finally, a discussion on possible future collaborations between Gilat and Spacenet was also placed on the agenda.

As usual, Gilat spared no effort in preparing for the meeting and set aside several days for discussing the relevant topics at hand. GE's decisions were liable to threaten the continued existence of Gilat, and we thus conducted simulation exercises that examined the following questions: What was really important to us? How do we expand our market share? And what were the practical alternatives for our continued operations under the changing circumstances? One possibility was mutual exclusivity, whereby Spacenet would be the sole distributor of our equipment: we would only sell to them, and they would stop working with our competitors. A second alternative was non-exclusivity, whereby each side would be able to sell our joint products to whomever they please and compete directly against one another; we knew that they would never agree to this. We also discussed how to extract a final round of orders out of Spacenet and guarantee specific marketing rights in certain countries. In addition, a vast array of other, less crucial matters were raised, such as whether Joshua would continue serving as Spacenet's vice president of marketing. In light of all of the above, we were leaning towards arriving at some sort of compromise with GE. Our characteristic fighting spirit had not disappeared overnight, but under the circumstances there appeared to be no other choice.

Furthermore, Amiram conducted an in-depth study of TurboSat: its technical attributes; Spacenet's problems completing the product; all the relevant sales and marketing issues *vis à vis* timetables; product development; and most importantly whether Spacenet could complete it without Gilat's hardware. Amiram's efforts were somewhat hampered by the fact that Spacenet restricted our access to all information concerning TurboSat's development. In fact, we were clueless as to how far the product had actually proceeded. Nevertheless, Amiram was ready for a comprehensive technical discussion with the Spacenet team and planned to emphasize Gilat's ability to help them develop TurboSat. We also constructed business models for various scenarios: Gilat purchasing Spacenet — not that such an option was on the table — and the consequences of turning Gilat into an outsourced producer that manufactures exclusively for Spacenet at extremely modest profit margins. Lastly, we put together a document that analyzed sales of the 19,000 units of the product that Gilat and Spacenet had sold over the past two years. Even to our surprise, the figures showed that Spacenet's sales team had only helped sell 16% (3,000 units) of the total; the rest was sold by Gilat.

In April 1997, we flew to London and headed straight for GE's luxurious offices in the City. The meeting was between two companies that at least on paper were still partners in a successful product, but there was much ill will festering on both sides. Gino opened the proceedings with an attempt to alleviate the heavy tension. "We are interested in continuing the partnership between us for obvious reasons: we have a mutual rival in the form of Hughes; we have shared customers that we are both committed to; and we have quite a bit of experience working together". His words, which were so typical of GE, sounded so convincing that I was momentarily convinced that Gino actually meant every word he said.

Following my own opening remarks — in which I shared Gino's sentiments — and the rest of the preliminary formalities, we proceeded to the regular updates. They reported on their acquisition of Tridom, a manufacturer of VSATs. The company was acquired by AT&T in 1988, but failed to take off. Spacenet acquired Tridom primarily because they feared that Hughes would gobble up the company's customers. Tridom's VSATs were sold in countries where Gilat had exclusive marketing rights. Therefore, Spacenet's plans to replace Tridom's product with our joint product were somewhat problematic. We patiently listened to their explanations about how Spacenet and Gilat would only benefit from the purchase of Tridom, without any attempt on our part to question their assessment. The Tridom report was followed by long-winded speech about GE and the internet, which we were already quite familiar with. We then delivered a brief presentation on our future products for the sake of fulfilling our contractual obligations, but divulged nothing beyond what was required.

Without any further ado, we then turned our attention to the first comprehensive discussion on TurboSat. Joe Chisholm, the proud father of the newborn baby, repeatedly reiterated the number of patents that they possessed, their incredible software capability, the new product's features, and the vast amount of resources that were earmarked for the project. By that point, Joe had worked himself into lather, so all it took were a couple of pointed remarks from Amiram to agitate Joe and ratchet up the decibel levels of the discussion. Amiram tried to explain that we could provide them with invaluable assistance in developing the product, but Joe turned down the offer with the flick of a wrist, which essentially negated the possibility that Gilat would collaborate on TurboSat.

I sensed that the moment of truth had arrived. The attempt to act as if everything is "business as usual" had failed and an explosion was imminent. Moments later, I chimed in with a cynical remark of my own that lit the fuse. Gino was stomping mad and raised his voice at me: "It's always about you and your product. I am sick and tired of hearing about your side all the time. Either you understand what you have to do, or..."

We were stunned. This was the first time that their teeth had been bared in such an explicit manner, and we felt as if the tiger was finally out of the cage. All the Gilat personnel got up and left the room in a demonstrative fashion. It was imperative that we let them know that they had crossed the line. While we were out, Joshua explained to Gino that this was not how a senior executive behaves, and Gino realized that he had overdone it. When we returned to the room a short while later, Gino looked as if he had seen a ghost and apologized.

A short marketing discussion on the topic of product positioning ensued, but everyone was obviously unsettled. Nonetheless, we carried on with the meeting. Perhaps all the attendees felt that we had to end the day on speaking terms and not in the throes of an all-out feud. Before leaving, we scheduled a meeting for the following day. In contrast to accepted protocol, no one initiated a joint dinner, as both sides would devote the evening hours to evaluating the situation and drawing conclusions about the future of the partnership.

Amiram and I left the building and wandered through the streets of London in an effort to digest what had happened and figure out where this was going. It was obvious that our worst-case scenarios were unfolding right before our very own eyes.

"What do you think they want?" I asked.

"The question is whether all of them want the same thing", Amiram replied. "Gino wants us to help finish the product and manufacture it for him because this will guarantee him a success. But Chisholm doesn't even want to hear about it. The very thought of Gilat getting involved in the development process drives him crazy. He is dead set against cooperating with us, and Gino can't twist his arm. Interestingly, Joe would be happy if we were to sell the product, as he has more faith in our marketing abilities than our technical skills. Regardless of their differences, there is no doubt that they are trying to force us to our knees".

"You're right", I answered, "but unfortunately we don't have a better alternative".

Needless to say, we didn't get much sleep that night.

The discussions the next day were anything but dull. They had done their homework and reached a couple of important decisions. At this stage of the game, Spacenet also wished to prevent an all-out war. They feared that all our energy and aggressiveness would be pointed at them. Consequently, they preferred to have us fill a marginal role in their own plans. When Gino explained to us how much they were interested in continuing the partnership, we could hardly believe that it was the same person that was "sick and tired" of us. In addition, he attempted to define Spacenet's minimum terms for any future collaboration: Spacenet would have to earn considerably more from the sale of the joint product, and we would have to completely abandon our marketing rights throughout the world. In return, they would be happy to let us manufacture the product for them.

Before we summed up the meeting, Gino presided over an interesting exercise. Each side listed what they believed to be the strengths of the other side as well as what they thought the other side would perceive to be its weaknesses. It was revealing to discover that Spacenet was well aware of the fact that we considered them a weak distributor which is unwilling to take risks as well as unfocused company with poor marketing skills. Meanwhile, we wrote that in their perception we were arrogant and greedy. Furthermore, we earn too much, so that the relationship is asymmetrical and unfair. The round of meetings concluded with a discussion on ideas for future cooperation, but it was evident to all of us that the summit had failed. War was in the air.

In the weeks that followed the London meeting, I filled my notebook with battle plans for withstanding the offensive that GE had in store for us. Our counter measures included plans for a new product that would not be connected to Spacenet; finding new strategic partners to replace them with; and even a preparing a first draft of a lawsuit against GE. It was clear that they would stop supporting us and our customers the moment the war broke out. As per Sun Tzu's sage advice in *The Art of War*, we planned to hit them with a well-timed assault at their most vulnerable spot. Until then, we continued to prepare for the confrontation.

That said, the battle plans didn't interfere with Gilat's daily operations, as we proceeded with business as usual – as if there was no war in the horizon. We landed major customers in new countries and increased sales to our regular customers. These developments reassured us that Gilat would not be abandoned by all our alliances once the war began.

We began to put our plans into action as the development of our substitute product got underway. The new product, which we dubbed "FlexSat" (Flexible Satellite), was designed to offer many more functions than our current product. Our general aim was to design a product that would be based on our hardware and completely independent of Spacenet's software. We conducted a search for potential partners and ultimately chose RAD Data Communications. Among the owners of RAD was Zohar Zisapel, my former commander in the Unit. A fine teacher and mentor, Zohar was also a good friend and my weekly tennis partner. I told Zohar about our predicament with the Americans, and he agreed to work with us right then and there. We reached an agreement on the terms of the deal within a few weeks. Zohar then introduced us to RAD's key players, and we immediately got cracking on the project.

By May 1997, Gilat and RAD had already devised a detailed plan for the development of a flexible product with all the features of our current product alongside a new feature in the form of telephony support. We planned to hit the market at a price of $1,995, one thousand dollars less than our regular product. In addition, we constructed a precise time table: the initial demonstration of the product was scheduled for the first quarter of 1998; we would start installing the system at our first customers during the next quarter; and by the third quarter, we would be selling production units. In addition, we positioned FlexSat *vis à vis* the other products on the market in an organized fashion and established a framework for migrating and acclimating existing customers to the new product. The smell of smoke in the trenches reinvigorated Gilat's management. Everyone was swept up in the excitement and wanted to be involved: to offer advice, enhance the product, and be a part of the new "shock troops". We debated the date of the product announcement and when to update our sales people. The last point was particularly crucial because once the sales people are aware of the plans, there's no turning back. Even if instructed otherwise, sales people only sell the latest product. We also decided who would be the first customers that Gilat would negotiate with. As usual, we quickly found a name: "Project Independence".

Relations with Spacenet steadily deteriorated. I maintained an open line of communication with Connely, but this was the only functioning outlet between the organizations. Oblivious to our battle plans, GE and Spacenet took measures of their own: Joshua was dismissed as vice president of Spacenet; they only talked to us about vital matters; and treated us like an outright competitor. Correspondingly, Gilat stopped searching for new customers for the joint product. Instead, we concentrated on repeat sales to existing customers, pushing our telephony products, and hunting for big opportunities outside the United States, namely all the areas in which we were not dependent on Spacenet.

We took the first blow of the battle during the third quarter of 1997. A number of analysts on Wall Street discovered that GE was working on a new product and even revealed its name. TurboSat could no longer be kept a secret, and the analysts began to confront us with difficult questions. As usual, we discussed everything in an open manner. During the mid 1997 quarterly teleconference, we even mentioned the possibility that the agreement between Gilat and Spacenet would be terminated at the end of 1998. Gilat's stock instantly plummeted, as there is nothing that investors hate more than risk. They assumed that Gilat was losing its prime ally and was thus about to enter a period of uncertainty. Consequently, many of our investors bailed out on us and rushed to sell their shares. Despite the vote of no confidence, we stuck to our guns.

Correspondingly, Spacenet was preparing for the official launch of TurboSat. We always had reliable sources in their corridors and managed to get our hands on their internal memos. These document included reports and analysis, which afforded us with a complete picture of the TurboSat's development: the product's capabilities at launch would be considerably less than what their sales people were currently pitching. However, they did a thorough job of positioning the product versus Gilat's existing products. Even though their internal memos admitted that their product was substantially inferior to our current product, they were convinced that their next generation would leave our product in the dust. In other words, Spacenet believed that they would make swift progress, while we would get bogged down and failed to upgrade our equipment.

According to Spacenet's timetable, they planned to initiate talks with their first customers in early 1998, but it was crystal clear they were lagging behind schedule. During the weeks that followed, suspicions began to seep into their own marketing memos that the product launch might be delayed. In fact, they even began to question whether the product would be ready at all. Consequently, we gradually came to believe that TurboSat may be a flop.

To begin with, we had little faith in Spacenet's marketing skills. The ineptitude of their sales people not only stemmed from their personal limitations. Sales people are the vanguard of any organization. In order to succeed — especially against an aggressive and successful rival like Hughes — the sales people must truly believe in their organization and take pride in its technology and products. Moreover, the sales process requires the support of every last member of the organization. Spacenet, however, never provided or, more importantly, knew how to provide this sort of unflinching, focused support. To make matters worse, the rest of the organization always accused the sales people of not doing enough: "The product is excellent but the sales people are running it into the ground..."

Above all, nothing bolsters an organization's morale more than the sweet smell of success. However, Spacenet rarely experienced the joy of victory; a slight edge in price, for example, was hardly enough for them to win the battle.

After thoroughly analyzing the situation that Spacenet was in, we decided that there was no reason to wage an all-out attack. Instead, we notified them that we would be prepared to manufacture TurboSat under certain conditions, but only once they had completed product development on their own. We also continued to keep an eye on their progress, or lack thereof.

Despite all the setbacks, Spacenet went ahead with the launching TurboSat. The announcement was accompanied by a huge public relations campaign, which proved, at least, Spacenet had a flair for public relations. The media was bombarded with a torrent of press releases, including the announcement of a huge deal with Enterprise, the car rental chain, for the sale of 1,500 units of TurboSat. The impression they made was that the Enterprise account was only the tip of the iceberg and that an incredible product was storming the market, without any intention of leaving prisoners...

The PR campaign indeed managed to arouse public attention. The trade press was flooded with articles on TurboSat, including streams of commentary by journalists and analysts on the relationship between Spacenet and Gilat. Our stock continued to drop; and worst of all, sales of the existing joint product came to a complete standstill. During a brief phone conversation, the Spacenet official that headed Project management told me that, "We're on separate paths now..."

Amid all the drama, we began to talk with Rite-Aid about renewing their contract, which was due to expire at the end of 1997. We were obviously familiar with Rite-Aid's hard negotiating style. How could we possibly forget the way they exploited the competition between Gilat/Spacenet and Hughes? It was only natural that they would try to take advantage of recent developments and play both sides off against each other in order to secure a substantial discount.

We reassembled our seasoned negotiating crew from the previous round in 1992: our mystery adviser, Joshua, Amiram, and I, along with the same cast of Spacenet representatives. Despite the tension between the two organizations, Spacenet had enough good sense to let us spearhead the talks. That said, even if we somehow managed to put aside our hard feelings, getting Rite-Aid to extend the contract was not going to be easy. We had to convince Rite-Aid that it was worth their while to stay with the old platform, despite the fact that the entire market couldn't stop talking about TurboSat. Moreover, we had to persuade them that our poor relations with Spacenet would not have an adverse effect on the product or the attendant services in the future.

The negotiations were tough, but we remained sharp and focused throughout. We offered them our most advanced model, of course. As part of the package, they would only have to replace the in-store units, while the antennae and the roof-top equipment would stay in place. The durability of the outdoor equipment saved both sides a great deal of money. Following a spate of dramatic twists and turns, our pricing won the day and they renewed the contract for another four years at excellent terms. "I don't even want to hear about Spacenet", Martin told me after we had shaken hands at the end of the negotiations. "As far as I am concerned, you are responsible for the system, and I hope that it continues to work as well as it has over these past few years".

Once again, the success with Rite-Aid testified to the fact that you can't replace the quality of a product and the relationships you have built over the course of a lifetime with a deck of slides about some new, unproven product, as promising as it may be.

After signing the Rite-Aid deal, we resumed our daily routine, while keeping a close track of developments on the Spacenet front. We continued to fight for deals that were not connected with Spacenet — the international market and telephony products — and our sales volume picked up at a nice pace. Moreover, we plowed ahead with the development of our new product. Unlike Spacenet, we managed to avoid leaking any details and all we divulged were a smattering of general statements about the new product.

In any event, Gilat was forced to wait and see how Spacenet's TurboSat would fare, and I took advantage of the down time by spending more time in Israel. At least my family benefited from the crisis.

9

Mergers and Acquisition

We were girding up for war when the winds blowing out of the corridors of Spacenet suddenly changed course. Not only did their rosy forecasts for 1997 fail to materialize, but their losses were much steeper than we expected. The situation at Tridom (the satellite manufacturer that Spacenet had recently acquired), was awful and trapped Spacenet like the Russians had done to Napoleon. Moreover, the completion of TurboSat was beset by constant delays. Worst of all was the loss of the Enterprise deal, which had been their pride and joy. The car-rental agency had patiently waited for TurboSat for months on end. But upon realizing that Spacenet was unable to provide so much as a demonstration of the new product, they decided to call the whole thing off and went to Hughes to buy their network . Spacenet had nothing to sell – and had nothing to show for their wonderful public relations campaign except yellowing newspaper stories and trade press articles..

On February 12, 1998, I received a most unexpected phone call from John Connely; over the past few months I had been the one initiating our conversations. His excuse for calling was to hear about my meeting with his boss, the president of GE Capita during a visit of high-ranking business executives in Israel. I heard that you met Gary Wendt", he opened. "What exactly did you guys talk about?"

I assumed that he was already well aware of the fact that I had vented to Wendt about my frustrations over Spacenet and the acrimonious events of the past year. In addition, I contended that Wendt's subordinates at Spacenet were making one mistake after another. Given the backdrop, I didn't want a long talk with Connely and gave him a curt review.

To my surprise, he began telling me about the severe

problems at Spacenet in an extraordinarily candid manner: "The Company is not meeting its financial commitments and is having difficulties developing TurboSat... I asked our CFO. to prepare an offer for you guys, which you'll soon be receiving. Check it out and let me know what you think. We want to sell you Spacenet in return for shares in Gilat".

Although we had raised the possibility so many times, I was caught completely off guard. "Look John", I replied, straining to conceal my astonishment and joy, "a lot of water has passed under the bridge these past few months and a great deal of damage has been done to the relationship. We will seriously consider any offer you send us., but don't be too surprised if the answer is no..." As my parting words echoed into the receiver, I was overcome with a sense of unadulterated joy, for there is nothing sweeter than the taste of victory.

As soon as I got off the phone, I burst into Amiram's office: "You won't believe who just called me", I exclaimed. "It was Connely, and he was begging us to buy Spacenet".

"It can't be!" said Amiram.

The seemingly inevitable showdown with GE had apparently been averted and a spontaneous party erupted at the Gilat offices that very night.

The proposal arrived several days later. By GE's standards, it was downright generous. They would sell us Spacenet for 30% of Gilat's shares and two of the five seats on our board of directors. The offer entailed real assets worth $85 million, including Tridom, and GE anticipated that the transaction would be executed at a value of around $200 million.

We poured over every last detail in the document. If this was their initial offer, then GE was clearly ready for serious negotiations and painful compromises. Best of all, this time around we weren't the ones feeling the heat. Needless to say, we agreed to enter negotiations.

The talks were set to begin on March 27, 1998, nearly a year after the ill-fated meeting in London. As usual, we did our homework. We sent GE a list of the topics to be discussed over the course of the negotiations: how the joint financial statements of Gilat and Spacenet would look in the aftermath of the deal; shedding production and administrative costs; positioning the products after the merger; our plans for replacing the equipment of Tridom's former customers with our own; the future of TurboSat (as correspondingly, negotiations were being held between Spacenet and the United States Postal Service over equipment for a system that would service tens of thousands of sites); management of Spacenet; the administration of Gilat after the transaction; possibilities for joint business development with GE; and, the steps to be taken before the transaction was consummated. Moreover, we provided them with a list of our non-negotiable conditions for the deal, which for a change were extremely one-sided in our favor.

We flew to New York for meetings at Manhattan's Sheraton Towers Hotel. GE was represented by John Connely, his CFO, and Gino, while I represented Gilat along with Amiram and Yoav. Although the cast was basically the same, the current talks and the London meeting were as different as night and day. Connely was extremely tense, while Gino had the look of a beaten man. They were encased in stuffy suits, while we sported casual wear and were quite relaxed.

Connely started the meeting. He repeatedly mentioned the word TurboSat. "We had the right idea, but Spacenet tried to create an exceptional product without the appropriate skills and knowledge. The acquisition of Tridom was also a mistake: their products are weak and unreliable; their customers call the support center four times more than our Gilat customers; and the service calls run much longer. The customers are unsatisfied, and we are at a loss for solutions".

Following what for GE and Spacenet was an embarrassing presentation on the current status quo, Connely got down to the nitty-gritty of the proposed deal. We were already quite familiar with the nuts and bolts of the offer, as we had analyzed it numerous times over the last month. This was followed by in-depth discussions on the topics of finance, operations, marketing, and sales. In addition, we raised the issue of joint ventures with GE. We naturally asked lots of questions to clarify certain matters. After three days of negotiations, we basically got what we wanted. Our biggest achievements were: the right to use GE's name for a period of three years; GE guaranteed to make up for the difference between the expected revenues for 1998, as per the original annual plan, and Spacenet's actual performance and to augment the financial 1999 results; and, last but not least, we were given *carte blance* over Spacenet and Gilat.

They wanted the deal badly, and we translated their desire into dollars and cents. However, the deal was not finalized on the spot, as we wanted some time to evaluate the offer before reaching a final decision. Nevertheless, we left the hotel with huge smiles wrapped around our faces, for Spacenet appeared to be ours for the taking.

Despite the need to think things through, convene the Gilat team, and reach a final decision regarding the Spacenet acquisition, I refused to put off my great dream: a month-long boat ride in the jungles of the Brazilian Amazon, which was planned for early April. I had organized a group of good friends (mostly from Gilat) and all my family members, we embarked on our journey right after the meetings with GE. From my standpoint, the timing was perfect. We were about to enter a completely different world where I would have more than enough time to brood over whether I was ready for the colossal task of merging Gilat and Spacenet into a single organization.

It was the most beautiful trip I have ever been on. We sailed down the Amazon on a yacht and explored the incredible jungles. Among our adventures was a torrential storm that lasted for hours; a heated battle against an army of marauding ants (which we barely managed to fend off), and myriad encounters with aquatic and land animals, many of which we had never even heard of before. We also ventured deep into the jungles on a fleet motorized canoes along the Amazon's tributaries. Throughout the journey, we made sure to find spots that afforded us with spectacular views of the sunset, sunrise, rare birds, and other incredible animals.

Even in the heart of the Amazon — home to perhaps the most enchanting places on Earth — I continued mulling over whether we could raise Spacenet out of the deep abyss into which it had fallen. Foremost among my concerns was whether it was possible to dispel the hatred and bridge the chasm that had grown between the organizations. I also tried to estimate the personal price that I would be forced to pay in order to realize this dream. It was clear that I would have to spend most of my time alone in the United States. My children were already in high school and it wouldn't be right to move the entire family to Virginia. The fact that I would have to be away from my family more often than not was indeed a heavy price to pay.

However, like any entrepreneur, I was fascinated by the challenge. The prospect of claiming the top industry spot in this market appeared to be seductively within my grasp. Moreover, I was captivated by the very idea that an Israeli company would swallow a larger American one and turn it into a powerhouse. This was an unprecedented feat, and I consequently felt as if we were on the verge of making history. Although Spacenet had more than its share of serious faults, it was rare for a company to acquire an organization that it was so familiar with. I wanted to become a 'gorilla,' a powerful and creative beast, and not a 'chimpanzee,' an inveterate imitator. In other words, I wanted to be the market leader; the one that takes the initiative and sets the pace. "Until this moment", I kept telling myself, "we were led by Hughes; perhaps now — by dint of the Spacenet merger — we could assume the lead".

I sat at the back of the boat for hours and immersed myself in thought. My fellow passengers, who were well aware of what I was going through, tried not to disturb me. Yet despite all my deliberations and against my better judgment, I returned home full of doubts and without a decision in hand.

While I explored the Amazon, Yoav received a mandate to run the negotiations by himself and proved to be at the top of his game. Pitiless and systematic, he didn't concede as much as one arable inch. Since he was among the most militant negotiators, each of his concessions was nearly unanimously accepted, and his reasoning was always convincing. Furtheremore, Yoav remained true to his convictions even in situations where he was at odds with a room full of opinionated people, including high-profile lawyers (each of whom charged Gilat hundreds of dollars per hour for their services). Yoav also traversed all the assorted mine fields along the way: the amount of shares that GE would receive; the purchase price that would be released to the press on the day of the announcement; the fees we would fork over to GE for using their satellites; and how to structure the transaction so that GE would be exempt from taxes. From the outset, Yoav made it abundantly clear that there were two issues that we were unwilling to compromise on: the TurboSat project would be discontinued; and Tridom would be shut down and all their customers' systems would be replaced with our equipment. Both of these conditions were hard pills for GE to swallow, but ultimately they had no choice but to concede to our conditions.

We also broached the topic of the contingency plans that both parties would adopt in the event that the Antitrust Division of the Department of Justice and the Federal Communications Commission (FCC) refused to authorize the transaction. However, since Hughes would still be bigger than the combined forces of Gilat and Spacenet after the merger, it appeared as if a veto was unlikely. Finally, over the course of the negotiations, we were surprised to see that against all odds, with the exception of Gino and a few others, no one at Spacenet had the faintest idea that a deal was in the making.

Even before the deal was signed, we began to think about the day after. We would have to assemble the employees of Spacenet, Gilat, and Tridom in order to explain to them the ramifications of the merger. The respective staffs would have to be reorganized, and a new management team would have to be recruited for Spacenet. Once the announcement was underway, we would have to touch base with the customers and worried investors to give them assurances that both of the companies were on solid ground. Finally we would have to explain the full implications of the acquisition to all the stakeholders, including all the painful measures that would be taken, such as shutting down product lines and people that would be sent home. We would also have to keep in constant touch with all the investors throughout the entire transition period. In addition, the organizations would have to carry on with their normal course of business, so that we would meet the quarterly financial targets and maintain our control over the entire joint operation. The first hours after the official announcement would determine the destiny of the entire merger.

There were indeed moments where I felt that we were losing our grip. In early August, Spacenet was closing in on the aforementioned gigantic deal with the United States Postal Service, who naturally wanted TurboSat, the product of the future. Spacenet had committed itself to the deal without so much as batting an eyelid, even though it was already quite obvious — at least to us — that TurboSat would never make it off the drawing board. To this very day, I can't understand how a huge and reputable company such as GE could commit itself to a deal worth hundreds of millions of dollars with one of the largest customers in the world when the product they were selling didn't exist and clearly never would. The decision makers were completely cut off from the people in the field, so that the instructions being passed along the chain of command were totally unhinged from reality.

If this was not enough, Tridom had recently developed a new product, which they had agreed to sell in substantial quantities to the Chinese. Before the acquisition, we were unaware of either the product or the agreement. GE begged us to pick up were Tridom left off, despite the fact that the new product was obviously not on our agenda. Needless to say, we were perplexed by GE's behavior. Only later did I discover that GE was then in the latter stages of negotiations of a locomotive deal with China, and they were worried that the cancellation of the Tridom contract would hurt their chances of landing the account. In any event, I promised Connely to consider the matter, and Yoav handed me the Tridom-China agreement file. After reading through hundreds of pages of the contracts, I decided that Gilat would refuse to supply the equipment required for there deal.

Once again, my notebook was bursting at the seams with battle scenarios, all of which were based on the assumption that the deal would ultimately fall through and Spacenet and Gilat would part ways. My plans included immediate measures for competing against Spacenet: steps for servicing our customers in the United States without the help of Spacenet; an aggressive sales pitch to our customers to go with Gilat after the seperation; accelerating the pace of FlexSat's development (even though it had become less of a priority given the abject failure of TurboSat); and locating new strategic partners. In other words, Gilat was on the verge of going solo.

The person that saved the day again was John Connely. By virtue of his wisdom and rich experience, he understood that we neither intended nor had any reason to back down. We stood our ground in the areas that were important to us and compromised wherever there was room for flexibility. In the end, GE caved in to most of our demands. The road to Spacenet was open, and we began to prepare for the signing of the agreement and the subsequent public relations campaign.

The most important part of any merger and acquisition is the message that is conveyed to the world. The message must be coherent, sharp, and unequivocal. In addition, the merger must contain a clear logic that can be articulated in one sentence. In our case, the message was as follows: "Vertical integration between a VSAT manufacturer and service provider". You absolutely cannot reveal so much as a hint of hesitation or uncertainty, as key investors, customers, and employees are liable to panic and abandon the company. The activities on the day of the announcement are akin to a major military operation. Everyone, from the general to the private, must know exactly what is expected of them and execute their role as flawlessly as a musician in a large orchestra. In other words, there is no room for improvisation, as everything must be executed in a precise and timely fashion.

The primary message that we sought to convey to the world was our connection to GE: The American giant was Gilat's parent company and largest shareholder; and our business cards were even adorned with their logos. Obviously, the link to such a reputable household name would only do us good. Throughout the negotiations, we insisted that they allow us to use their name during the next three years. Not many people in the United States were familiar with the name Gilat, whereas the name GE opened doors. It was also incumbent upon us to emphasize a couple of other advantages that the acquisition afforded us: service infrastructure in the United States, Europe, and Latin America; approximately 120 new customers throughout the world, which formerly belonged to Tridom; full possession of all the international marketing rights for every single one of our products (the majority of the marketing rights previously belonged to Spacenet); a bundle of orders; and last but not least, Spacenet's TurboSat technology was now in our hands. Although we already knew that there wasn't much behind those words, the rest of the industry still believed that it was the ultimate product and was anxiously awaiting its arrival.

We planned every last detail of the acquisition announcement in advance: the announcement to the press; a presentation for the employees; a teleconference with the mavens of the capital market; and messages to be discussed with analysts and customers. All the people that were assigned parts in this grand co-production were given detailed scripts. In addition, they attended practice question-and-answer sessions and took part in a full-dress rehearsal. We also tried to foresee and prepare ourselves for every possible contingency. Clearly, the day of the announcement was of immense importance to us.

The announcement was set for the 26th of September. I slept like a baby the night before and got up in calm, refreshed, and confident state of mind. A final briefing was held at 8:00 AM, and the announcement was released to the press at 8:45 AM. As the announcement was issued, I called several of our most important customers and investors, but didn't catch any of them at their desks — apparently it was too early in the morning.

By 9:00 am, all of Spacenet's employees were assembled in a hotel near the company's offices. Connely opened with a speech that was short and to the point. We had agreed to refer to the reorganization as a 'merger' in order to help Spacenet's employees digest the news. However, by his third sentence, Connely referred to it as a 'acquisition.'

Connely then gave me the floor, and I opened my speech with a brief personal note: "Spacenet and I go back a lot longer than most of the people sitting in the audience, as I have been wandering your corridors since 1987... I have gone through the best and worst years of my life with Spacenet", I added, "and I am ready to usher in a new era". Thereafter, I surveyed the situation at Gilat: its products, major customers, and plans for the future. I recounted our struggles to acquire customers for our telephony products and even provided them with a live update of a huge telephony deal that we had landed in Kazakhstan at that very moment. Spacenet's employees also heard about the secret behind Gilat's success: the lowest cost producer, dedication to quality and reliability, strategic partners, and a reputation for loyalty to our customers. "Gilat", I told them, without any effort to conceal my pride, "is the leader in market share: We are in first place in telephony; and together with Spacenet, we are in second place in the VSAT market". I explained to them the logic behind the merger and the objectives that we had set for ourselves: to become the world leader in the VSAT field; to reach a market cap of $1 billion; to create value for both our shareholders and employees, by distributing options to the latter; and to set the tone throughout the industry in all that concerns technological innovation.

I also highlighted the cultural aspects of the deal: "Unlike GE and GTE, Gilat focuses on the same field as you folks here in Virginia. Despite its small size, Gilat is highly focused and capable with a strong tendency for taking on opportunities. It takes great pride in its accomplishments and possesses a tremendous desire to win.

Furtheremore, our culture is based on the open door approach".
Accordingly, I gave all Spacenet's employees my email address
and told them that they could write to me on any topic. "You
can send me any email you like to **yoel@gilat.com**. I'm not
promising an answer the same day", I smiled. "In all likelihood,
the response will arrive after my next flight".

I informed them that I would personally head the transition
team and summarized my role: "I am in charge of the merger, and
I will be situating myself right here in Virginia. The merger with
Spacenet is currently the most important topic on Gilat's agenda,
and I will provide a personal example by allocating most of my
time to the topic. Together we will become a focused team and a
global factor in our field. GE plus Gilat".

The time for questions arrived, and the audience was far
from shy. I was inundated with questions on the nature of the
relationship with GE. For example, someone asked us to what
extent GE would be involved in the management of Gilat? In
response, Connely emphasized the fact that the company was our
responsibility, not theirs. He also informed the audience that he
would be serving as an active member of Gilat's board of directors,
but nothing more. Of course, I was asked whether we were planning
to let go of employees; and if so, how many? I obviously gave a
general and noncommittal response. Moreover, I was asked if we
would continue to provide the same health care and fringe benefits
that the staff had enjoyed until then.

After the meeting, Connely and I held a teleconference with
members of the investment community. Wall Street was apparently
optimistic about the deal, as by the afternoonGilat's stock rose by
12%.

Notwithstanding all the action, I waited with bated breath for all
the meetings to end, so that I could at long last take a look at the
exalted TurboSat, which had aroused so much fear in us. After
years of exclusion, I was the first person from Gilat to step foot in
Spacenet's laboratories. I wandered through the rooms in search
of the legendary product. Finally, the lab manager took me to a
room and pointed to eight, gray computer boxes that were tucked
away in the corner. "These are the units", he said.

"That's it?" I shrieked, unable to contain my shock.

"No, here are the circuit boards of the hub cards", he
replied and handed me five boards that were etched out by hand,

with numerous corrections.

I nearly fainted on the spot. I was expecting a sparkling, state-of-the-art system, which was capable of landing the space shuttle. Instead, I was gaping at several ordinary but abandoned units which lacked so much as a hint of the tens of millions of dollars that were invested in the project, or the wild dreams that were predicated on its success. Given the irreconcilable gap that stood between the grandiose vision and the meek reality, it was indeed an incredible surprise. GE had signed contracts worth hundreds of millions of dollars and these grey boxes were all it had managed to come up with? How could the heads of such a large company be convinced by a few engineers who believed that they could do it all? How could experienced marketing personnel get swept away by this mirage and sell a product that doesn't exist? And how could Gino, the smart and talented president of the company, believe that this was his ticket to eternity?

I refused to believe that these worthless boxes discarded on the floor were all that Spacenet had to show for a visionary project worth millions of dollars.

Although the deal was slated to be sealed in another three months, we were already the *de facto* owners. I set up shop in a small room near the copying machine. The door was almost always open, and anyone passing by, could — and usually did — exchanged a couple of words with me. At times it was a nuisance, but it was well worth it, as it reinforced my message concerning the new management style that we were trying to introduce. Likewise, more of our people started moving into the building. Ilan Kaplan, who was brought in to run the technical marketing group, notified everyone via email of his arrival and that he would be getting down to business at once. However, Spacenet's lawyers voiced their opposition and pointed to the fact that the deal was still not complete. We were indeed formally forbidden to start running the company, but we were not to be denied...

To begin with, we decided to replace most of the senior executives at Spacenet. We wanted people who were intimately familiar with the market and who would bring an aggressive attitude to Spacenet. It was only natural, then, that at the time our top candidates — Shelly Rivkin and David Shiff — were both employed at Hughes. Rivkin, our candidate for president, was a pleasant, older man with grey hair. He was a classic salesman and had a great deal of experience in manufacturing. Over the years, we had lost many a deal to Hughes on account of his efforts. In addition, he had a sister living in Israel. Shelly was presently heading the groups that manufactured Hughes' infrastructure for cellular equipment. The division was in decline, and the offer to run Spacenet, instead of Gino, was intriguing. Shelly and I hit it off from the get-go, and it was easy persuading him to leave Hughes.

David Shiff was a harder sell. He was the most accomplished sales person in the industry and was the one who closed most of Hughes' big deals. Every time we competed head to head against David, we were dragged into a lengthy war of attrition. He's a sharp, handsome, and charismatic man, as well as an elegant speaker, who is endowed with impressive presentation skills. Consequently, he is a natural at building relationships. To top of it all off, David is a proud Jew who was on the constant lookout for an Israeli bride…

We had already tried to lure him over to Gilat before we acquired Spacenet, but failed. "You don't stand a chance against us", he once told me. "I know what our next product is going to be and the one after that as well, while you guys are bogged down by Spacenet…" The balance of power, though, had shifted, and we applied heavy pressure on Shiff to come aboard. He vacillated and, as could be expected out of a shrewd operator like David, conducted drawn-out negotiations with us over the terms of his employment agreement, primarily the options. Upon hearing that Rivkin had already signed on, he decided to join us as well. Both of them began their new jobs at Spacenet towards the end of the year. As the one who was most responsible for their recruitment, I felt that we had added two star players to the roster who would lead Spacenet .

A great deal of time and effort was invested in the meetings with Spacenet's staff. These meetings were aimed at inculcating our vision and culture into the employees' consciousness and coping with the most pressing problems on the agenda. We brought over a group of Israelis who integrated themselves into the organization's middle management ranks and contributed immensely to the assimilation of Gilat's aggressive culture.

However, we quickly came to realize that the veteran employees weren't exactly thrilled with the changes. As far as they were concerned, we were attempting to dictate unfamiliar business norms to them. I learned an especially valuable lesson from the departure of Steve Angel, one of Spacenet's veteran employees and a personal friend. I got to know Steve over the course of our shared flights and visits to various sites and customers. He was a highly-experienced technical worker who comported himself in a direct manner. One day, without any advanced notice, Steve tendered his resignation. I couldn't get over the shock, as these sorts of things never happened at Gilat. Our employees always expressed their frustration well before they reached the boiling point, which provided us with enough time to tend to their problems and keep them in the company.

I invited Steve for breakfast in order to find out what had come over him, and relentlessly pounded away at him, without holding anything back: "Why didn't you say a word especially after all we have been through together?"

"What do you want from me?" he gaped. "I'm an American that thinks differently from you Israelis. For me, it's just a job. I never agreed to devote my life to this place, and I'm not accustomed to working so hard. I admire and respect you guys a great deal and wish you the best of luck".

Steve later returned to work with us at StarBand, but it wasn't the same.

In any event, the exchange with Steve really opened my eyes to the fact that not everything that was in our best interests was necessarily in the best interests of our new employees.

Insofar as coping with daunting work loads was concerned, the merger process was one of the most difficult periods of my life. I laughed it off and told everyone that my contract with Gilat entitles me to five hours of sleep a night and one meal a day. What most sticks out in my mind from this period is an image of myself at Reagan National Airport in Washington. I am in a suit and tie, schlepping a suitcase, and running to catch a flight, while simultaneously holding a conversation on my cell phone. During the early stages of the merger, I flew to at least two meetings a week with customers, held countless telephone conversations, and received about one hundred emails a day. There were very few moments of personal satisfaction. One of those moments was waiting for me when I returned home following the acquisition announcement. Upon entering the house, I found a letter from my beloved wife Simona on the table:

"Everyone occasionally gets excited about something or another. One person is fascinated for thirty minutes, another for thirty days, but an individual that remains captivated for thirty years is sure to become a success story... Your passion has never waned. Only yesterday, this huge accomplishment (the merger) was thought to be beyond reach, but by virtue of your passion and talent you have conquered this summit as well. All that is left for me to do is to wish you continued success and hope that you will continue and enjoy your next quests".

There were also several other moments of grace during these pressure-filled days. I first felt the power that our new position afforded us with during a meeting with a potential customer: Cumberland Farms, a New England-based company that owned a chain of 600 stores in gas stations throughout the country. As usual, we were competing head to head against Hughes. I sat infront of Cumberland's president, vice president of IT, and their communication people, who bombarded us with questions, but our story was beyond reproach: Like Hughes, the Gilat-Spacenet tandem constituted one entity that supplied both equipment and services. We were flexible, had prestige customers, and were willing to go the extra mile to land an account. The Cumberland team was quite impressed by our ties with GE. However, what made the deal for us was the fact that I — the CEO of the parent company — personally attended the meeting. My presence in their office testified to the importance that we placed on the deal, whereas their contact person at Hughes was merely a local sales person. I referred to the Cumberland meeting during the next staff meeting at Spacenet. In my estimation, the landing of the Cumberland deal constituted the turning point in the making of the merger.

Following the Cumberland meeting, we made another senior-level appointment at Spacenet, but this time the individual came from within the organization. Diane, Spacenet's former director of marketing, was charged with overseeing the company's investor relations. Diane has a strong financial background, an impressive appearance, and a gift for cultivating relationships. Her acceptance of the position improved the quality of my life. Investors consistently complained that we did not pay enough attention to their needs and that we were taking them for granted. While their first complaint was legitimate, they were off-base with respect to our professed arrogance. We were simply busting our tails to ensure the success of the business itself, so that we were left with little time to address their questions and issues. Until then, our investor relations effort was limited to stop-gap measures, but once Diane got on the job, we had a senior executive with all the time in the world to talk with the investors, prepare for the quarterly conference calls, take initiative, and find new investors. She did a wonderful job and the results were quite evident, as our stock steadily improved.

Company moral was climbing as well. We landed new customers, upgraded our service to existing customers, and the value of our options steadily rose. There was a true sense of unity throughout the organization. The new Israeli recruits set a personal example and their commitment left a visible mark on the organization. A new Spacenet was taking form before our very eyes.

Inevitably, there were also many trials and tribulations along the way. A new VSAT product featuring a completely new version of software was released to the market, and we installed the new system at Rite-Aid, the United States Postal Service, and other select customers. In the past, we had phased in new products by first installing them at a few sites. Only once the initial sites were stabilized would we install the rest of the network. However, this time around the pace of installations was murderous, as we furnished nearly a thousand new sites a month at the Postal Service and several hundred at Rite-Aid. Everything was proceeding according to plans, when a series of crashes completely shut down the transfer of data at both Rite-Aid and the Postal Service in one fell swoop. I was sure the screams emanating from our customer's mouths would be heard as far away as Israel.

The entire company made a concerted effort to solve the problem. Given the epic dimensions of the system failure and the fact that I was working out of Virginia, I decided to personally manage the crisis and presided over two meetings a day. As usual, the Israelis claimed that the Americans don't know what they're doing, while the Americans complained that the Israeli equipment doesn't work and that the Israelis weren't keeping them in the loop. I rushed over a large group of engineers from Israel, and all of us crawled under the hood to find out what went wrong. We temporarily reverted to the previous software version; this emergency measure guaranteed relative quiet, but severely hindered the system's overall performance. The employees immersed themselves in the never-ending task of repairing one bug after another until the crisis finally ended.

This was just the opportunity that Hughes was waiting for. Even after losing deals, Hughes continued to regularly keep in touch with the customers. Once the crises erupted, they waited for the moment the customer would throw in the towel. Some of our people were incensed by Hughes' behavior, and I attempted to calm them down. "There is no reason to get mad at them", I said. "The best course of action you can take is to concentrate on repairing the glitches. I guarantee you that a week after the systems are up and running, the customers will have already forgotten about Hughes". However, it was easier said than done, as sometimes it took us weeks to overcome the problems. The customers were on the brink of despair and we nearly joined them, but we gradually stabilized the systems. From the emergency room, we were transferred to the recovery room and from there to the ward, before finally being released.

Once we got over the hump, the pace of installations improved by leaps and bounds. From 5,000 installations per year we rose to over 20,000. We contrived a sophisticated installations procedure: A pilot group consisting of our own staff would install the customer's first sites, run its applications, and work out all the kinks. The group would also involve the customer in the installation process and demonstrate that the system was indeed executing all the applications that were promised. Once everything was in order, independent contractors would complete the rest of the job. These same independent companies also installed Hughes' equipment, and they informed us that we were installing more sites than our arch rivals.

Spacenet's 1998 Christmas party, the first one that I participated in, was rather low key. Gino summed up his tenure in Mclean, Virginia and thanked the employees for all the good times they shared. I got to meet the employees' spouses and attempted to breathe some life into the party. There were raffles, a festive meal, some token dancing, and an abundance of polite conversation. As soon as the party was over, I took off for Israel in order to get in a couple of days with the family

The New Year also meant that the time had come to submit the annual report to the shareholders. "The strategy of integrating the Spacenet people into Gilat is commensurate with Gilat's strategy itself", Amiram and I wrote. "Add strong leadership and a touch of market savvy to our outstanding technological capacity, and mix it all with Gilat's entrepreneurial spirit…"

We indeed began to reap the fruits of our concerted efforts.

10

Leaving the Competition in the Dust

By November 1998, the efforts to merge Gilat and Spacenet were in full swing. While I was buying necessaties in one of the shopping centers in McLean, I received a call from Yoav on my mobile. "All the investors and analysts are clamoring to hear about the merger with Spacenet", he informed me. "At least twenty people have called me".

"If so", I immediately responded, "let's execute another offering. Instead of setting up update meetings, we'll issue shares and raise money..."

"Great idea", Yoav signed off and immediately began to organize the offering.

Within days, Yoav had completed the structure of the offering: two lead bankers — Merrill Lynch and Goldman Sachs — and three secondary bankers — Oppenheimer, Lehman Brothers, and Salomon Smith Barney. The offering, which sought to raise between $200 and $300 million dollars, was enormous by any standards. At the time, it was the largest offering ever executed by an Israeli company. We received the blessings of our board of directors and hit the road.

As noted earlier, the story is the most important element of a successful offering and we had all the reasons in the world to be proud of ourselves. 1998 was a banner year. Sales totaled $155 million, and Gilat was the undisputed leader of the telephony market; in this year we enjoyed 60% worldwide market share of this product. In the data communications market, we had quickly narrowed the once-formidable gap between Hughes and Gilat to a mere seven percent: 47% versus 40%. And all this before we even began to take into account the sales of our new subsidiary,

Spacenet.

From one of the smallest communications hardware manufacturers in the world, Gilat rapidly expanded into a leading company with a successful product. Following the merger, Gilat also provided communication services to large organizations the world over and closed deals worth millions of dollars with these customers, without any negotiation: We were now simply taking orders, not selling the company; a big difference. Few Israeli companies could claim to have come so far so fast.

In contrast to the technical investment language of the previous prospectus, the current edition was written in plain English. The prospectus featured a brief history of the company and its founders, as well as information about our major customers: the United States Postal Service, BP (British Petroleum), John Deere, the First National Bank of the United States, Rite-Aid, Peugeot, Citroën, and Telkom South Africa. We obviously highlighted the merger with Spacenet, which provided us with new distribution channels and many new customers. However, the part of the acquisition that merited the most attention in the prospectus was the fact that the mighty GE was now Gilat's primary shareholder, now holding some 30% of our shares.

The prospectus concluded with a slew of impressive figures: Since Gilat's establishment in 1987, sales had consistently grown, but the real upswing began in the late 1990s. From $24 million in 1995, Gilat's sales had skyrocketed to $130 million in 1997. Last but not least, the combined sales of Gilat and Spacenet during the first nine months of 1998 had surpassed the $170 million mark.

Every prospectus is legally obligated to cite the risks that the company faces. We noted the fact that the acquisition of Spacenet had exposed us to many new dangers: doubts as to whether the merger would be consummated; Spacenet's history of large losses; and the many new obligations that Gilat assumed as a result of the merger. The prospectus also referred to the historic dangers with Gilat always had to contend: whether the company would maintain its focus notwithstanding enormous growth; its dependence on a handful of large customers; and the need to constantly develop and launch new products.

The offering itself was carried out in an exemplary fashion. Unlike the previous round, the current offering was big enough to merit the undivided attention of all the underwriters, as an issue of $300 million translated into a commission of $15 million, a fat paycheck even for the most prestigious investment banks in the world.

The investors hounded us with requests for meetings. In order to meet the demand, we split into two teams — I personally comprised the first team and Yoav and Diane formed the second — and rented private jets to shuttle us from meeting to meeting. We worked extremely hard: two weeks of non-stop presentations from dawn to dusk. Our eyes were bloodshot by the end of each day, and we were developing other symptoms of acute sleep deprivation.

Two of the meetings stood out in particular. The first was actually a two-stage process with Paul Krieger, a big-time investor who specialized in high-tech companies. The first meeting took place six months before the offering. "I don't expect you to invest in us now", I told him. "All I want to do is tell you our story and ask that you keep track of us from here o. If we manage to meet our benchmarks, then you'll get in whenever you see fit".

Paul was extremely impressed, as nobody had ever presented him with such an offer before. When I reached San Francisco during the course of the road show, Paul invited me to dinner. He wasn't accompanied by any bankers or analysts, and the meeting was practically a friendly chat. In fact, Paul barely even talked about the offering. Among the topics we discussed was Iridium's massive public offering several days earlier. Paul was the investor that had single-handedly managed to lower their stock's value by 15% and was quite proud of himself. Thereafter, the conversation shifted to the topic of Gilat. "I tracked your company for the past six months", he said, "and I intend on making a substantial investment during the offering. I appreciate the way you treated me, and it's going to pay off for you guys in a big way..." Paul indeed ordered 20% of the shares that were offered — an investment worth tens millions of dollars — and thus became one of Gilat's principal shareholders.

The second meeting that has remained etched in my mind was with Oscar Castro, who had already purchased a nice chunk of Gilat's shares during our IPO. He had held on to the shares for quite some time before selling them at an excellent return. Since our first meeting, I had kept in constant touch with him, for Oscar was a real aficionado of the data communications industry and always had a great deal to say about each of Gilat's major moves. The meeting took place in the luxurious offices of a new, San Francisco-based fund that Oscar was working for. As soon as I arrived, Castro and his four colleagues attacked with a list of hostile questions and claims. Castro contended that the partnership with Spacenet "is a defensive merger and not an offensive one". In investors' slang, this means that we bought a company whose base profitability was lower than our own. Therefore, in his opinion, the motives behind the acquisition were defensive: a compulsory integration between an equipment supplier and service provider in order to preserve market share. By that point in the meeting, Oscar had become quite vocal: "We have known each other a long time Yoel, and this is the first time I am telling you in no uncertain terms: you're making a mistake here that is going to undermine the profitability of your company. Not only are we not going to buy shares, but we're going to unload the stock we're holding onto".

This was the most humiliating moment in what was otherwise a very successful road show. Naturally, not all meetings are going to end with orders, and you certainly can't please all the investors all the time. However, coming from an old, respected acquaintance like Oscar made it difficult not to take the criticism seriously and personally. I drew on every possible argument in my repertoire in an effort to refute their arguments and defend our decisions, but they were unconvinced. Throughout the rest of the road show, I kept thinking back on that meeting, when the stock rose in value and when it dropped before the issue. They were right, but we didn't see it coming. Given our personal history with Spacenet and the emotions involved, it was perhaps impossible for us to analyze or comprehend the deal in such an objective manner.

I was in Milan when the offering came to a close in February 1999. Gilat's stock had indeed come a long way since the announcement of Sapacenet acquisition. In August 1998, the price of our share was $32; and by year's end, following the announcement of the merger, the price had climbed to $40. Some two months later, at the height of the road show, the stock peaked at $67. In other words, Gilat's value had soared to $1.3 billion! The stock then dropped over the next two days before closing the issue at $57. This was a bit disappointing considering the fact that it had hit the $67 mark only a few days earlier. Nonetheless, the offering was still an enormous success, as the stock rose from $47 on the eve of the road show to a final issuing price of $57 dollars, and we raised another $311 million. Like any successful offering, the issuers, investors, and bankers were all satisfied.

Eleven years ago, each of Gilat's five founders had paid 200 shekels (about $125 back in 1987) for half a million shares of a company that no one had ever heard of. After the offering, each one of us was worth over $25 million. We didn't let the money go to our heads; none of us bought a fancy Porsche or other toys. We continued to plow straight ahead toward new targets — another customer, another technological advance. We continued to sit through late-night marathon sessions, pile up frequent-flyer miles, and cope with an endless string of demands and mishaps. All of the founders were fatigued, but we carried on with the long sojourn towards our dream of becoming the leader of the field. Translating the success into money was important, but it was not the be all and end all. We still weren't ready to step out of the tunnel that we had entered over ten years before.

These were the gung-ho days of the dot-com bubble in which the model and philosophy of the "new economy" was taking form. The new economy was predicated on information technology, the internet, and globalization. These new ideas attracted a great deal of public exposure and influenced the outlook of large swathes of the finance and business worlds. As a result, the market was being flooded by a new species of companies, each trying to raise the banner of the "new economy". Obviously, these developments also had a profound impact on Gilat's operations.

The basic premise of the "new economy" was that companies that managed to construct and utilize new networks before the rest of the competition would dominate the twenty-first century. Consequently, what was previously considered sound corporate policy — such as the ability to attract investment, wisely managing the company's cash flow, and controlled growth — was cast aside as part of the mad dash to reach the market first. The prevailing attitude was that the quicker a company positions itself with the right product, the greater its long-term value. Accordingly, many start-up companies attracted exorbitant sums for their stocks, experienced unbridled growth, and rapidly bypassed the established companies in terms of market capitliazation, which had attained their position after years of hard work and sound investment. This entire period was reminiscent of the land grabs of the 1800s, as a host of companies raced out into the frontier to claim their stakes.

Gilat had exactly what these 'new economy' companies needed: a unique technology that would allow for the rapid deployment of networks which could connect these companies to the rest of the world. Furthermore, our technologies were not dependent on ground-based communication lines and were reasonably priced. These businesses were so well financed and in such a rush to deploy their communication networks that the price of the equipment was not the main issue. We were sure that the "new economy" would lead us straight to the coveted home consumer market. And, for all practical purposes, Gilat was positioned as the proverbial gate-keeper to such networks for companies of all stripes that were racing to grab a piece of the "new economy'.

We convened an intra-company conference entitled "Gilat in the Era of the New Economy". I ran a slide show on the strategy of network-based eBusinesses and delivered a passionate speech on the principles that undergirded the new way of thinking: "These are dynamic businesses which take the initiative, and their goal is to establish far-reaching communication networks as quickly as possible. They are capable of raising money relatively easily, and their decision-making process is rapid".

"And therefore the risk is also higher", Amiram interjected.

"True", I answered, "but if we believe that their business model is sound — and their investors undoubtedly have faith in their ability — then we are faced with a huge opportunity, which could very well constitute a new, fast-growth business segment. I suggest that we take the bull by the horns before Hughes does".

Amiram, who is always more skeptical and cautious than I am, was also in favor of the idea. However, John Connely, who represented GE — Gilat's largest stockholder after the Spacenet merger — was extremely wary: "I agree with the general idea, but we had better think long and hard about each of the potential customers before entering any sort of agreement with them. The strength of the deal is also its weakness. If we choose the wrong companies, it could get ugly…"

Throughout the dot-com era, we were courted by hosts of companies. However, we zeroed in on those companies that in our estimation offered added value and were involved in markets that would generate the most opportunities for us. In early 1998, we started working with a company called ZapMe! The company and Lance Mortensen, its founder and CEO, made quite an impression on us. It supplied schools with computer packages, each of which included fifteen terminals, a laser printer, an installation program, and a satellite communication system for connecting to the internet both during and after school hours. The network offered pupils, parents, and teachers user-friendly access to an array of computer tools and a high-speed internet hookup. ZapMe! was the largest provider of these sort of services in the United States, and no less than thirteen thousand schools signed up for the new service. Gilat was an ideal communication provider for ZapMe!, as we were capable of quickly hooking up thousands of schools that lacked any other means for connecting to a high-speed internet service provider.

What made ZapMe! unique was that it was offering a network, internet service provider, browser, and content provider all under one roof. Although ZapMe! did not create content on its own, it enabled other programmers to transfer large quantities of educational material to the installed schools. In addition, the millions of students using its service received their own email address, and ZapMe!'s home page served as the exclusive home page for all the schools. Both students and educators alike lavished the company with praise. It was indeed a beautiful dream that featured an exciting technology with vast potential.

Before closing the deal with ZapMe!, we visited the schools and were impressed by the way the children took to the system. The business model was clear: the computers would be provided free of charge in return for advertising space on the interface screens and the ads would constantly change. The business model roused the interest of large organizations and important advertisers. Many investors and companies, including large firms such as Sylvan Learning, Dell, Toshiba, and eventually Gilat, invested in ZapMe!. In 1999, they executed an IPO and the value of its stock more than doubled relative to the price we paid for its shares.

After ZapMe!, we moved on to a company called AccentHealth. The company produced a quality show on health news and other medical topics in the 'healthy lifestyle' genre, which it screened on televisions and VCRs that it had installed in over 10,000 waiting rooms in medical clinics throughout the United States. AccentHealth contracted CNN to produce one new episode per month. Twelve minutes of every programming hour were allotted to advertisements, which were viewed by tens of millions of people. Since the audience was highly-segmented, advertisers were willing to pay handsome fees for thirty second slots.

AccentHealth's main problem was logistical. Once a month, its messengers distributed ten thousand tapes to the various clinics. The method was expensive and did not scale: many tapes failed to reach their destination; some of the televisions didn't work; and the company lacked an effective method to prove to advertisers how many people actually watched their commercials. Obviously, these drawbacks severely damaged its profit margins.

The company's management longed for a system that would allow them to replace the video tape with electronic file delivery. This would enable them to distribute their content to the clinics via a network for hassle-free display on the television monitors. They also needed a system that would verify whether each computer was running the correct file and that the televisions were working. Lastly, they wanted to enable the patients and medical staff to surf the internet via their website. Unlike many of the other companies in the fledgling dot-com world, AccentHealth had a solid business model, a large professional staff, and an annual turnover worth over millions of dollars.

The competition over AccentHealth's ten thousand sites once again put us against Hughes. AccentHealth was cognizant of their power and of how badly both of the two rivals wanted the deal. The most important issue from AccentHealth's standpoint was not money, but adapting the system to meet their exact specifications. Once they saw the networks that we were already operating for other customers, they fell into our hands and an agreement was signed by early 1999.

These were glorious days for Gilat, as there was a true sense of excitement, especially at Spacenet. The work never ended and our future was looking bright. We had orders for about 20,000 sites, including 7,000 for the United States Postal Service and thousands of installations for ZapMe! and AccentHealth. Moreover, Gilat was set to replace 6,000 of Tridom's old terminals.

The organization was growing at a frenzied pace. We invested considerable amounts of time, effort, and money on the construction of new provisioning systems. For the first time in our history, we were facing a situation in which we had more than enough sales lined up, and the only factor holding us back was the limitations of our installation capacity. We savored the moment, for we knew that good times such as these were unlikely to repeat themselves.

That said, our situation was not exactly a bed of roses. Hughes was well aware of the power rising out of Zion and fought us at every turn. The theater of operations turned to the large oil companies, which were consolidating- saw Shell merge with Amoco and BP unite with Texaco. These mergers complicated matters, as both Gilat/Spacenet and Hughes had installed thousands of sites for these companies: we had 6,000 sites installed at Shell, and Hughes had about 7,000 sites at their new partner, Amoco; we had 1500 sites at BP, while Hughes had about 5,000 at Texaco. Each of the companies informed us that after the mergers they intended on working with only one supplier: Gilat or Hughes.

Shell was the first to act. They let both competitors know that they would go with the supplier that offered the best price. Each side lowered their prices until the deal no longer made economic sense for either of the rivals. It was clear to us that Hughes was dead set on offering the lowest price, come what may, as they were behaving as if their very existence was on the line. In contrast, we had an enormous quantity of sites to install, even without the Shell deal, and did not feel as though we had to beat Hughes at all costs. Therefore, once the prices had dipped below the breakeven point, we decided to draw the line. As a result, Hughes landed the Shell account, and both sides got ready for the battle over BP.

BP had new technical demands, so that the competition over their account was not only a matter of price. Hughes opened with an aggressive sales campaign, and we established a sales force that was headed by Shelly Rivkin and David Shiff, Spacenet's new senior executives who had crossed over from Hughes and were thus familiar with the customer's decision makers from their days at the 'evil empire.' BP naturally enjoyed the battle, and they were not the only ones. The analysts on Wall Street were also thirsting for a bloodbath and placed great importance on the competition over BP. An especially diligent analyst, John Coates of Salomon Smith and Barney, called up the purchasing people at BP, who informed him that they were leaning towards Gilat. To our astonishment, Coates published a report in which he authoritatively declared that

Gilat would win the deal.

I was fuming mad and gave Coates a ring. "You are causing us direct damage. There is nothing to publish until the customer makes a final decision. If we lose, you will have played a major role in the outcome".

"I'm only doing my job" was all Coates had to say for himself.

In any event, Hughes took the hint. The next day they hopped on a plane to England and basically set up camp at BP's headquarters. An agreement was hammered out two days later, as Hughes agreed to drop their price by another whopping 20%. "You can't beat a price like that", the BP executives apologized to us. "Hughes offered us the discount on the condition that we sign the contract right there and then, and we couldn't refuse". In sum, Hughes was willing to lose a serious amount of money, as long as they prevented us from reaping yet another success.

The news of Hughes' victory was released to the press within hours, and Gilat's stock immediately plummeted by 12%. "How can an analyst publish a prediction you're going to win a big deal", Paul Krieger assaulted me over the phone", and two days later you guys end up losing? You've lost control of the situation!" For perhaps the first time in my life, I was speechless. All I managed to do was clear my throat with a faint cough.

Although no company likes to lose two major deals back to back, we didn't let these setbacks get us down. Notwithstanding the irritating defeats, our customer base was growing at an accelerated pace, and we were indeed enjoying a banner year. In fact, the entire market was taking off, as industry-wide sales rose from 81,000 new sites in 1998 to 130,000 in 1999. The services that we provided our customers were first-rate. Our installation and maintenance procedures were among the best our industry has ever seen. In addition, we astounded our customers by meeting all our commitments on installation timetables, levels of service, and maintenance. Consequently, most of our customers agreed to give us favorable reviews, and nothing makes a better impression on a potential customer than a favorable recommendation from a competitor.

Our biggest coup during that period was the Dollar General account. Dollar General is a gigantic discount store chain with over 7,500 locations. Our people did a stand-up job reeling in this prize fish. For example, we located the decision makers at Dollar General; installed equipment in their houses (which enabled them to work from home); and introduced them to several of our satisfied customers. This particular account was a huge accomplishment for us, for it marked the first time that we ever managed to land a deal in which our price offer was higher than the competition's. Despite the steeper price tag, Dollar General was well aware of the advantages of doing business with Gilat.

Once again, it was difficult to hide our satisfaction with the year-end report of Simon Bull of COMSYS:
"One of the things that have characterized the market over the last few years is the cut-throat competition between Gilat and Hughes. In 1999, Gilat managed to surpass Hughes for the first time in its history, as it secured control over 50% of the world-wide market share *vis à vis* only 48% for Hughes"...

"Until 1994, Hughes completely dominated the market. From that year onwards, Gilat's growth was pronounced, as it seized significant swathes of market share from the other players in the industry…(I)ts victory was first and foremost psychological".

Once again, Simon praised us for our phenomenal performance, especially against a tough competitor like Hughes. He reemphasized the fact that we had continuously developed new products and lowered our prices. In the telephony field, Simon couldn't help but notice that our market share was about 70%: "Gilat is leaving everyone in the dust and is the undisputed leader in this market segment".

As far as we were concerned, these accomplishments were considerably more than just psychological victories. We had been striving to reach the top spot in our field since the company's establishment some ten years back, so this moment was one of the highpoints in the history of Gilat.

Hughes refused to take the report lying down. To begin with, they exerted immense amounts of pressure on COMSYS to closet the report before it was published. Secondly, the day before Simon's report hit the newsstands, they hit us with a highly publicized patent infringement suit, which caused quite a stir in the market. Furthermore, on the day that Simon's study hit the press, Hughes released what for them was an unprecedented document entitled, "Hughes' Response to the COMSYS Report". The response basically consisted of a three-pronged attack against Simon's research:

- First, Hughes attempted to refute the amount of orders that was cited in the report. They contended that the report ignored many of the orders they received for upgrading existing sites.
- Hughes claimed to have recounted the existing terminals. According to their tally, they accounted for 54% of the sales compared to only 45% for Gilat. However, Simon contended that Hughes had added a substantial amount of orders to their sales totals, which he conscientiously omitted from his report.
- Lastly, Hughes also calculated both companies' revenues from VSAT sales. According to their estimates, their income from the field was over half a billion dollars, whereas Gilat made do with a little over $300 million.

In any event, Simon's report was published and attracted a great deal of attention throughout the industry, while the Hughes response failed to make much of an impact. Moreover, the lawsuit never reached the courts and ended a year later in a low key compromise. Even though they didn't deserve it, we paid Hughes a small sum of money and the settlement failed to make any waves. Nothing could stand in the way of our sweet victory celebrations.

At the time — as well as to this very day — many people asked me how an Israeli company managed to reach the top spot. In a nutshell, it's all a matter of gaining an advantage: holding a gun in a knife fight. If a company can create a winning set up, it will win. We worked hard to improve our products, reduce their price, and build a reputation as a highly-driven company that loyally serves its customers. In turn, our customers knew that our equipment did not break down and that we provided our distribution channels with all the support they needed.

Once Gilat acquired Spacenet, we were primed for a major breakthrough. From that moment on, we had total control over the products, the sales process, and market positioning, and this enabled us to influence the way the public perceived the company. Our ability to focus the entire organization on the main goals, ignore petty problems and foster a true team spirit, as well as get the organization to believe in itself— what appeared to be an impossible task against a rival like Hughes, especially after years in which Spacenet had been mired in a losing culture — were all responsible for Gilat's ascent.

Furthermore, you have to know how to choose your battles. In a competitive market no single company is going to sweep up all the deals. Consequently, a company must find the way to land the right deals and concede the wrong ones without losing too much sleep over these supposed losses. Market share is usually the product of a handful of key customers. Therefore, it is incumbent on the organization to concentrate on the crucial deals.

Finally, your entire staff must be totally committed to the process: the management team, which establishes the company's strategy and objectives; the marketing and sales people, who do everything in their power to land the deals; the engineers and development people, who enhance the product value and create advantages *vis à vis* the competition; and the service and support staff who convey the company's commitment to the customer by means of their relations with and efforts on behalf of the customers.

Of course, it's easier to create a new market and dominate it from the outset, but this was not the situation that Gilat found itself in. We were forced to embark on a difficult and indirect road packed with formidable rivals and dangerous obstacles. Nonetheless, we always believed that we would ultimately reap the fruit of our efforts.

By the end of 1999 we did, all our dreams had come true.

11

A Star is Born

Rarely does a high-tech company have the opportunity to burst out of its present framework and immerse itself in a new, innovative paradigm that promises to change the world.

The reason for such an abrupt change is likely to be either defensive or offensive. On the one hand, it may come as a response to a rival that has adopted measures that are likely to afford the latter a competitive advantage. On the other hand, the shift may result from a huge opportunity that the company had come across. In Gilat's case, the transformation stemmed from both offensive and defensive factors.

By mid 1999, the dot-com bubble had grown enormously. A host of new ideas and industries were taking off, including the high-speed internet market. Everywhere you went people were talking about cable modems and high-speed internet. The first experiments were underway announcing the dawn of a new era that would completely change the world.

While keeping our eyes open, Gilat also strode into this wonderful world in search of new opportunities. After the success of the Spacenet merger, we felt as if the industry was expecting something big out of us — that we would launch some grand vision. Like all revolutionary ideas, our new product practically popped out of thin air. We launched a high-speed communications service for the home consumer, which was entirely independent of cable infrastructures or any other ground-based infrastructure. By means of a small satellite dish mounted on a roof, customers would have access to a high-speed internet connection and hundreds of television channels. This was a significant breakthrough, especially for people living in remote, sparsely-populated regions. Until then, the chances that, say, an Indian village in the Andes Mountains or an isolated community in Australia or China had of being connected to the internet were far-fetched. No one was willing to bear the excessive costs of laying down the necessary phone lines or cables. Therefore, our new service was likely to have a profound impact on people's lifestyles. It was indeed a far-reaching vision, the likes of which no other satellite company had conceived by then. From a business standpoint, we hoped that once the amount of units sold reached a critical mass, Gilat would be able to expand its manufacturing capacity and lower the price, so that we could even compete with the telecommunication and cable companies for rural and suburban areas.

The opening shot for this new market territory was fired by the competition, as an initiative unleashed by Hughes hit us like a ton of bricks. On June 21, 1999, AOL and Hughes called a dramatic, joint press conference. AOL, the world's largest online and information provider, which traded on Wall Street at a market cap of about $100 billion, was joining forces with our arch rival. In what was indeed a polished and impressive performance, the two giants illustrated a new world in which AOL would sell a high-speed internet service that was based on Hughes' one-way satellite system. Customers would connect to the internet via a telephone hookup to AOL, but the information from the internet would be transmitted via a small dish that would be connected to their personal computers via an affordable communication card. The new service would enable data to be transferred at least twenty times faster than a regular phone line connection, and the user could access the internet in a straight-forward, user-friendly manner. The service was slated to begin during the last quarter of 1999 and would be available throughout the United States by 2000. Existing AOL subscribers would only have to add $14.95 a month to their basic monthly package alongside a one-time payment of $295 for the equipment.

A revolution was in the making!

As more details of their plan were released, we realized that our position was deteriorating rapidly. Not only would the service be sold through the lethally efficient sales channels of AOL, but by large chain stores as well. Moreover, AOL would invest no less than $1.5 billion in Hughes, which would use the funds to purchase equipment, and mount a huge sales campaign and keep down the initial sales price for the first 500,000 subscribers, until the economies of scale kicked in.

The nightmare wasn't over yet. They talked about developing a special browser for the service — an improved version of Netscape, which AOL also owned. Moreover, the two new partners explained how their future service would quickly spread from the United States to Latin America and Asia. Last but not least, they predicted that they would sign 1.5 million subscribers within three years.

Whoever heard the news — consumers, investors, potential customers, and of course the competition — had no reason to doubt that these two huge and reputable companies would indeed fulfill this earth-shattering plan and meet all their ambitious timetables.

The press conference was broadcast live on the internet, so that we heard the admiring questions of the analysts and reporters as well as the confident answers of AOL's and Hughes' executives. Every question and answer constituted another blow. However, the effect was not limited to the psychological realm. While the press conference was still in progress, we received reports from Wall Street that our stock had begun to decline. We were shocked. I don't remember ever feeling so helpless, for the two giants were hijacking our dream in broad daylight. In other words, Hughes was going to use that $1.5 billion to seal us off from our true goal: to penetrate the desirable yet vaguely defined American home-consumer market.

This was one of the darkest moments in the history of Gilat. Not only were the founders and senior executives frightened, but the despair percolated through the corridors to the offices and labs. We feared that the AOL-Hughes joint venture would turn us into a small niche company, which specializes in providing satellite communication services to a few large companies and selling telephony services to godforsaken regions on the edge of the world.

Several days after the press conference, we went ahead with a regular, pre-planned all-hands meeting at Gilat. At these sorts of meetings, the entire company is assembled and we report on the company's performance, plans, and objectives. This forum enabled us to let the employees know what was expected of them, while providing them with a platform for voicing their opinions to management. However, the subjects that we presented at this particular meeting were no longer relevant, as the main topic had changed overnight. People looked me in the eye and demanded answers:

What is the significance of AOL's and Hughes' announcement? To what extent does this narrow our market potential? Can we stop their 'story?' And finally, the ultimate question: should we start worrying about our jobs?

For perhaps the first time, I was unable to calm their fears.

I was preoccupied by the competition's new service for days and nights on end. We tried to determine what Gilat's relative advantage was and asked ourselves if it was imperative to come up with an even more revolutionary offer. However, even if we came up with a fabulous idea, how would we contend with the power that was being brought to bear on us? In other words, how would we form a coalition with the combined power of an AOL and Hughes? The chips appeared to be stacked against us.

July 13, 1999. I remember that day as if it were yesterday. It was a Saturday morning, and I was in my McLean.apartment the company kept for our Israeli employees. There were usually several people camping out at the flat, but this time I was all alone. I held a long and depressing telephone conversation with my wife. Being so far away from home was taking its toll on the entire family. "Do me a favor", Simona lashed out at me. "Use that creative mind of yours to figure out a saner routine. Take some of the load off, and spend more time at home…"

"I'll think about", I told her before saying goodbye. Once again, I found myself caught between a rock and a hard place. How can I reduce my work load in light of the new competitive threat against Gilat? Again, I asked myself whether the time had come to concede some ground.

And then, out of the blue, the idea hit me like a bolt of lightening: In contrast to the one-way product that Hughes and AOL were offering, why not launch a two-way satellite product? Our service would not need any phone lines whatsoever. Like Hughes, we would offer an affordable price by manufacturing large quantities and attracting investors and dominant strategic partners. Perhaps Microsoft, AOL's arch enemy, or Echostar, Hughes' traditional rival, would be willing to consider a joint venture; and GE, Dell, or Intel might also be interested in getting in on the action. I immediately asked myself a series of questions: "Can we execute the product strategy at price low enough to compete with

AOL-Hughes? Is there a realistic shot of convincing any of the aforementioned power-houses to join us? Is this sort of plan likely to reach the magnitude of our competition's plan? Is it realistic or am I day dreaming?

Above all, I was amazed by the power of the idea's simplicity. As I sat in that empty apartment, I was getting filled with a sense of confidence. An overwhelmingly clear and focused vision — a grand plan that could hit the target like a laser beam — had taken shape before my very eyes.

I put down three sentences on three separate lines: "A high-speed, two-way satellite network for the consumer market".

"One dish for both internet and television".
"A million subscribers by the end of 2002".

I sat at the table and went over the lines again and again and was pleased with what I had written.

I took out a block of white paper, which is still in my possession, and wrote down a headline in huge letters that took up the entire length of the first page: "Gilat's Strategy for a Broadband Internet Connectivity for the Home consumer". Without batting an eyelid, I continued to map out the plan:

* Two-way, broadband communication for the home. One single dish for both the internet and television. One million subscribers by 2002.

• Service: to be run entirely by Gilat: installations, maintenance, service, and customer care.

• Potential partners: GE, Microsoft, Echostar, Dell, and Intel.

• Price: $49-$69 per month.

• The product: a VSAT; an attractive box; a 90 x 60 centimeter antenna; a kit with the necessary accessories for self-installation; and a wide array of applications.

• Revenue streams are the same as the internet model: subscription fees, advertising, content, and portal. We will have to secure external financing in order to fund the satellite capacity segment and infrastructure and to set up the new organization, as there is no way to integrate the plan within Gilat's existing model. Consequently, attracting strategic investors is an absolute must.• Priorities: a name for the service and product; positioning the service within the framework of Gilat's and our partners' product lines; recruiting a president and other executives to run the new company's operations, installations, and maintenance.

• Conclusion: The biggest opportunity Gilat has ever had. We've got to get moving at once, before AOL and Hughes gather momentum. It is essential that we tell our own story, namely the introduction of two-way satellite communications for the domestic market, with which to detonate Hughes and AOL's story.

• Final word: We can do this!

I put down the pen, turned on the computer, and typed the presentation. I then drafted an understated email message and sent it to the inner circle: Amiram, Joshua, Yoav, and Simona. The day had flown by; and before I knew it, it was already late at night. By the time I settled into bed, I knew that I had earned my daily bread...

Simona came to work on Sunday morning (in Israel, the work week starts on Sunday) and turned on her computer. She knew that a message from her husband would be waiting in the inbox, but was probably anticipating a response to her request that I spend more time with the family. She printed the file I sent, read it, and immediately rushed over to Amiram: "Did you see this?"

"I don't know what to do with it", Amiram mumbled. "I don't know if this idea will work..."

Neither did Simona. The news was not exactly fit her dream of a 'saner' life. "We're not exactly heading in the right direction", she thought to herself.

From that point on nothing could have stopped me. My notebook was filling up with ideas on the organizational charts, the business model, the product's development cycle, and logistical matters. I also got ready to break the news to GE and John Connely. The meeting with Connely would focus on presenting the vision, Hughes and AOL's possible reactions to our initiative, and preliminary marketing ideas. Furthermore, I immediately established a small team of people to whom I explained the idea. I didn't have to explain myself too much, for they were instantly captured by the vision. Everyone I spoke to reacted as if this was exactly what they were waiting for. I could feel the excitement in the air. Ori Gilliam, who joined Gilat during the Rite-Aid period, assumed responsibility for the operations, and Yossi Gal, a top-notch engineer, who relocated to the United States and integrated himself into the Spacenet system, took charge of the technical aspects of the services. I set up meetings with GE and Echostar and looked for a way to get to Microsoft. We hired a consultancy to analyze the market demand and quickly formulated the first business model. It was obvious that we would need hundreds of millions of dollars in revenues just to breakeven. However, a negative cash flow during this period, amid the new economy, was not necessarily a liability; in fact, many dot-com era entrepreneurs probably considered it an advantage.

Connely was enthusiastic, but immediately made it clear to me that GE wouldn't invest in the project. Thereafter, I set out for the first meeting with Echostar, a large satellite operator and provider of satellite television services. I met with Mark Jackson, who was head of the company's Transmission & Satellite Services and Broadcast & Interactive Data Units. He asked many good questions, but was non-committal. During the meeting Charlie Ergen, the CEO and owner of the company, stepped in and apologized for not being able to stay, as he had a plane to catch for Washington.

Since I also had to get back to Washington, I immediately bought a ticket on his flight. Against my habit, I purchased a first class ticket in order to sit next to Charlie. Throughout the entire four-hour flight, I didn't leave him alone for a minute. We got to know each other and our ways of thinking. It was the beginning of a friendship. Charlie gave me an invaluable lesson on two-way communication and the internet in a world where television is transmitted via satellites. In addition, Charlie intimated that he would not be the first to join the project, but if we generated momentum Echostar would also jump on the bandwagon. We parted ways in Washington and agreed to meet again soon.

Notwithstanding the prowess and prestige of Echostar, our main objective was to forge a coalition with Microsoft that would serve as a counterweight against the combined forces of AOL and Hughes. A partnership with the titans of Microsoft would clearly change the balance of power and vastly improve our chances of transforming the vision into reality. However, infiltrating such a large organization was no easy task, especially considering the fact that, save for their local sales representative in Israel, we had no contacts at Microsoft.

Following a myriad of failed attempts to breach the ranks of their senior management, someone told us that Harel Kodesh, who served with us in the Unit, was Microsoft's vice president of consumer appliances (to include devices like the Palm Pilot). We turned to Harel, and he immediately offered us his assistance. He gave us a complete rundown of who's who at Microsoft and told us which division we had to penetrate in order to make headway. Furthermore, he put us in touch with just the right man: Jon DeVaan. Among the leading developers of the Office program, at the time Jon was then in charge of MSN internet access at Microsoft. I gave him a ring, and he was very polite. At the end of the conversation, he told me that he would send a team to Spacenet in order to study the topic. From my standpoint, this was a major step forward.

As usual, we did our homework. The three Microsoft representatives who came to Virginia were impressed with the product and the vision and asked us to demonstrate the product in their labs. Several days later, we gave a demonstration of the product in Redmond (Microsoft's headquarters), and it passed the test with flying colors. Microsoft responded by giving us a long due-diligence list of information we needed to provide. Moreover, John invited us to send a delegation to Redmond for a comprehensive technical meeting, to which we dispatched the company's top engineers.

By early October 1999, Gilat had clearly gotten past the test phases of the 'courtship,' as we had proven to Microsoft that we were capable of getting the job done in a timely fashion. As a result, Jon invited us to a pivotal executive meeting in Redmond in which we would be given an opportunity to present our plan before Microsoft's decision makers. We couldn't have asked for anything more.

Amiram and I flew out to Redmond. Before the meeting with the company's executives, we stopped by Harel's office for a preparatory discussion. Harel shared with us everything he could about the organization's internal politics and decision-making process; as we expected, reaching decisions was long and grueling. Moreover, he told us how he thought Jon would behave at the meeting. From Harel's, we hustled over to the building in which the meeting was held.

The visit to Microsoft was a moving experience in its own right. Their campus is about the size of a mid-sized college and is dotted with dozens of dormitory-size buildings; little wonder that it's referred to as a "campus". Each building houses a different product group. People get around the campus using an internal bus system. The work environment is tremendous. In the entrance to the building that Jon DeVaan presided over, we saw an employee choir practicing for some event, and a delivery man bringing a stack of pizzas to a group that was celebrating the completion of some project. It was a youthful, colorful, and winning environment. I got a firsthand look at why Microsoft was (at the time) the king of the world.

The meeting itself was somewhat bizarre for my taste. Eight people were waiting for us in the room. Throughout the discussion, however, people were constantly coming and going — this is apparently their style. Jon was nice to us, but his assistants spoke in an aggressive tone and bombarded us with questions: "Who are you guys? What have you done until now? How many customers do you have? What is your business model?"

The barrage continued even when the discussion turned to the technology: "How many users can the system handle? What is the economic rational behind the plan? What are the problems that can be expected during installation? How many work stations will the service center have? What will the price per terminal be if the units are manufactured in large quantities? And once you reach your manufacturing goals, how much will you charge for the service per month? How do you envision the breakdown of responsibilities between Microsoft and Gilat?"

To this point, we had anticipated all the questions in advance, so that it wasn't all too difficult coming up with satisfactory answers. However, just as we were getting comfortable, a crushing question burst out of a dark corner of the room: "Are you guys capable of producing a million terminals in the upcoming year?"

I thought for a second before answering: "Not a million,

but we can definitely manufacture a quarter of a million. By the following year, our capacity will reach a million units". The person that asked the question was not pleased with my answer, and I wondered if this would spoil our chances...

For the next two and a half hours, Amiram tried to explain to them the nature of satellite transmissions. He underscored the fact that the system was designed to transmit and receive large amounts of data at any given moment, so that we were quite capable of handling many customers at once. They weren't too interested in these details and continued to mercilessly assault us with questions. Consequently, we didn't have a clue as to whether they were impressed. In any event, Amiram and I made excellent use of our usual Gilat approach: one spoke while the other thought. Whenever we were presented with a difficult question, we exchanged a couple of words in Hebrew before answering. Suddenly, the discussion came to a close, as everyone except Jon left the room. "You did well", he told us. "Give us some time, and we'll get back to you". After hours of fielding questions, we were relieved that the meeting was finally over.

Simultaneous to our courtship of Microsoft, we also conducted a limited dialogue with AOL. Our good friend, Yossi Vardi — one of the pioneers of the Israeli high-tech industry and among the founders of Mirabilis, the company that invented ICQ (the popular messages program) — introduced us to David Colburn, AOL's all-powerful negotiator, and we offered them a deal that was similar to the one that we were negotiating with Microsoft.

Notwithstanding the negotiations with AOL and although we wanted to keep our options open, most our energy was invested on Microsoft. At the end of October 1999, we again met with Jon DeVaan, at Telecom Geneva. Jon refused to commit, and the conversation was confined to general topics. He explained to us Microsoft's way of thinking and informed us that a decision would be reached by the end of November.

A couple of days later, we decided to unveil our new strategy to the world. We had some hesitations over whether this was the right moment, but we felt that the time had come to throw a monkey wrench into Hughes' story. In a teleconference with the analysts, we presented the idea, the motivation behind the product, and the means for realizing the dream. Furthermore, we explained why our product was superior to that of our rivals. Wall Street was not only intrigued, but demanded an in-depth report of our plans. The analysts lavished us with praise: "Superstar", wrote John Coates of Salomon Smith Barney; "A look into the future of broadband internet", was Goldman Sachs' headline; and "a stake under the tent and a pleasant surprise", wrote Merrill Lynch. As a result of the rave reviews, our stock rose by $10 in one day and soared to a high of $85. "We have left the Earth's orbit", one of our employees told me. "I hope the landing won't be too painful", I replied.

At the end of November, we received the joyous news that Microsoft wanted in on the product and that they were interested in opening negotiations. We felt like miners who had struck gold and celebrated the remarkable turnaround in our fortunes. Only five months ago, Hughes had delivered a powerful right hook that sent us sprawling to the canvass. However, we were back on our feet and the momentum had began to shift in our favor, as we seemed to be on the verge of landing a potent partner for our new endeavor. Microsoft sent us a detailed, voluminous contract written by the best lawyers in the world. It took me an entire weekend just to read through all two hundred pages and get a feel for what they wanted. There were several pages on the equipment, technical aspects, internet services, and their terms for using the MSN portal. They also included an investment agreement between Microsoft and the new company, which had yet to be named. Furthermore, they demanded that Gilat fully guarantee all the new company's operations.

Joshua presided over the negotiations along with our attorney Gene Kleinhandler. It's not easy arguing with such a huge organization, as Microsoft is tough. However, to be fair, they conducted themselves in a logical and acceptable manner. They asked for exclusivity *vis à vis* their primary rivals (AOL and Yahoo), a concession to distribute the product in other countries (in the end, they only got Mexico), and expansive veto rights over business decisions, including the sale of the company. In return, they were willing to invest $50 million for a 26% stake in the new company. The negotiation teams made headway, but had yet to produce a signed contract. As usual, the main problem was attracting the attention of the company's decision makers.

Over the course of December, we transformed the business plan into a dynamic document. The plan described the size of the market, the rise of cable modems and high-speed internet, and the potential of the satellite market. We prepared a positioning strategy, battle strategies, and detailed lists of the potential distribution channels (strategic partners, retail outlets, and domestic internet service and satellite television providers). In addition, the plan included a section on procedures, various elements of the service and organization, and an estimate of the amount of money that we would need to get the entire project up and running. Finally, we decided to call the company 'Gilat-to-Home'. Once the plan was complete, we presented it to the public. The 'story' was a success, as financial investors were excited about the new concept. Nonetheless, the puzzle was still missing two crucial pieces: strategic partners who would be willing to invest in the new project; and no less importantly, someone to actually head the company.

The name Zur Feldman was first brought to our attention by Yossi Vardi during the TELECOM '99 exhibition in Geneva. After selling ICQ for hundreds of millions of dollars, Yossi became the undisputed guru of the Israeli high-tech industry. He stopped by our booth, examined the products, heard our plans, assessed their potential, and gave us some juicy advice. Before he left, we asked him if he knew of anyone that could run the new company: "I have an outstanding Israeli candidate named Zur Feldman, but there's no chance that you guys will manage to recruit him".

Zur's fate was sealed at that very moment. We tracked him down and heard that he was planning to visit Israel in December 1999. Amiram and I quickly took the initiative and invited him for a talk. Zur showed up and charmed both of us off of our feet. A veteran of an elite IDF unit, Zur had already spent many years in the United States, where he had accumulated vast experience in the consumer market, including a long career as the head of operations at Packard-Bell. There was no mistaking his outstanding personal attributes. When Zur understood what we were getting at, he switched roles and began interviewing us. Although he agreed to take a copy of the business plan, he seemed somewhat amused by our offer. In fact, Zur left us with the impression that he wasn't all that interested in our proposal and that he had simply stopped by to meet a couple of fellows with similar backgrounds.

So, I was quite surprised when Zur called me up a couple of days later and told me that he liked the plan — further proof that the business plan is an important component of any new venture, especially when you're dealing with someone that knows how to read one. The next step of our courtship was an invitation to a meeting on the launching of Gilat-to-Home in Latin America, which was called for January 2000 in Florida. We held two intensive days of discussions on how to tap the vast potential of the Latin American market. Zur was impressed, and I then invited him to McLean in order to check out the operations and meet our people.

Zur took me up on my offer and spent a day at the Spacenet offices. Over the course of dinner, he provided me with an in-depth prognosis of our endeavor. He explained to me that the first 10,000 sites would seal our fate. More specifically, our ability to draw lessons from the initial problems, particularly the complaints fielded by the call center, and translate these into improved user experience that would be in the service future. "Half of the problems can usually be repaired over the phone", he emphasized. "But based on my experience with PCs, I estimate that most of the problems will come from the computers. Therefore, the strong link between the product and computers used for internet access will prove to be a disadvantage".

Zur then explained to me some of the problems that the PC industry was having with maintenance and warranties. Although he presented methods for solving these problems, Zur had doubts as to whether Gilat could contend with them. "Will your development people accept the authority of an American company, even if it happens to be your subsidiary?" he asked. He then went into great detail about the home consumer market, especially the problem of sales returns. Moreover, Zur taught me how to launch a product and emphasized the importance of a brand name. Until I met Zur, I thought that I already knew everything, but our conversation left me with the sense that what he had forgotten more than I will ever know. On each of these topics, he had an informed opinion which he articulated in an eloquent manner. As we parted ways, he slapped me on the shoulder and told me: "You have a long road ahead of you Yoel. I wish you the best of luck".

From the time we spent together, I discovered that Zur places supreme importance on values, friendship, and loyalty. His stellar character together with his administrative know-how, understanding of the market, and the positive aspects of his Israeli (*tzaber*) mentality formed a winning combination that was a cut above the rest. Consequently, I decided that I had to make every effort to bring him to Gilat. We sent Zur for interviews with Microsoft and Brian Friedman of Furman Selz, which was slated to be our only outside investor. Needless to say, Zur merited the high esteem of all his interviewers. Finally, I even flew out to California to meet his wife Anat, in order to convince her that we were a nice bunch of guys…

I wasn't sure if Zur would agree to join us until the very last minute. When I finally received word that he was signing on, I was absolutely elated. The hiring of Zur Feldman as the CEO of Gilat-at-Home was one of the better decisions I ever made. After years of working together, I am convinced that all the superlatives that I attributed to him were right on the mark. Zur is undoubtedly one of the best people that I ever had the honor of working with, and he quickly became one of my best friends. Our loyalty to one another over the course of our joint endeavors was special and rare. I enjoy hearing his voice and his optimistic perspective on everything under the sun. Last but not least, I admire the way he always gets the best out of both himself and the others around him.

As the new millennium kicked off, the negotiations with Microsoft picked up steam. The main bone of contention was the product's cost, as they strongly demanded a lower price. We ultimately reached the time-tested compromise whereby the price would be reduced as the sales increased. The sides also haggled over the monthly cost of the service, mutual exclusivity, and the extent of Gilat's influence over the marketing, which incidentally turned out to be minimal.

At the time of the negotiations, we examined additional marketing outlets and attempted to discern the implications should Echostar decide to join in.

Joshua and Gene constantly kept me abreast of the talks with Microsoft. During one particularly rough stretch of the negotiations, I was forced to rent a private jet and fly to Redmond for dinner with Jon DeVaan in an attempt to resolve the crisis. Immediately after the meeting, I got back on the jet for a redeye flight to Washington in order to make it on time for an early-morning meeting with the Postmaster General.

To the credit of the Microsoft people, it must be said that

they were aggressive yet fair. In contrast to their reputation as rough negotiators, the degree to which they leveraged their power was quite reasonable. After four months of long and tiring negotiations, we finally reached an agreement and the announcement was released to the press on February 16:

> "Microsoft Corp and Gilat Satellite Networks Ltd. today announced plans to provide the first consumer two-way satellite broadband offering designed to improve Internet connection speed and user experience across America. This marks the first time that two companies have teamed up to offer consumers high-speed Internet access via two-way satellite, which is especially exciting for people who do not have access to any other broadband connectivity solutions. Trials of the two-way satellite service have begun, and wide availability of (the) service is expected by the end of 2000. "

The press release also informed the public of the establishment of the new company, Gilat-to-Home, in which Microsoft was investing $50 million in return for 26% of the company's shares. It also made note of Zur Feldman's appointment as the company's CEO. Richard Belluzzo, Microsoft's vice president for the Consumer Group, was quoted as saying that, "This offering helps us deliver the Everyday Web by making high-speed access a reality for more consumers and joining forces with an industry leader like Gilat makes this possible". I also chimed in with a statement of my own: "We've said from the outset that one of the most important aspects for launching Gilat-To-Home is finding a strong Internet brand that would provide rapid access to the consumer. MSN, with its market leadership and high customer satisfaction, is the perfect partner with which to build Gilat-To-Home".

There was one more bombshell in our press release: The product "will be available directly from Microsoft as well as... RadioShacks throughout the United States...With more than 7,000 RadioShack stores located within five minutes of 94 percent of U.S. households and businesses, the retailer will be ready to demonstrate, offer and install this national broadband solution to all interested U.S. consumers by the end of 2000".

Not only were hundreds of articles published in newspapers, magazines, and websites, but, for the first time since Gilat was founded, we were also making headlines. The news caused quite a stir on the market, as industry and financial analysts disseminated their forecasts throughout the world: "A satellite covers a huge area", a trade journal quoted Lee Hungean, an analyst at a well known reaearch firm. "The deployment can be carried out quite rapidly. Deploying the system before the construction of a high-speed ground-based network may constitute an advantage..." Ty Carmanel of Credit Suisse could not contain his excitement: "The competition will find it very difficult to array themselves in a competition versus Microsoft and Gilat..." All the important trade journals wrote about our new product. The argument can be made that the very fact a high-speed internet service can be accessed via satellite was brought to the public's attention by Gilat.

The name 'Gilat' was on everyone's lips, and my inbox exploded with emails from various organizations all over the world. The the demand for my time left me gasping for breath.

On February 20, less than a week after the announcement of the deal with Microsoft, a crucial phone call arrived from Mark Jackson of Echostar: "Charlie wants to cut a deal with you guys. He was really impressed with your agreement with RadioShack. Come over at once for negotiations. We want to announce a deal in three days".

I flew to Echostar's offices in Denver with Joshua and Zur, for two days of intensive discussions. While the talks with Microsoft lasted four months and the agreement encompassed hundreds of pages, the Echostar deal was done in two days and was articulated in a memorandum of understanding two and a half pages long. Every contentious issue was solved in a swift and painful manner. We would express our reservations, and Charlie either accepted or rejected them right then and there . If we agreed, the negotiations would continue; if we stood our ground, Echostar would have sent us packing with a stern warning: "Should you have any second thoughts and return to the negotiating table, you can expect even less favorable terms than the offer you walked away from".

The news of the partnership and Echostar's investment in Gilat-to-Home was released to the press on February 23. The announcement was made during the annual convention of Echostar's dealers at the Adam's Mark Hotel in Denver. From our standpoint, the timing was perfect. Echostar's announcement helped us maintain our momentum and bolstered our status as the hottest goods on the market. Many other announcements were also made at the convention, but ours easily attracted the most attention. After unveiling the news, Charlie invited me onto the podium. Wearing an Echostar shirt, I explained the strategic implications of the deal for both Echostar and Gilat, and the significance of the product for the American home consumer. We then proceeded to Gilat-to-Home's booth in order to demonstrate the product to the dealers. A lively crowd congested around the booth and bombarded us with questions.

All the industry's top analysts were on hand, and they lavished our latest move with unequivocal praise: "Another huge victory for Gilat", said Rob Kaimowitz of Furman Selz; "Microsoft and Echostar — more solid penetration points for Gilat", wrote Tim Luke of Lehman; and John Coates of Salomon Smith Barney offered us his "congratulations".

The shares of both companies skyrocketed. On the day of the announcement, Echostar's stock soared by over $20 to $120 and Gilat's stock rose by $8 to $168. The number of articles in the press continued to grow, and we lost track of the number of inquiries coming our way. On February 28, we published the tremendous financial results for 1999 (the same year in which we snatched away the market leadership from Hughes) and that very night we raised $350 million in overnight convertible bonds.

February 2000 marked the highpoint for Gilat. It was the pinnacle of a long journey that had begun fourteen years earlier. When the five founders entered the tunnel, we didn't have much to offer. There were some vague ideas and directions, but nothing concrete. However, what we did have was a vision, a team culture, a wonderful friendship, and a strong desire to win. It was these very assets that enabled us to marshal a huge, concerted effort. Now the moment had finally arrived when we could say that, 'We did it.' The screens on the floor of the Stock Exchange were proof of our ascendance. On February, Gilat — G for Gidi, Y for Yoel, L for Levinberg, and T for Tirosh — was trading at over $4 billion market cap, the peak value for a company that started out in a studio apartment in north Tel-Aviv. We were on the summit for but one fleeting moment. The moment was too short for my taste, but it was all ours. We earned it in the trenches by dint of our wherewithal to infiltrate the right place at the right time. Gilat had proven our theory about 'a gun in a knife fight".

As these lines are being written, I am no longer at Gilat. Several years have passed since I left the company. Nevertheless, what John Connely, the senior executive at GE, told Yoav as we reached our apex will accompany me for many years to come: "No other company has yet to accomplish what you guys did during the first quarter of 2000…"

On February 18, we installed the first two units of our new product. One unit was installed in my house in McLean and the second at the home of one of the employees. The first hundred units were installed at the homes of Gilat's and Spacenet's employees. These units served as a sort of test lab, which enabled us to get the service up and running. Thereafter, we installed units at the homes of senior executives at Microsoft and Echostar and recruited lists of friends and family members that would get to test the service in the coming weeks. Meanwhile, we trained installation companies and prepared for the deployment of thousands of units in the months ahead.

As usual, everything worked according to plan at the initial sites, which were located at the homes of our most patient employees and installed by our top people. However, problems began to surface during the following weeks, the biggest of which inevitably transpired at the homes of top executives at Microsoft and Echostar. In general, the units were taking too long to install. There were also a few bizarre incidents: Damage was caused to one house while the installer was inserting the cables, while another rep fell into the living room after the roof gave in beneath his feet.

Like any new network, the regular crashes began after a few hundred installations, and the service was down for many long hours. Once again, we returned to the days of cleaning the bugs that hampered the launching of the Rite-Aid network, but this time we were dealing with an entirely new product. We received impatient calls from Microsoft and an invitation to an emergency meeting at Echostar. The new employees, who were being absorbed into the newly-created company at a breakneck pace, started to lose faith in the network. Once again we bore witness to the difference between American employees — who tend to lose their bearings when things don't go according to plan — and Israelis — who improvise, persist, and keep on trying until they find a solution. As usual, we concentrated on repairing the defects and entered the text-book crisis mode: we held a daily meeting and flew over engineers and other professionals from Israel to the United States. Zur took full charge of the crisis and kept his calmness even during the most trying moments.

During this period, we encountered one of the most riveting phenomena of the high-tech world: the spawning of cult-like cultures around new technologies. During the initial stages of the launching of a new product, the most sophisticated users — many of whom are *not* employees and have no vested interest in the product — ravenously probe the system for every possible feature and use. Our own employees, programmers from Microsoft, technical people from Echostar, and assorted application developers, as well as those computer geeks and technology freaks that banged on our doors to receive the service first, all served as beneficent hackers. They ran every possible application and downloaded so much data that they shattered every traffic model that we had designed. Their tinkering compelled us to set up a "traffic police" and develop monitoring and control tools that would enable us to supervise the amount of bandwidth allotted to each user.

The most problematic application was the Napster (a program for downloading large files, primarily films and music), which accounted for no less than 40% of our traffic. Since the network was designed for ordinary browser use, we — and for that matter all other internet providers — constantly adjusted the system in order to meet the users' changing needs.

Despite the difficulties, the product attracted a passionate following on the internet. Dozens of forums and newsgroups discussed our product and sent us recommendations for improving the service. People even wrote programs that improved the system's performance and allowed others to use their software for free. Websites were established with recommendations and tips on how to get the most out of our service, and some of the web authors even asked to be compensated for their advice...

The most impressive example of customer initiative first came to my attention in an email that was sent to me by one of our employees: "Yoel, open this", he wrote me. "It's incredible". Unable to resist, I checked out the website and couldn't believe my own eyes. Macintosh computers make up only a small percentage of the domestic PC market. Therefore, from an economic standpoint, it isn't worth going through all the trouble to build a framework for the Mac. However, the dedicated Mac user who built this site described, step-by-step, how to connect our product to the Macintosh. He explained what hardware and software was needed and provided explanations with colorful illustrations. In fact, his documentation style and graphics would not have embarrassed any of our documentation books. Furthermore, he formed a discussion group and assisted any Mac owner that wanted to use our service. If Gilat would have prepared a manual for connecting Macs to our service, the expenses would have probably run into the many tens of thousands of dollars… I was absolutely astonished by the voluntary enterprise of the computer geeks.

Our initial users undoubtedly enhanced the product. Information that passed by word of mouth, in closed and open forums, contributed immensely to the creation of the new medium.

In April, I installed a unit at my bother Arnon's cabin in Lake Tahoe, Nevada. He sent me an email with his impressions:

"Hi dear brother,

I am sitting here in our incredible cabin and for the first time in our history in Tahoe we are "properly" connected to the world. We came to Tahoe yesterday and I run to the new computer to find out how this baby is behaving and how good is the invention. I opened the MSN and immediately read about the raid for Elian Gonzales from his relative's home in Miami.
Since this write up included voice clips I clicked on those and actually heard the reports from Clinton and others. I sat in owe and it took me some time to digest the feeling that there is no limit of man's inventions. Next was logging onto the server at work and receiving my emails here at the cabin.

In short, I was playing with this new tool for hours enjoying the freedom of being part of the cyber community. It felt great. The connection works flawlessly and I can't tell the difference between my cable modem at home and my Gilat 2 Home here.

I then remembered a conversation between the two of us about one

or two years ago in which you told me about the plan to come out with a satellite connection to the net. At that time I mentioned that I would be happy to use one. The conversation was filed away and low and behold a few years passed and the thought coalesced to a real system that I am sure will concur the world (at least where no good communication exists). I am proud to use the system that you and your company conceived, created and executed.
Thank you for the opportunity to have one of the early systems I am sure we will enjoy it for many years to come.

Yours

Arnon   "

In June, we prepared for an exhibition of satellite television dealers in Las Vegas. The show features scores of exhibitors and is attended by thousands of dealers, as well as many journalists and analysts. We decided to take part in the show in order to demonstrate the service, educate the market, and sign up distributors. Moreover, we wanted to stress the fact that we were the first ones to release a working product. We knew that Hughes would also be participating in the show and exhibiting their competing product, which was introduced after ours. Gilat, Echostar, and one of the large distributors all demonstrated our product in their respective booths. We prepared a five-minute presentation and managed to put together a modest document to hand out to visitors.

Gilat was the most prominent exhibitor at the show. Despite the poor location of our exhibit (due to the fact that we registered late), every day about a thousand people passed through our booth. Every fifteen minutes, fifty people squeezed into our small booth (all of 20 square meters) and watched our presentation. The flood of registrants was so high that our database crashed, and we were forced to manually register many of the visitors. The passionate conversations with the dealers were indicative of the immense excitement that our new product aroused. The exhibition's most memorable moment took place at the cafeteria. As I left the registrar and turned to sit down with a few of my guys, one of the visitors at the exhibition came up to me and asked if we were from Gilat-to-Home. "Yes", I said.

"And what's your position?" he continued.

"I'm the chairman of the company", I blushed.

"How do you guys dare use a name like Gilat-to-Home?" he shouted at me. "How do you expect me to sell a service with that sort of a name? Who here has ever heard of Gilat? Haven't you ever heard of the concept of a 'brand name?' You guys have got to change the name!"

I was taken back by his impudence yet charmed by his concern, involvement, and desire to succeed. "Okay", I told him, "we'll change the name".

"Thanks", he said and kindly allowed me to tend to my lunch.

Inspired by the gung-ho distributor, we embarked on a brand development process, which above all entailed finding a new name for Gilat-to-Home. Zur had me read a thick book on creating brands, and I discovered that the Coca-Cola brand name is worth much more than the company's market value… In addition, we hired a prestigious positioning consultancy to spearhead the entire process and explain to us the principles behind the art of branding, including how to choose a name, conduct a market study, and cement a brand on the market. We also held a long discussion with them on the positioning strategies that Hughes and AOL might adopt. Our consultants' main premise was that, "Products are built in a factory — brands are built in the mind…" Similarly, the book contended that a brand is the promise of experience or a lifestyle, as well as the essence that bonds an organization to its customer or end user.

The positioning consultancy conducted a market study on 609 people, some of whom subscribed to the service. As expected, the results were extremely positive. The respondents pointed to the following advantages: speed; one price policy; the guarantee that they would always be connected (namely, users did not have to waste time dialing up the server); and the fact that the service had no connection whatsoever to the telephone and cable companies. The primary obstacles that were noted were the expensive one-time charge, the monthly fees, and the customers' satisfaction with their current service provider (which was typically good).

Naturally, the name-changing process was the climax of the entire brand development enterprise, and we even convened a special forum to discuss the issue. Several possible names were suggested, one of which was StarBand. I wasn't thrilled with the name, but most of the participants liked it. The moderator tried to weaken my resistance with a bit of humor: "When I spoke to Yoel about the name, he asked me 'If not Gilat-to-Home then Gilat-to-What?'" Everyone laughed, but I still wasn't sold on the name. To make matters worse, I was the only Israeli at the discussion because Zur had rushed off to be with his son, who was bitten by a snake and hospitalized. Consequently, I found myself pitted against a host of Americans who were in favor of the name. Before making a final decision, I consulted with my friends at Gilat and we weighed all the options. On the one hand, we can't tell them what to call the company, for they are the ones who would actually have to go out and sell the brand to their fellow Americans. On the other hand, StarBand may have suited the American audience, but the name was stripped of the Gilat spirit, which was so important to us. Against our intuition, we ultimately agreed to go with StarBand.

The day after the exhibition in Las Vegas, I wrote in my notebook that "the story is at its peak. We have to take StarBand public". Despite the fact that about 120 people were already working at the company and some 2,000 sites had been installed, StarBand was still in its infancy. Everything else being equal, it is usually easier to go public before you get bogged down by the company's actual performance and when all you have to sell is a 'story.' Once the company has a few quarters under its belt, some of the customers are bitter and the organization is primarily judged by its financial results. It took me over a month to convince Zur, Brian, and the boards of directors of StarBand and Gilat that the time was ripe for a public offering. However, once I had obtained the go-ahead, we rolled up our sleeves and the first draft of the prospectus was ready within six weeks.

This entire period was quite hectic and, of course, there were difficulties. For example, there was a problem with double IP addresses in the system, and the units at the homes of Charlie Ergen and Jon DeVaan, of all people, only worked intermittently… However, as is our custom, we continued to plow straight ahead.

Whereas StarBand was forging ahead, we were receiving reports of a complete standstill on the other side of the battle lines. On the day of their joint news conference, AOL and Hughes appeared to have the next big hit, while we appeared to be history. However, the tide had suddenly turned. From the moment the market heard of our new venture, AOL and Hughes were stopped in their tracks. Although they barely had a product, their brand was already *passé*. Needless to say, we were overwhelmingly pleased with these developments, as we had managed to derail their story and deliver a death blow to their product. The entire episode was further proof of the tremendous impact that a news story can have on a company's fortunes. The story is indeed the engine behind the wheels of industry.

We started working on the presentation for StarBand's IPO, which was scheduled for November. The presentation reflected the great demand that we anticipated for our product. If everything went according to plan, by the time of the offering RadioShack, Echostar, and our own advertising campaigns would already be in full swing. We positioned ourselves as an internet infrastructure company, which was planning a new satellite system that would reach millions of customers in the immediate future. The IPO's stated objectives were to finance the installation of the first wave of units and to plan and launch a state-of-the-art satellite system, which promised to be more efficient and to substantially lower the market price of the service.

We prepared an updated business model whereby we undertook to connect 25,000 subscribers by the end of the year, 250,000 by December 2001, and one million by the end of 2002. In addition, we set up a meeting with the representatives of the six largest investment banks on Wall Street. Yoav and Brian skillfully presided over the negotiations with the banks, each of which spared no effort to win the account . All the offers that we received from the rival banks placed the value of the company before the IPO at between \$2 and \$2.5 billion! Even we were surprised by the results. The story was indeed at its height, and we felt like the kings of the world.

On November 5, 2000, StarBand was officially launched at a most impressive ceremony in Washington. We demonstrated the service and explained its latent potential to the adoring crowd, which was comprised of scores of reporters, analysts, partners, employees, and friends. Moving speeches were given by David Trachtenberg, StarBand's new president, Zur, and I. However, the representative of an Indian tribe living at the bottom of the Grand Canyon stole the show. In a complicated logistical operation, StarBand installed several stations in the reservation's schools and public institutions. The representative explained the significance of the internet revolution for her village's residents, who didn't believe that they would ever be connected to the internet. In fact, the tribe was flabbergasted by the radio and television broadcasts as well as the enormous learning opportunities that were suddenly available to them for the first time. Many people in the audience were moved to tears by her speech

Yet another precedent was set the next day, as Gilat made it to the front page of the Washington Post for the first time in our history. Under the headline "Adding a New Channel to the Internet", Peter S. Goodman wrote the following story:

> "The first thing that happened after the high-speed Internet arrived in this Indian village was that some people started listening to the radio.
> An unremarkable occurrence, until one considers that the Havasupai Indian reservation sits at the bottom of the Grand Canyon, a two-hour drive and an eight mile walk from anything resembling a town. Its squat wooden houses are encased by the canyon walls. Radio never reached here before…"

That same day, two Washington television stations covered the story. One of the reports showed how we had installed the terminals in the reservation, and the second explained the technology's latent potential.

Not bad for a small company from Israel.

12

The Clear Sky Gets Cloudy

In the beginning of November 2000, we were on top of the world. We were being courted and complimented by investors and analysts; all the important newspapers were writing about Gilat's vision. Our dream of reaching the stars seemed as close as ever, and we naively believed that nothing could stop us.

However, only three weeks later, the world came to a halt. Nothing had prepared us for this eventuality. The pundits declared that the "internet bubble had burst", and "the new economy had reached the end of its line". Before we knew it, all our operations had been hit. The first sign of trouble surfaced on the Stock Market, where all the dot-com stocks took a sharp dive, but we maintained our cool. As high-tech veterans, we had grown accustomed to this sort of decline — precipitous as it may have been — and were certain that it would be followed by a swift recovery. to our dismay this was not the case: We failed to see the writing on the wall. The second sign was even more ominous: investment capital began to dry up. The first to have their faucets shut were the dot-com companies. Despite these developments, the dot-coms continued to burn up what little cash they had left at a reckless pace. "How Long can they Keep it Up?" screamed a headline in the *Wall Street Journal*.

Investors made it quite clear that they had stopped looking for investment opportunities. "A structural change is transpiring", Kent of Wellington, a leading institutional fund, told me. "This is no passing phase". I may have heard what he said, but am not too sure that I actually listened to his words and I certainly did not internalize them. Several weeks later, I asked Kent to invest in StarBand and then he really let me have it: "Are you crazy? You still don't understand what is happening to the market?" At long last, the message started seeping in.

The crisis caught us at the top of our game. A the time, we were number one in the world in terms of market share; selling equipment and providing services across five continents; and building new companies that promised to bring the revelation of high-speed internet to the domestic consumer. We had access to all the human and financial resources that we needed in order to ratchet up the pace of our growth and deployment. Gilat was sprinting towards the goal of annual sales in excess of $500 million, but at such break-neck speeds that any stick in the wheels was liable to end in disaster.

Only two months earlier, the future had seemed so bright. Within half a year of its establishment, StarBand was already dwarfing Gilat, and we disseminated its prospectus to the public. The prospectus was graced by the biggest names on Wall Street — Morgan Stanley, Merrill Lynch, and Salomon Smith Barney, names which any company would be proud to include on its prospectus. We were pitching a company whose initial pre-money valuation was $2.5 billion. Since Gilat held some 40% of StarBand's shares, its own value soared by about $1 billion. However, Gilat's stock dropped as soon as the prospectus was released. The reason was rather obvious: many investors decided to sell their shares in Gilat so that they could use the proceeds to purchase our latest hit — StarBand. "Why stay with the equipment manufacturer", they reasoned, "when the very same people are offering such a riveting story…" We felt as if Frankenstein's monster had turned on its master. StarBand's mercurial rise forced Gilat to start contending with an image problem: Gilat endeavored to become a full-fledged multinational corporation, but were we a manufacturer or a service provider?

We subsequently invited a group of managers and external consultants for a discussion on Gilat's positioning, and the consultants recommended that we change the name and logo. However, we adamantly refused, for it is not easy parting ways with a name that had accompanied us for thirteen years. In addition, the advisors formulated a new positioning strategy: "Gilat is enriching communication at work and at home; paving the way for a new lifestyle; offering a wide array of possibilities; liberating customers from other information infrastructures; and transmiting an aura of innovation that is changing the way the world communicates". In other words, Gilat is the living room of tomorrow.

We adopted this positioning strategy and gave a demonstration of the product and service at my house in McLean. The show consisted of a high-resolution plasma screen, a superb sound system, and five hundred of Echostar's television channels. The system served as both a computer and television. Everything was interactive, and all the manifold services could be accessed via a single remote control. The stunning demonstration featured a scene from the movie Apollo 13: the shuttle lifting off into the clear blue skies, leaving an impressive trail of fire in its wake. The camera then instantly shifted to a close up of a woman in the crowd with tears in her eyes. Last and not least, all this was transmitted via the internet and was entirely independent of television stations. In essence, we were unveiling the dawn of a new era, and the slogan that would embody this entire vision was, "Gilat — Communications without Boundaries".

The most glaring sign that the bubble was about to burst was the sudden turnaround in our relationship with AOL, which at the time was the undisputed champion of the internet world. During this same period, AOL announced its mega-merger with Time Warner, which possessed an unrivaled treasure trove of media content. Consequently, many experts considered the new combination to be the leading company of the twenty-first century. In contrast to Microsoft, AOL was focused entirely on the internet;Gilat and StarBand couldn't hope for a better partner than Time Warner-AOL.

AOL contacted us in October 2000 and asked us to come to their offices and give a presentation on Gilat and StarBand. We had put quite an effort into the presentation and by the time we arrived at AOL's legendary headquarters in Dulles, VA — a half hour drive from our offices — I could feel the butterflies in my stomach. The room was packed with people: twenty AOL representatives versus five from Gilat. From the questions they raised, we could tell that they were very impressed. On the other hand, people were constantly coming and going, mobile phones were ringing, and the actual decision makers were only present for part of the meeting. Therefore, we were worried that the idea wouldn't catch on among the company's upper echelons.

After the meeting, we sat down with David Colburn, AOL's

shrewd chief negotiator, and Jay Rappaport, David's deputy who was responsible for deals in the United States. We discussed a colossal investment of $600 million in StarBand. I felt like Alice in Wonderland, as the deal was too good to be true. The price that AOL would pay for the shares would be a little less than the price of the offering scheduled for November, so that it stood to turn a profit right after the issue.

In turn, Gilat/StarBand would use the cash to subsidize new customers' equipment. During that period, it was standard practice for companies to subsidize the price of its products to acquire subscribers – the so-called Subscriber Acquisition Cost.. Our thinking was that if subscribers signed long-term agreements for broadband internet service, the equipment would be sold to them for considerably less than its actual cost and the balance would eventually be covered by the monthly service payments. Besides the equipment, the AOL people asked that we allocate a significant portion of their investment to advertising. Both sides also spoke of mutual exclusivity, without detracting from their relationship with Hughes or from our relationship with Microsoft. In addition, they raised the issue of collaborating with us on the internet service that we were providing to schools with ZapMe!. They hoped to outfit every child that used the service with an AOL email address and to sign a similar deal in Europe and Japan. We also discussed the development of a user-friendly satellite browser that would be predicated on the Netscape technology, which also belonged to AOL.

Both parties agreed to a series of follow-up meetings, and they appointed a full-time project coordinator in order to guarantee the necessary attention of the relevant AOL executives. David and Jay understood the time pressure that we were under due to StarBand's imminent IPO and thus made every effort to push the project forward. The title they chose for the next meeting was, "Look what AOL can do for You…" We left their offices is a state of ecstasy. Only a year and a half ago, they were Hughes' partners, and it now appeared as if we were on the verge of doing a deal with them. If the negotiations panned out, StarBand would have two 'minor' shareholders in the form of Microsoft and AOL. By dint of the huge amounts of money that were expected to flow into StarBand's coffers, we would be able to underwrite the acquisition of hundreds of thousands of new customers. Moreover,

Time Warner's rich inventory of media content would improve our service by leaps and bounds. Needless to say, our bankers were also ecstatic over the prospects of a partnership with AOL-Time Warner, as this was our ticket to the next level.

The next day, we sent David and Jay a one-page proposal, which summarized the understanding that had been reached during the meeting. However, it took them a month to get back to us; during that month the stock market deteriorated further. Consequently, what was good in October was no longer good enough for November, and their counter-offer was completely different than the one we had rushed over to them. Despite the changes, the agreement was still reasonable, and we were eager to consummate the deal and get the ball rolling. During that same month, they also conducted a comprehensive background check for the purpose of determining whether the two companies were indeed compatible. Their study included a thorough examination of StarBand's business plan and the agreement with Microsoft; StarBand passed the test with flying colors. Thereafter, a series of technical discussions were held on the browser.

During the weeks that followed, AOL suggested that the service be inaugurated in Europe, a peripheral market in which their rival Microsoft was not active. We agreed to begin in Europe and failed to realize what a mistake this was. In essence, they wanted to buy time until it became clear just how bleak the situation on Wall Street really was. This strategy enabled them to keep open the option of a deal with Gilat, without having to make a serious commitment. Unfortunately for us, the capital market continued its steady decline over the course of the negotiations.

AOL's revised draft concerning the American market arrived on January 23, 2001. The terms were awful, and I had reservations on practically every line of the contract. To begin with, they wanted a trilateral agreement with Echostar. Secondly, the original investment of $600 million had whittled down to a mere $150 million. In addition, they suddenly demanded extensive stock options, which in our opinion were entirely unwarranted. Finally, they spelled out their final decision regarding the entire issue of marketing cooperation in a single word: "no".

Breaking my habit of brief replies, I responded to their counter-offer with an email that was a page and a half in length and rather violent. David Colburn's response was fast in coming and no less hostile. His letter primarily dealt with macro topics, but it contained the following unequivocal message: "Friends, take it or leave it". I then turned to Jon DeVaan of Microsoft for some informal advice. After filling him in on our dialogue with AOL, I asked Jon if Microsoft was interested in a similar deal. Jon mulled it over for a moment and answered that there was a distinct possibility, but it would entail an immense lobbying effort on my part in the corridors of Microsoft.

Following my chat with Jon, I got back to David and told him that we were reopening talks with Microsoft on a similar deal. David was outraged. On February 10 he sent me an improved draft and all that remained were a few minor details to sort out.

However, the Stock Market soon took an abrupt turn for the worse, which marked the beginning of a tailspin that would last for two whole years. From that point on, we hardly managed to get hold of the AOL execs on the phone, and the drafts that arrived kept getting worse and worse. Every single understanding that we somehow managed to ring out of them vanished after a couple of hours, and the newest draft offer was always less appealing than its predecessor. AOL was angling for a one-sided agreement that would only obligate StarBand and oust Microsoft from the picture. At a certain stage of the talks, they even notified us that AOL reserved the right to unilaterally terminate the negotiations at any point in time.

To add insult to injury, the AOL executives started behaving like gangsters. I recall one particular occasion in which I was on a hike in the Galilee, and David was supposed to give me a ring at 5:00 pm. We were in an area with poor reception, so I hurried to an area where we could hold an uninterrupted conversation. David indeed called at 5:00 sharp, but his opening words left a bitter aftertaste: "Hi Yoel. You have two minutes for this conversation…".

I had never come across such heavy-handed negotiating tactics and felt like calling everything off. In fact, everyone at AOL opened their conversations with the same line, as this was apparently their way of conducting negotiations. Meetings were postponed or canceled altogether, and they didn't bother returning telephone calls or emails. Our allies in their corridors tried to help us, but the entire process was degrading and, ultimately, fruitless. For the first time in the history of the company, we started to get a taste for the bitterness of defeat.

By the spring of 2000, the entire business world came to a screeching halt. The most prominent manifestation of this development was the shortage of cash, and the first to feel the brunt were the dot-com companies, including the eBusinesses that we worked with. ZapMe! was not only hampered by the cash crunch, but found itself trapped in a raging political storm. A prominent coalition of activists embarked on a public crusade against the company in order to prevent their "children from being exposed to advertisements in school". The ZapMe! people tried to put up a fight; at one point, they even looked into the possibility of switching to a model without advertisements, which would be funded by federal grants and sponsorships from large companies like Ford. Despite the problems, AOL was still eager to work with ZapMe!, as they wanted to furnish their own email addresses to the two million pupils who already had email courtesy of ZapMe!. We also thought that the company had great potential and that they could help us bring our technology to schools, as well as internet cafes throughout the world in areas without communication infrastructures. Therefore, we didn't want to stand on the side and watch ZapMe! keel over due to a lack of funds. As a result, Gilat decided to acquire a majority stake in the company for a considerable sum of money. Only later, when we were desperately strapped for cash ourselves, did we realize what a mistake it was.

Another company that saw its cash reserves dry up was AccentHealth — the company that wanted to install thousands of monitors in clinics throughout the United States. As noted earlier, we really believed in their vision and, following a slugfest with Hughes, we ultimately landed the account. In the aftermath of the Stock Market's collapse, however, AccentHealth experienced many difficulties. Its management tried to blame us for their troubles, and there were indeed technical problems. However, the majority of them stemmed from their own logistical flaws and not our network. Towards the end of 2000, after we had already installed 1,550 units we were left with no choice but to pull the plug on an exciting project that was supposed to consist of ten thousand sites.

The situation at other companies we worked with was no better. They all cut back their level of operations, and the first ones went under in the beginning of 2001. Within a few years, the network-based businesses model (whereby a company's value is determined by the number of people using their network instead of the traditional benchmarks of revenue and expense) was a thing of the past.

For some reason, the crisis had yet to hit Latin America with full force. Gilat always enjoyed a great deal of success south of the Rio Grande. Our aggressive sales people blanketed the entire continent, and everyone knew who we were. We established extensive telephony networks in Peru and Columbia, installed tens of thousands of terminals in Brazil, and continued to operate a modest service-based business in Argentina that we had acquired from Spacenet. Therefore, it was only natural that we started to develop a counterpart to StarBand in Latin America. The idea of StarBand Latin America was conceived at a media and internet conference that was initiated by Goldman Sachs in early 2000. Everyone at the conference talked about South America's infrastructure problems and the need for broadband, and we already had exactly what the doctor ordered: a new, fully-operational, and reliable solution which offered interactivity and enabled information to be disseminated in a rapid yet convenient manner. Following the conference, the media tycoon Rupert Murdoch invited us to a meeting on his empire's Latin American operations. Murdoch was interested in working with us, and his people asked us for a detailed proposal. We also met with all the continent's large internet providers and television distributors. Insofar as financing our Latin American enterprises was concerned, we received an investment offer from a large investment bank, but we quickly turned it down. In addition, we had reached the advanced stages of our negotiations with Microsoft on the Latin American market. All the market studies we conducted pointed to the tremendous potential that the continent held in store for StarBand.

StarBand continued to expend a great deal of time and effort on consolidating its service, and we thus took great pride in showcasing our achievements in the United States to our Latin American hosts. As noted, there is nothing quite as attractive as the sweet smell of success, and we were indeed courted by a host of South American service providers and strategic partners. In August, I met with Jaime Chico Pardo, the CEO of TELMEX, the largest telecom firm in Latin America and the primary communication service provider in Mexico and other countries as well.

Jaime had heard about Gilat and StarBand and asked for a comprehensive presentation on our technologies and business opportunities in the fields of telephony and the internet. The meeting was scheduled to last an hour, but we ended up sitting with Jaime for three hours. He was extremely interested, asked excellent questions, and examined several business alternatives. All of TELMEX's executives participated in the meeting, along with their key procurement and technical people. We hammered out a huge equipment deal, which indeed panned out, and discussed joint ventures and investment opportunities in both Latin America and the United States. TELMEX worked extensively with Microsoft, and Jaime dazzled us with stories about his meetings with Bill Gates. We then set up a work group and immediately began to lay the groundwork for the new partnership. By the end of the meeting, we were on cloud nine.

The capital market was also intrigued by our potential in South America. Blackstone, one of the largest investment funds in the world, even tired to pressure us into letting them invest in our Latin American operations. A Taiwanese executive, who managed a fund worth hundreds of millions of dollars, also displayed an interest in StarBand Latin America. He stopped by for breakfast at my home in McLean, saw the demonstration of the home entertainment system, and couldn't stop raving about it. "We have only one request", he told me after the meal. "We want to invest at least $75 million". However, at the time, we were at the height of our negotiations with TELMEX, so I refused to commit. "I'll think it over and get back to you", I answered.

We repeated the classic mistake of refusing money. In fact, we were so choosy about the investors for StarBand Latin America that we ended up missing the train. According to our estimates, the subsidiary was worth about $300 million on the day it was founded. In practice, though, the amount of capital we raised did not even befit a company worth $100 million. By the time we were ready to accept the original terms, the investor had lowered his assessment of the company's value and reduced his offer accordingly. We simultaneously held negotiations with several large financial partners and strategic partners, some of whom competed against each other. As a result, the dialogue was complicated and the horse trading occasionally got bogged down by ulterior motives. The negotiations with AOL over our Latin American operations are an excellent example of what went wrong: AOL had recently penetrated into Latin America with the declared intention of conquering the market for itself and wanted us to work exclusively with them. Consequently, all the other potential investors felt intimidated by the internet giant. TELMEX and Microsoft thus also tried to pull us into their orbit and prevent us from doing business with others. We found ourselves caught in a tug of war and tried to maneuver our way between all the aggressive suitors…

Amid all the wheeling and dealing, the capital market finally hit rock bottom. A telephone conversation with TELMEX was the first sign that the rules of the game had changed: "Investment — no; strategic relations — yes". However, we weren't alert enough and failed to discern the warning that was latent in this statement, namely that all the initial investment offers would be whisked off the table. Within a matter of weeks, the financial investors gradually stiffened their terms. In addition, our strategic partners were forced to contend with their own problems, so that we were left out to dry.

By the time we started to comprehend the extent of the decline, it was already too late. We were prepared to revert to options that we had previously written off as insufficient, but they were no longer on the table. The most common excuse for the delays was that the managers were waiting for the approval of the board of directors, which naturally failed to materialize. Moreover, everyone suddenly became obsessed with what others were doing, as investors were afraid to take the initiative. Our Latin American dream had started to turn sour.

Despite the writing on the wall, we had difficulties coming to grips with the new status quo because from our standpoint everything was fine: the customers were pleased and the demand for our products and services was very high. Our main problem was the rate at which we were using up our cash. Since StarBand was subsidizing equipment sites, it accrued a debt of about $300 on each installation. Consequently, we found ourselves up against a strange conundrum: demand was enormous, but the more it grew the greater the strain on our cash flow. We anxiously waited for the investors to pour in money and cover our debts, but nothing came of all their promises. Many long months were to pass before it dawned on us that we had missed the next train as well.

More than anything else, our vision was blurred by our skyrocketing sales. At the end of 2000, the demand for StarBand had reached unprecedented heights: Microsoft announced their relationship with RadioShack; and within a span of two weeks, Echostar ordered 20,000 terminals. Soon, orders soared from several dozen a day to thousands per month. Furthermore, StarBand was talking to several chain stores, such as Best Buy and Circuit City, about having them market the service, and we ran an advertising campaign under the slogan, "Just Look Up..". An on-line sales outlet was launched on StarBand's website, which raked in orders for another 5,000 terminals within a few days. The forecasts that arrived from the market and StarBand's order department surpassed all our expectations. Finally, AOL was exerting pressure on us to commit to supplying hundreds of thousands of units in 2001.

As a result, we assumed that we would sell whatever we managed to produce. We had already manufactured 120,000 units in the year 2000 and planned to produce another 300,000 units in 2001. In order to meet our production targets, we ordered large volumes of equipment and took commitments of hundreds of millions of dollars with our suppliers. We were banking on the money from the large investors and StarBand's IPO, but the investors were waffling and the offering was postponed. The market had internalized everything that had transpired on Wall Street, and the bankers thus constantly lowered the value of the offering. Under the circumstances, we had no choice but to consent to their requests. The value of the company still stood at $2.5 billion in September 2000, within two months it had dipped to a little over $1 billion dollars. By December, we had given up on the entire idea of going public, as it became obvious that, even at the reduced valuation, none of the investors were interested in new offerings.

StarBand, which had hoped to raise $400 million with which to pay back its debt to Gilat and build up a critical mass of subscribers, came up empty-handed. If StarBand had gone public a month earlier, we would have raised hundreds of millions of dollars. But this time around, luck wasn't on our side and we essentially blew our big chance by a hairsbreadth. This was also a personal setback for us, as our five previous offerings had all, at the very least, met our expectations. Consequently, the failure of the StarBand IPO had rudely changed our theory that we were somehow immune to the cycles of Wall Street.

StarBand rapidly burnt through its money. The demand from the field continued to grow, and the company continued to stock up. As a result, we turned to a broad range of potential investors in an effort to raise capital for StarBand.

Despite the fact that that the global crisis had slowly made its way to the continent we still believed in our ability to raise money for our Latin American operations. We attempted to convince strategic partners, like Boeing and Lockheed Martin, to invest in StarBand Latin America. However, the investors that evaluated our Latin American operations were actually interested in investing in the United States. All the investors we solicited kept asking the same unanswerable question: "If the situation is so good, why aren't your current investors raising their stakes? What happened to the deep pockets of Microsoft and Echostar?" It turned out that the very fact that we had turned to these organizations damaged our chances of raising money in Latin America. "If the United States is now off limits to investors", they asserted, "why take a risk on Latin America?"

On the heels of these defeats, we rushed to Redmond, the stronghold of Microsoft, where the entire story with AOL came back to haunt us. When we were at the height of our success, we should have continued to foster our relations with the key people at Microsoft and work with them on joint products. Now when we needed Microsoft most, we suddenly came to the realization that we did not have enough supporters in Redmond. As usual, Jon DeVaan tried to lend us a hand, but he was no longer active: and the people calling the shots — other managers who did not share his excitement over StarBand to begin with — turned us down. "First raise money from others…", they told us.

Left with few other alternatives, we headed out to Echostar's headquarters in Denver. Echostar had invested $50 million in StarBand, but we had already spent the money. Charlie Ergen gave us all the time we needed to state our case. He made an honest effort to understand the changes that we had incorporated into our economic model in light of the financial crisis and asked piercing questions on StarBand's ability to survive in a world bereft of external capital. We put together a comprehensive presentation with explanations on every facet of StarBand's expenditures and how an increase in subscribers affected our cash-flow cycle. We attempted to prove to Charlie that one hundred thousand subscribers constituted our breakeven point — a target which in those days still appeared to be well within our reach — and once we reached that benchmark everything would work itself out.

Charlie promised to think it over, but it was obvious that we had failed to convince him that we were a solid investment. I had done everything possible to cultivate my relationship with Charlie, who I held in the highest regard. He started out in the early 1970s selling antennas for large satellites and built up the company with his own bare hands. As the business flourished, Charlie purchased several large communication satellites and transformed Echostar into a $20 billion empire. I had counted on his help, but came away disappointed.

The stark reality began to sink in during the flight from Denver back to McLean. Amiram and I looked at one another and asked ourselves if we were capable of guaranteeing StarBand's survival.

We continued to make heroic efforts to raise money in a world that no longer cared for 'stories' and was solely interested in results. We felt as if we were stuck in the mud.

Alongside the dramatic race for money, I was swept up, against my will, in yet another drama: a struggle between different groups within the organization. Each unit was charged with different tasks: there was the core business unit, which sold data and telephony networks throughout the world; Spacenet, which sold services in the United States; a group that sold equipment in Latin America; a team that sold equipment and services in Europe; and now StarBand — both the US and Latin American groups — had been thrown into the mix. Each of the groups was independent and tended to its own matters. Of course, there was also headquarters in Israel, which handled development, manufacturing, marketing, and business development.

Despite our phenomenal growth, all systems continued to operate like clockwork. Even when the machinery creaked, everything worked; everyone understood their role and cooperated. Consequently, it was easy getting messages across to the entire organization. Amiram and I dedicated quite a bit of time to visiting the various offices, keeping our people up-to-date, and holding review meetings and personal conversations. We periodically convened company-wide update meetings, and the unit heads were on good terms with one another. Gilat possessed a passionate culture that was grounded on unity and responsibility. The unity was expressed by the willingness of all our employees to help each other out, while the emphasis on meeting targets was indicative of the sense of responsibility that united the entire organization.

On the very day the dot-com bubble burst, we started having problems running the organization. It became increasingly difficult to meet sales targets, and the pitch of the creaks in the machinery intensified. In accordance with the old Hebrew proverb "The destitute of your own city come before the destitute of your neighbor", every internal unit was only concerned with its own results. The fact that a substantial portion of the compensation was based on commissions only aggravated matters.

The most contentious issue was commissions on deals that spanned several geographic regions. These issues had always existed, but what was once a slight headache had deteriorated into a chronic migraine. Moreover, the problem of internal prioritization of resources turned into a critical issue. The intensity of the claims and complaints that I received in my email reached new heights. The internal politics, which of course no organization can escape from entirely, had spun out of control and turned into a severe company-wide phenomena.

The first major crack involved the core-products sales force. They vehemently contended that they had not been receiving enough attention from management and that the R&D people were practically ignoring them. Unlike the past, when the entire organization would focus on a large deal, it had indeed become rather difficult to grab management's attention and secure the necessary resources. They argued that their ability to cultivate customers, land deals, and develop new markets had been seriously hampered, as reaching these goals naturally require technological advances, marketing focus, and a great deal of support from management.

There was no shortage of these problems. During our annual sales meeting, the Chinese group described a huge potential deal with the Chinese Ministry of Water Resources that had gone up in smoke. The Ministry was interested in expanding their network for measuring flood information throughout the country. They turned to our Chinese sales people with a list of specifications and expected a comprehensive demonstration within several weeks. The sales people subsequently forwarded the specifications to R&D

and underscored the tight time schedules involved. However, the development groups were preoccupied with other projects and missed the deadline. This marked the first time that Gilat had failed to meet a commitment because our development people were stretched too thin. With tears in their eyes, the Chinese described how they lost the deal. Moreover, immense damage had been caused to the reputation of Gilat and our sales people in China.

The second rift was an outright feud between Spacenet and StarBand. This episode was perhaps the most personally frustrating, considering all the energy I had expended. The two companies resided in adjacent buildings, and Spacenet's marketing and sales department occupied the top floor of StarBand's building. When StarBand was first launched, it relied on Spacenet for many services. The latter operated the network for StarBand's subscribers and also offered computer and logistical support to them. Within a short period of time, though, StarBand had rapidly grown into a company with over 300 people —compared to Gilat's 2,000 — and established all the departments it needed in order to operate as a fully independent company. At the outset, StarBand's operations department worked out of Atlanta and was primarily comprised of the original Tridom group, which did a wonderful job. However, the seething historical animosity between Tridom and Spacenet also managed to sour the relations between the latter and StarBand. Before Gilat acquired Spacenet, Tridom had been acquired by GE, which then merged Tridom with its other subsidiary, Spacenet. During the merger process, the two organizations became embroiled in an ugly struggle to prove their technological and operational superiority to the new bosses at GE, and I never managed to mend the deep rift between the two.

The StarBand-Spacenet dispute was further intesified by the establishment of a strong operations group at StarBand, which was headed by two Israelis who had previously worked at Spacenet. Not only did StarBand — the rising star — feel absolutely independent of Spacenet, but felt the same way towards Gilat as well. Spacenet had a difficult time seeing StarBand spread its wings and garner resources from Gilat, and these jealousies steadily deteriorated into bitter power struggles.

Furthermore, turf battles arose between Spacenet and StarBand over the gray areas of operational and marketing rights. On the face of things, there appeared to be a clear and logical division of duties between the two organizations: one catered to the private and public sectors, while the other catered to the consumer market. However, what happens when a company wants to connect the network to its employees' homes? Does the business go to StarBand or Spacenet? Naturally, egos clashed and the turf wars and personal jealousies became a deadly combination.

Zur Feldman — who is superb at managing relations and imparting values to his staff — did his best under trying conditions, but even he occasionally lost his temper. That said, the Spacenet people were much more vocal. I increasingly found myself forced into the role of kindergarden teacher, and both sides realized that I was fed up with the situation. Although I believed that the vision and common good would ultimately prevail, the reality out in the field didn't match my expectations. I remember internal discussions at Spacenet in which I was accused of personally identifying with StarBand and of always taking their side. "Who do they think they are?" they lashed out at me. "We have been in this business twenty years, and they barely have a year under their belts. The milk on their lips has yet to dry…" This was all well and true, but from my standpoint the most important barometer was the present results, and there was no denying that StarBand was doing a standup job. Nevertheless, I felt like a father torn between two sons…

Power struggles also reared their ugly heads in Latin America, where the services and equipment groups started to compete directly against each other. Although I couldn't believe my own two eyes, the two units occasionally even attempted to inflict damage on one another. Although there was a very strong personal element to this feud, the primary motive, as usual, was money. The struggle over commissions got so out of hand that we were forced to unite the two operations and subordinated one group to the other. Only once these stern measures were in place did we manage to clarify the division of responsibilities between the two warring factions.

Last but not least, there were the problems surrounding the development unit. For many years, Gilat's R&D department was the strongest component in the company. During Gilat's first years, the development teams were run by Amiram, whose superb business acumen galvanized the entire department. Moreover, the department's cohesion was bolstered by the fact that its key players and group leaders were veterans of the same unit in the IDF's Military

Intelligence Corps and had thus worked together for years. This robust culture was also instilled in the new recruits. On the one hand, the development staff displayed wonderful technical skills and innovation, met its deadlines, and developed products with the best cost-efficiency ratios in the industry. On the other hand, they were arrogant: they acted as if they knew it all; treated the customers like 'monkeys;' and were condescending to the other employees, especially the marketing people. As a rule, strong R&D departments have a profound impact on a company and its priorities. If its people want to develop a certain product or feature, it will get done immediately and at practically no additional expense. However, if they are against a certain project, the development will lag on for years and cost a fortune.

As such, the most frustrating collision involved Gilat's development unit and StarBand. At their peak, the StarBand people legitimately considered themselves Gilat's main customers. StarBand's executives came to Israel on a regular basis for discussions on the product, and were occasionally accompanied by people from Microsoft or Echostar. Once in a while, the StarBand team — most of whom were Americans — had to resort to pressure or other tactics to persuade R&D to develop a certain function, and this drove them berserk. Zur, an Israeli and also at heart, understood the feelings of the Israeli engineers and tried to calm his people down. However, the rest of StarBand's management had a hard time appreciating the Israeli mentality, and this mini-culture clash led to incredibly embarrassing situations — heated discussions, ulterior motives, and bulling tactics —which were practically unheard of at Gilat. "It all started", some smart guys from R&D needled me, "when you agreed to change the name from 'Gilat-to-Home' to 'StarBand'".

Despite the hostilities, our R&D people maintained their cool. Under the guidance of Amiram, who made a huge effort to calm both sides, the development group did what they felt was in the company's best interests. One of the better ideas at the time was to send some of our R&D people to StarBand in order to get a firsthand look at their problems.

In addition, there was a struggle between the product management groups in Tel-Aviv and the sales people in Latin America. The Israeli telephony group claimed that the sales people didn't understand what they were selling, "for if they did, they wouldn't be selling products that don't exist". Moreover, they complained that the sales group was keeping them out of the loop: the sales people were neither consulting with the main office nor showing them the proposals. On the other hand, the sales group in Latin America, which was run by two aggressive Israelis, justifiably claimed that, "the view from Tel-Aviv is distorted". In other words, the people in Israel don't understand what Latin America is all about and that the support staff should be closer to the customer.

As a result of these feuds, my email folder, which earned the nickname 'internal politics' nearly burst from the constant postings.

By the beginning of March 2001, we were well aware of the storm clouds brewing above. The efforts to recruit investors for StarBand, both in the States and Latin America, were still dragging along. Some of our negotiating partners still seemed genuinely interested, but no real progress had been made, and we started to doubt that the talks would end any time soon.

We conducted an in-depth examination of our sales, the rate at which we were burning cash, and the dynamics of the market. Among the sober conclusions that we reached was that while our sales volume remained high, growth may be slower than we had projected. These figures compelled us to re-assess our forecasts for the upcoming quarters, and we began to contemplate what would happen if some of the big projects that we were banking on fell through. The fact that we lacked much of a backup plan for these sorts of contingencies was highly indicative that our pride over our accomplishments of the past few years had blinded us. that we had suffered from during the past few years.

The picture that was unfolding was getting gloomier by the day. Given the extensive changes in the market, there was little chance of meeting the targets and staying within our budget. Worst of all, the pace at which we were expending cash accelerated and our reserves were running low. I started to come to the realization that we may have to abandon the original plan and that we may even be galloping straight into a brick wall.

We thus held a series of emergency meetings with each unit and attempted to update our yearly forecasts and develop contingency plans. I also turned to an option that had always paid dividends in the past. My role at Gilat was always that of player-coach. Whenever we found ourselves in a bind, I would assume the point guard slot. In late February-early March, while Zur and the rest of the StarBand team made a heroic effort to keep the ship afloat, I took a desperate stab at closing the AOL deal. For quite sometime, I still believed we could turn the AOL situation around and that this would constitute not just a rescue but the deal would catapult us to the next level. I simply couldn't contemplate the fact that Gilat was digging itself into a hole.

By now, all the personal doubts that tend to accompany crises situations were out in the open: "Can an entrepreneur really run a company from day one until the point where it has reached Gilat's current size? For that matter, can the same group of founders run the same company for fifteen years? Am I capable of seeing things for what they are? In other words, after all these years, is my hand still on the pulse of the industry and organization? And am I capable of accepting criticism and navigating the ship through the storm?"

Overwrought with fear, I endured many a sleepless night second guessing my decisions. "Was it a mistake to drag Gilat into the StarBand adventure? Would Gilat have really lost its competitive edge had StarBand not been established?

I slowly arrived at the conclusion that the time had come to hit the breaks, even though it was abundantly clear that our ability to keep fighting on all fronts would be compromised once the world realized that we had come to a halt. The public backlash would severely limit our ability to raise capital for both the United States and Latin American chapters of StarBand. Moreover, the pace at which orders were flowing in and StarBand was installing units would invariably slow down; the upside is that this would reduce the burn rate through our scarce remaining funds.

Any public company that doubts it will meet its stated forecasts and objectives must issue a public profit warning. The purpose of such a caveat is to provide a clear signal to shareholders and potential investors that the company may miss its targets. My gut instinct, which had admittedly lost some of its edge over the past few years, told me that a profit warning — and regrettably, we were drawing closer to that stage every day — could have lethal consequences. At best, we would go through a rough period of one or two years until we recovered. At worst, the profit warning would precipitate a tailspin whose end I didn't dare contemplate.

Nonetheless, I still harbored faint hopes that we would do the impossible: meet our production and financial commitments and hammer out a deal with AOL.

We had somehow managed to make headway with the AOL negotiations. However, the internet giant was well aware of the fact that we lacked any semblance of leverage whatsoever and fully exploited our weaknesses. The draft agreements became ever worse from one version to the next. The conversations with David Colburn and his underlings may have been pleasant, but the printed words stung. We even tried to coax a fair deal out of AOL by spending a fortune on advertisements on their websites, but with each passing day they became less and less committed.

Two days before the teleconference in which we were scheduled to confirm the forecasts that we had prepared for the present year, we finally extracted a final version of the agreement out of AOL. The agreement was blatantly one-sided and humiliating, but this was to be expected of talks in which a party with its hands tied behind its back finds itself at the mercy of a strong and wily negotiating partner. Given the circumstances, the battle was over before it started. In any event, we convened a meeting of StarBand's board of directors in order to discuss the deal. Echostar had serious doubts as to whether we should sign it, and Charlie asked for more time to mull it over. Microsoft wasn't thrilled either, but Jon DeVaan understood that we were left with no choice. The board approved the deal, and we signed on the dotted line. Since the news was of utmost importance to StarBand and Gilat, we asked our negotiating partners at AOL for permission to announce the deal at the teleconference the next day. They turned to their supervisors, who responded with an emphatic NO. The agreement wasn't binding on AOL and it was far from clear as to whether AOL would accompany Gilat to the next level

On March 11, 2001, Gilat was forced to issue the first profit warning in its history: "We have met our sales forecast for 2000, but will be substantially lowering our expectations for 2001".

The business world was stunned by the news. At the next teleconference with our investors, we tried to calm their fears. We presented a series of new deals — foremost among them, the contract for 7,500 sites that we had signed with Dollar General — and tried to emphasize StarBand's enormous potential, despite the current difficulties raising money. However, by that point, no one listened. The analysts, including our good friends, battered us with a torrent of harsh and unpleasant questions.

That very day, Gilat's stock collapsed from $36 to $14 per share. The company's stock had thus regressed to its value at the time of its IPO some eight years back. Both the electronic and print media attempted to figure out were we had gone wrong and mercilessly pointed the blame at us. "The Dream is as Far Away as Ever", the headlines screamed. The death spiral had begun.

13

The Death Spiral

The profit warning triggered a raging fire, which consumed everything in its path. Gilat barely left the headlines. In fact, the extent of our press coverage was similar to our situation four months before, except that now we were tumbling down a steep slope, desperately trying to grasp on to something to stop the descent. Reporters from Israel's two primary television stations demanded to enter our building and threatened to film the complex from the outside and tell the public that Gilat's management is denying them access.

GE's John Connely, who did not attend the board meeting, was stunned and demanded explanations. Meanwhile, we began to receive reports from our sales people of confused customers, and deals that were on the verge of being signed were put on hold. The employees were also worried. Our friends greeted us with sorrowful faces, expressed their sorrow, and tried to console us. Like everyone else, we tried to figure out what had gone wrong.

The company was consuming more cash than it was making. In fact, the rate at which we were burning up cash constituted a threat to our continued existence. It became abundantly clear that unless we implemented a series of drastic steps, we would run out of money and wouldn't be able to finance our daily operations, including the payroll. As a result, we repeatedly reviewed our sales forecasts for the coming year in an effort to adjust the expenditures to the level of income in an effort to stop the bleeding. Much to our dismay, we discovered that our budgeted revenues did not materialize. Consequently, there was no choice but to implement drastic cutbacks in our daily expenses. In fact, the dreaded moment which we had been desperately trying to prevent was upon us: we would have to let go of employees.

Over 2,000 people were employed at Gilat in the beginning of 2001. After heart-wrenching discussions, we decided to dismiss about 400 of them. They were all good people, and some of them had practically been with us from the outset. There was also quite a bit of dithering over how to carry out the entire process. Should we dismiss the employees all at once or gradually, over the course of a year, with the hope that things would turnaround and we wouldn't have to go through with the plan? In the end, it was Irit, the company's vice president for human resources, who laid down the rule: "One fell swoop beats an ongoing crusade…"

At a general assembly for all our employees, Amiram surveyed the difficult situation with a grim look on his face. "I'm not saying that we are not to blame", Amiram said, in reference to both of us, "but the economic downturn in the global market has also left its mark on us. The dot-com bubble has burst, and the crisis has hurt the telecom companies. We have no choice but to adjust to the new reality". Amiram then presented the new work plan whereby Gilat would shift the focus back to its core businesses and ratchet down its involvement with StarBand and the domestic consumer market. This was followed by a survey of the sales and expense forecasts. Amiram then shifted the focus to a lengthy explanation of the company's advantages and explained why Gilat had a good shot at enduring the storm. He concluded his words in typical Gilat fashion: "What's important is not the size of the dog, but the power of its bite".

As soon as Amiram finished, he was forced to contend with a fusillade of difficult questions:

"Can you promise us that after these measures are taken, the ship will right itself?"

"No", Amiram replied. "All I can promise is that we will do our best".

"Will there be another round of cutbacks?"

"I don't know. I hope not".

"And what will happen if the darkest scenario comes to pass?"

"We'll cross that bridge when we get there", Amiram answered. "But I assure you that we are implementing this very painful cutback in order to decrease the likelihood of that".

The meeting ended with a penetrating remark by one of the company's most loyal employees: "Enough with the apologetics

. I want to see a knive between the teeth…"

Parting ways with the dismissed employees was a harrowing experience, as one-fifth of Gilat's staff was sent home. I recalled the scenes that I had witnessed at Spacenet only a short while back: the cartons stacked with the belongings of workers who had just been relieved of their duties; and the security guards that accompanied them out of the building without even letting them remove their personal files from their computers. Disgusted by these scenes, I vowed that Gilat would behave differently. Every worker that was issued his walking papers stayed on for another two months. We tried to find jobs for some of them at other companies, but it wasn't easy, as Gilat was hardly the only company that was in trouble. In addition, I spoke with many of the people we let go on an individual basis. To my relief, the employees understood that we simply had no choice but to streamline the staff, and they appreciated the fact that we behaved like human beings. They parted ways with tears in their eyes, wished us the best of luck, and let me know that, if called upon, they would be happy to return.

During the second quarter of 2001, we found ourselves in a frantic and heroic race to meet our sales targets. The entire organization focused on several large deals. Every vice-president took personal responsibility over a deal or two, and we held meetings on potential deals twice a week. In addition, we prepared for what we considered to be a critical trip, which was devoted to raising capital for StarBand. We lined up a four day stretch of intensive, full-day meetings at Microsoft, Echostar, Rupert Murdoch's News Corporation, and AOL.

Before the road trip in mid April, we touched base with Len Roberts, the chairman and CEO at RadioShack. We filled him in on the situation and asked him to help us out with Microsoft. He promised to try and help, but wasn't very optimistic: "Hang in there guys, it's rough out there…"

Early Monday morning, we touched down in Seattle — the first stop on our country-wide tour —for a meeting with Microsoft. Our delegation included Zur, Amiram and myself. Jon DeVaan was no longer at Microsoft, and we were welcomed into the conference room by his replacement Ted Kummert and three of his people. The hosts viewed our comprehensive slideshow, and responded with questions. The delicate matter of the deal with AOL was raised towards the end. "Why'd you do it?" they asked. "Didn't you realize who you were dealing with?"

"We wanted to create a standard", we replied, "and hoped that AOL would serve as an excellent distribution channel. They promised us the world, and we also wanted to get Hughes out of the picture". It was a difficult and most unpleasant moment; we didn't have much to say, and they sensed it. Microsoft was clearly disappointed with our misguided step, and the unspoken message of the meeting was that we should have made every effort to hammer out a deal with them first.

In any event, we offered to sell them the network that StarBand operated for RadioShack and asked them to continue investing in StarBand. They promised to have an answer for both requests before our meeting with Echostar the next day, but the tone throughout the meeting did not bode well.

We gave Microsoft a call as soon as we arrived in Denver; and as we suspected, our salvation would not be coming from Redmond: "We've decided not to invest any more in StarBand", Ted Kummert said. "However, we are prepared to buy the RadioShack network. The proceeds from the sale will buy you guys some time. We want to continue working with you, and we'll be in touch…"

Upon receiving the news, we rushed over to the meeting with Charlie, who gave us a warm welcome. Charlie had many questions in store for us, and his focus was on trying to understand two critical issues: our technical limitations *vis à vis* high-speed internet services that are delivered via cable modems and phone wires; and the economic model of our service in a world bereft of external funding. Armed with a host of slides and all the right answers, we tried to convince Charlie that StarBand could get through the difficult crisis and ultimately prosper. We did a terrific job of holding onto Charlie's attention throughout the meeting. At times he was excited and at other moments he was criticizing us, but he was as sharp as a knife from beginning to end. He asked for some time to think things over, but his parting words were less than encouraging: "Although I'm intrigued by the topic, I'm not sure that I am ready to investment more money in StarBand. Keep me posted on your meetings with Murdoch and AOL, and we'll take it from there".

Without momentum, nothing moves. If there's no pressure on the investor or buyer, then why rush into things? From Charlie's standpoint, the further StarBand deteriorated, the better the terms that he could secure. The road trip was half-way through, and there were still no solutions or money in sight.

During the overnight flight to New York, Amiram and I retraced Charlie's questions and our answers. We then mended a couple of small holes that we discovered in our model and fine-tuned the presentation for the next meetings.

On Wednesday morning, we entered the New York offices of the News Corporation for a meeting with Rupert Murdoch and his vice presidents of finance and technology. The entire business world knew that both Murdoch and Microsoft were thinking about buying Hughes. The media tycoon responded to our basic presentation with a spate of questions and subsequently interrogated us about Hughes. Thereafter, we presented him a world in which every satellite television operator could also provide homes with high-speed internet services. Murdoch, who holds the global leadership in the field — he is the satellite television service provider in England, France, Italy, Latin America, and Asia — was excited: "You guys are very convincing".

As the meeting drew to a close, Murdoch surprised us with the following question: "So what do you guys want?"

"To begin with, a modest investment in StarBand", we answered.

"There is a 90% chance that we'll do it. In fact, we're prepared to start the due diligence meetings today". Murdoch restored the color to our faces, as finally there was a glimmer of hope that some help was on its way.

By Thursday afternoon, we were in Virginia for a meeting with David Colburn and his host of advisors at AOL. My relationship with David had nearly been destroyed, and a testy dialogue ensued. They accused us of failing to meet the targets that we had committed to. In contrast, we claimed that there would not have been any delays if they had signed the contract on the agreed-upon date. The entire atmosphere was poisoned from the start and no one actually listened to what the other had to say. Amiram and I left their offices with the feeling that we had wasted our time.

We returned to Israel with mixed feelings. Gilat continued

to focus on its core business. Thanks to a stand-up effort, we nearly met the financial targets that we had set for ourselves. However, we incurred yet another blow at the end of the quarter: Echostar informed us its dealers would stop selling the StarBand service due to all sorts of(what in our mind were non-existant) technical problems; this would stop until Echostar's management had a chance to "look into the matter". As a result, the pace of StarBand's installations dramatically fell, and the downward spiral continued.

The third quarter of 2001 got off on the right foot. Echostar's Mark Jackson called and asked us what we wanted in return for a controlling interest in StarBand. Since it was abundantly clear that Echostar had the superior hand, we were forced to set our terms with our backs to the wall. We asked that Echostar invest an appreciable sum in StarBand and ensure that the latter repay its debt to Gilat, even if it took a while. In addition, we asked Echostar to launch a satellite that was specifically designated for StarBand, which would considerably improve its profitability. Finally, we insisted that the entire transaction be executed based on StarBand's present value. We started exchanging emails on the topic, and all the top executives at Echostar, Gilat, and StarBand were involved in the preliminary talks. In the end, Charlie picked up the phone and invited us to Denver: "I am going to give you two days of my life. We'll either reach an agreement, or part as friends".

We obviously accepted the invitation. In early July, Yoav, Gene, and I arrived in Denver for two days of intensive negotiations. The talks centered on the following topics: operational issues; marketing rights; the prices that StarBand and Echostar would charge each other for their services; the amount of the investment; the composition of the board of directors and shareholdings; the status of the minority shareholders, including a small company named Microsoft; StarBand's operations in Latin America; and, of course, the deployment of the new satellite.

The negotiations were business-like and the atmosphere was pleasant, as Charlie was less aggressive than usual. He invested all the time that was needed to reach an understanding. He didn't take advantage of our weaknesses, and only pressured us on issues that he considered to be paramount. For example, Charlie demanded that StarBand's board of directors be comprised exclusively of representatives from Gilat and Echostar. Similarly, he haggled over the ownership stakes for each of the potential scenarios that were discussed and was inflexible on all that concerned the operation and financing of the satellite. From my standpoint, the satellite was the most impressive part of the entire deal because Echostar was committing itself to an investment of around $300 million. It is worth noting that we spent hours discussing technical matters, including the structure and deployment of the satellite, but the negotiations over how much the satellite would cost StarBand took less than five minutes! Within two days, the sides managed to draft mutually acceptable document.

Nevertheless, there were several crises over the course of our 48 hours in Denver. For example, a heated exchange erupted towards the end of the first night around the rights in Mexico. Moreover, our attempts to convince Microsoft, over the phone to relinquish their seats on the board of directors were filled with difficulties, as Microsoft doesn't like to take a back seat to anyone. Notwithstanding the flair ups, both parties signed the heads of agreement document before we left Denver, and the definitive agreement was finalized within two weeks.

The deal was announced on July 11. Echostar offered the public a detailed explanation of the agreement and declared that they supported our marketing plans. As we expected, the deal received excellent reviews from the analysts, who managed to put their finger on our motives: "Gilat is putting up a hungry baby for adoption". We really felt as if we were giving up our child, but we knew the parents and hoped that it would be in good hands... Gilat's stock immediately shot up by 20% to $12 per share. The market reacted well, our employees' confidence improved, and we believed that the company was back on the right track. Although we were well aware of just how difficult it had become to advance deals and sell goods, we hoped to close a couple of big deals in September, which would help us meet our financial goals.

Like hundreds of millions of people throughout the world, our hearts skipped a beat at the sight of the two planes slamming into the Twin Towers. The entire business world was paralyzed, and we were in absolute shock. We spent the first few days after the attack trying to figure out the significance of the tragedy and its ramifications on our own operations.

9/11/2001 cast a shadow of doubt over the entire business

world. All transactions in the United States were put on hold. As far as Gilat and StarBand were concerned, postponements came pouring in from every conceivable direction, and the money that was supposed to be invested in StarBand had yet to arrive. In the immediate aftermath of 9/11, all air travel to the United States was suspended. When the flights resumed, I traveled to several large customers and partners — including Charlie from Echostar — aboard completely empty commercial flights. We examined the possibility of closing several of the deals that were already in the making, but I left all the meetings in a depressed state of mind. Budgets were frozen on every level, as were all the existing plans. "It'll take time", I was told at each of my destinations. "All our priorities have changed".

Naturally, no deals were signed.

The flood waters were already reaching our shoulders, and I had no choice but to confess to Charlie the full gravity of our situation. I then asked him to purchase 15,000 units over the course of that quarter in order to reduce our towering stock, enable us to meet our sales forecasts, and provide us with some much-needed cash. He patiently listened, but his "no" was resounding. "Buckle down", he cautioned. "It's not going to get better anytime soon".

I returned to Israel in a somber mood.

From a personal standpoint, one of the most trying moments took place towards the end of September 2001 at the annual toast with the entire staff in honor of the Jewish New Year. "I have nothing to say", was the same response I had for everyone that asked me to give a few words. However, the employees wouldn't take no for an answer. "You have no choice", they insisted. "Everyone wants to know what's going on. You can't hide".

As I got up to speak before hundreds of anxious employees, I remembered other gatherings at which the employees evinced a fighting spirit and their eyes glimmered with boundless hope. Those days, which were not so far way, seemed like centuries ago. The truth was that I really didn't have much to say: "Today I am not a man of revelations. The situation throughout the world and in our own market is steadily deteriorating. It is obvious that we are not living in a vacuum. There are a couple of large deals on our sights, but at the moment the momentum is working against us, as deals are constantly being pushed off". Nonetheless, I tried to soften the difficult tidings with some positive news. "After the attack on the Trade Center, New York's entire communications network was down, and the only means of communication that remained in service was Gilat's terminals, which were connected to our satellite system at the fifty branches of the Postal Service in the metropolitan area. Our equipment continued to work flawlessly, despite the fact that it was being used for many tasks that the system wasn't originally designed for". However, my stories failed to brighten up the mood that filled the room. I didn't mince words: "If the tide doesn't turn soon, we will not be able to meet the targets that we have set for ourselves". The ramifications of another disappointing quarter were clear to all. After my impromptu speech, many of the employees astonished me by coming up and shaking my hand without uttering so much as a word. I stood there with tears in my eyes and felt like the captain of a ship caught in a savage storm, whose entire crew continues to stand behind him.

The death spiral extended into the fourth quarter. On October 3, Gilat issued a another profit warning in which we were forced to report that our sales were a whopping 40% lower than expected. Moreover, the warning also divulged the following setbacks: the damage that had been done to our reputation; the fact that our network-based customers had steadily vanished off the face of the earth; and the state of our stock, which continued to plummet. Within hours after the warning was released, our stock tanked yet again, from $5 to $3.5. During a short and painful teleconference with the analysts, I tried to put the best spin on things. I informed them of the completion of StarBand's fundraising round with Echostar and of a large deal in Peru worth $27 million. I also made note of the fact that Gilat had managed to cut its expenditures by $5 million per quarter. Finally, I told them about our plans to develop new applications for communications backup which had become a key issue for large organizations in the aftermath of 9/11. However, the analysts focused on the figures that appeared on the profit warning and demanded clear answers to their piercing questions. To make matters worse, for the first time analyst reports were being published with recommendations to "sell" shares in Gilat. We took it hard, and the atmosphere in our offices could be summarized in one word: depression.

Once again, we initiated a series of meetings aimed at preparing new financial forecasts and further cutbacks. Upon making the agonizing decisions, we held another company-wide meeting in which we informed the employees of all the measures that we planned to take, including the decision to suspend part of our operations. Furthermore, there were more heart-wrenching scenes of another 400 dedicated employees that would not be coming back to work. This time the dismissals left us with no choice but to suspend our plans for developing and marketing an inexpensive, efficient product for the US domestic market. In sum, we were caught in a vicious cycle that repeatedly forced us to simultaneously reduce our expenditures and stabilize our sales in order to win back the public's confidence.

Two weeks later, Echostar announced that it was buying Hughes. Like the rest of the world, we heard about it in the news. The press had a field day, as a host of teleconferences and interviews were held with all the factors involved. The Israeli press naturally tried to discern the consequences of the deal on Gilat. "Life Buoy or Hangman's Noose?" the headlines asked. Against my habit and in contrast to the education I received in the unit, I succumbed to the pressure of the journalists and granted interviews to *Globes* (Israel's business daily) and *Haaretz* (Israel's most respected daily paper). I wanted to give the public my own take on the situation and respond to a row of negative headlines and articles. I attempted to present the company's years of feast and famine from our own perspective and reiterated the fact that we were still the market leader. I also spoke about the opening of a new domestic market and the profits that we continued to rake in from the sale of telephony products in developing countries. Above all, I wanted to explain why Gilat still had a bright future, and why our technology was superior to that of the competition. As usual, the journalists had their own ideas of what was newsworthy, and not everything that I said merited the proper attention in the articles.

In December, we held negotiations with some of the leading satellite companies: The discussions with Intelsat were remarkably pleasant due to their laid-back culture and the fact that both parties shared a similar strategic outlook. Talks were also held with SES, the world's premier satellite company. After GTE sold Spacenet to GE in 1994, SES purchased Americom from GE and thereby also acquired a 25% ownership stake in Gilat. The discussions centered around the establishment of joint ventures along the lines of StarBand's collaborations in Europe and Latin America. The talks with Intelsat advanced to the point in which they were interested in purchasing Spacenet's operations unit. Furthermore, we began a new dialogue with Echostar on technological cooperation and the development of joint products.

Given the sudden flurry of negotiations, Gilat's management split up into several negotiating teams: I presided over the contacts with Intelsat and Echostar regarding the home consumer market, while Amiram and Joshua negotiated with SES and Alcatel, the French communications giant, on the establishment of a joint venture in Europe. The three of us laid down our coach's whistle and suited up as players. We invested a great deal of energy on developing new ideas, which did not really suit our official work plan. Although we felt as if we were steering Gilat away from its declared areas of focus, we knew that if we clung on to our old principles, we risked losing everything.

Gilat also had to start coping with a new time bomb: In February 2000, — when we were at our peak — we sold $350 million worth in bonds that were due to mature in 2005. At the time, the value of the company's stock was over $150 per share. In addition to the interest, the bond holders received an option to convert the bonds into shares at a value of 20% more than the purchase price; in other words, over $180 per share. The analysts, who suddenly realized that our stock had tanked to $3, demanded to know how Gilat was going to generate $350 million in order to pay off these bonds in 2005.

In an effort to allay these fears, Gilat's senior executives granted interviews to one of the Israeli papers, but the attempt backfired, as the editors gave the interview the following headline: "No Israeli Company has Paid its Bond Debt". Of course, the quote was taken out of its context, but the damage had been done. In any event, the entire bond issue constituted a serious threat to Gilat's existence.

The fourth quarter of 2001 was decent. We met the reduced targets that we had set, and the losses tailed off a bit. In addition, a couple of large deals with strategic partners, such as Intelsat and SES, appeared to be coming along. We wanted to believe that the worst was already behind us.

2002 opened with a burst activity. Intelsat informed us that they wanted to conclude the negotiations and get our joint ventures — service providers catering to the United States and

Latin America — up and running. Meetings were set and Gilat's executives went to Washington to try and close the deal. The talks with Echostar also gathered steam, and I met with Charlie about once a month. Charlie's vision of uniting his satellite television empire and his fleet of powerful satellites with control over the satellite-based high-speed internet industry — or what he referred to as his "everything connects" strategy — appeared to be close to fruition. Nonetheless, I decided not to tell him about the Intelsat partnership until it was a done deal.

In the meantime, StarBand was fighting for its life; as things stood, it would run out of money in April. In January, however, we were still optimistic that Echostar would invest an additional sum in StarBand or bring in new investors. An interesting situation had developed whereby I was holding advanced negotiations with Charlie, while Echostar was simultaneously throwing a monkey wrench into the works by neglecting StarBand. We naturally brought up this issue, but Echostar claimed that they first had to determine the implications of their merger with Hughes, if and when that panned out.

The next month our situation took an abrupt turn for the worse. Early one morning, I was stirred awake by a call from the Intelsat representatives who informed me that their investment bankers did not approve the deal. "You have to be nuts to work with Gilat now", the bankers reprimanded them. The Intelsat reps didn't stop apologizing and asked us to try and talk with the bankers — the very same bankers who only a year ago had begged us to let them underwrite StarBand's IPO.

Troubles, so they say, always come in pairs, and Echostar began to adopt an adversarial approach to StarBand, as Charlie's proposed merger with Hughes was still waiting for the approval of the American anti-trust authorities. By means of a roundabout logic, Echostar tried to persuade the authorities that the merger was the only feasible economic model for providing satellite-based internet services. They pointed to StarBand's shaky state as cutting proof of their claim, even though we well knew that they were largely responsible for its woes. Consequently, they stopped payment on their $10 million debt to StarBand — under the pretense that StarBand also owned them money — and were thus in our view, in violation of their agreement with StarBand.

Although I was quickly running out of options, Amiram

and Joshua managed to make progress with SES. In fact, the two sides agreed to launch a joint venture in Europe at the beginning of the next quarter.

That said, the market for our core products was still weak due to the uncertain state of our primary customers: the large communication network operators. We didn't even manage to overcome the lowest hurdle that we had set for the first quarter of 2002, and the future was looking less and less promising.

The death blow was delivered during the second quarter of 2002.

At the beginning of the quarter, there was still room for optimism, as we announced the deal in Europe with SES. The astonished business world received the news with joy, but we found ourselves increasingly bogged down on the American front.

Charlie hammered the final nail in StarBand's coffin during an analyst quarterly teleconference with Echostar management in May. Resorting to his sophisticated explanations, he claimed that in light of StarBand's failure to secure a critical mass of subscribers Echostar had no choice but to go ahead with the merger with Hughes and wash its hands of StarBand. In his opinion, our economic model was predicated on at least several hundred thousand subscriptions and simply didn't work when there were only tens of thousands.

We felt that Charlie was twisting the facts and that every word he uttered was an affront to our good name. The StarBand management and its staff saw these events unfold in stunned disbelief. Ties between the two organizations were completely severed after it became evident that Echostar had billed StarBand's subscribers, but had refrained from forwarding StarBand its share of the revenues. Consequently, StarBand lost its primary source of revenues and was rendered devoid of cash. StarBand turned to the courts and filed for an injunction that would force Echostar to fork over the subscription fees. However, Echostar mounted an impressive battery of lawyers, and the court rejected our request. Left with no other choice, on May 31, 2002 — as a present for my fiftieth birthday — StarBand filed for bankruptcy in the Federal courts.

The Israeli press jumped on the news like vultures gathering around a dying zebra. "Is Gilat going Bankrupt?" the headlines screamed, and the reaction of the analysts was also severe.

Consequently, our stock dipped below the $1 mark for the first time in its history, and we feared that the SEC would revoke Gilat's standing as a public company.

Only three years earlier, we were the hottest thing on the market. Our stock soared to $180 per share, and Gilat was worth in excess of $4 billion. Analysts and investors courted us, and large companies sought joint ventures. Where are we now?

In September 2002, there was $90 million left in Gilat's bank account. One of the options that stood out our disposal was to continue running the company with the hope that we would manage to earn enough money by March 2005 in order to pay off the above-mentioned $350 million bond debt. However, we realized that this was a treacherous path. So long as there was still a substantial amount of cash in the company's coffers, our best course of action seemed to be a major restructuring aimed at turning the company around, with the hopes of convincing the bondholders to convert their bonds into shares. However, this option also meant ceding control of Gilat to the bondholders. For the founders, who had managed the company since the day it was established and always worked with a supportive board of directors, it was indeed a gut-wrenching decision. As sad as it was, we made the decision without thinking twice, for any other route was liable to threaten the very existence of Gilat.

In essence, we embarked on what is known as "a reorganization of the capital structure", or Chapter 11 as it is classified in bankruptcy law. We interviewed candidates with experience in guiding this sort of process and chose a group that included a handful of Israelis, who we felt we could work with. Unfortunately, they presented themselves as the advisors of the board of directors, and not the management. The advisors turned up everywhere: they attended every important meeting and visited all the subsidiaries. Moreover, they coaxed us into preparing a new business plan and started giving orders to executives and employees alike. In essence, they nearly took over the company, and the confrontations with them were thus unavoidable. Every time a conflict arose, they would claim that they were appointed by the board of directors, and not the company's managerment, so that only the board of directors was authorized to tell them what to do. We eventually fired them, but the very decision to hire them and give them a free hand constituted yet another mistake in our fall from grace.

We continued to take a pounding during the following months. In the beginning of July 2002, the Columbian government notified us that they were "abandoning" the $67 million bid that we had won and that the entire matter would be passed on to the next government, which would be elected in August. "Are Gilat's customers voting with their feet?" the papers and analysts asked.

Our competitors smelled blood and consequently did everything in their power to exploit our weakness. For example, some of them sent letters to the prospects over whom we were competing depicting Gilat as a company on the verge of collapse. They highlighted negative articles that had appeared in the Israeli press and distorted news stories they had gleaned from the news agencies. The letters implied that Gilat was already bankrupt, had no resources with which to extricate itself from its current predicament, and was basically on its last legs. The most glaring example of this sort of tactic was disseminated by none other than Hughes. Our arch rival took steps to obfuscate and confuse the lines between StarBand and Gilat to give the impression that Gilat was also going under. Gilat was clearly on the defensive. We attempted to explain the difference between StarBand and Gilat and present the latter in a positive light, but we felt as if we were chasing our own shadow. The wolf pack had begun to tail the injured herd…

In September, we absorbed one of the most excruciating blows of that entire period. Over the past few years, we had lured away many of Hughes' customers. Just that previous year, we nabbed four of their customers, foremost among them was one of the crown jewels of the Hughes empire: the Holiday Inn chain, with 2,200 hotels in the United States alone. Hughes struck back with everything they had, and Rite-Aid was one of their main targets.

At the time, the drug store chain was also immersed in a difficult reorganization process. Criminal charges were brought against Martin Grass, the son of the chain's founder and my closest ally at Rite-Aid, who left the company in a rush. *The Wall Street Journal* ran daily reports on the developments at Rite-Aid. Amid all the commotion, the chain's management was replaced, including all the people we had worked with, to exclude the low-level technical staff.

From Gilat's standpoint, the key player at Rite-Aid was now Don Davis, the new senior vice-president of information services. Davis' career at Rite-Aid began when the company acquired the chain that he was working for. At first, he had a hard time finding his place in the organization, but after the purge of the company's senior management ranks Don's status markedly improved. He had worked with Hughes in the past and reached the conclusion that he had enough power to throw us out and bring in our arch enemy. He conducted a detailed technical evaluation and comparison of all the products on the market and subsequently released updated specifications, which in our view favored Hughes. Nonetheless, we exerted a superhuman effort to hold on to them. I traveled to Rite-Aid's headquarters in Harrisburg, PA three times and met with their management. They were all new people who had no fond memories of Gilat.

I sat with Davis for hours and attempted to convince him to continue with Gilat. "As far as we are concerned, Rite-Aid is a flagship customer", I said. "No other company will offer you the same sort of commitment that you have been receiving from us". However, I felt as if I was talking to the wall. Even if I didn't always manage to convince a customer to buy our products, I never failed to cultivate a relationship — that is, until I met Don Davis. He neither reacted to nor took into account any of my arguments. Under the façade of "impartial" procurement, we were led into a dead-end street. The technical staff wanted to continue working with us, but Davis was clearly the one calling the shots. Upon presenting the recomendation to his management, he passionately argued in favor of dumping us. "Given their financial problems", he contended, "it would be a risk to continue working with Gilat".

The defeat stemmed from the combination of our obvious woes and our inability to build a relationship with him, which in the not-so-distant past was one of our areas of expertise. The actual financial damage that we incurred paled in comparison to the moral blow of losing a flagship customer. I took the loss personally, for this was the company which had furnished us with the story that enabled us to blaze our way to the IPO ten years earlier. Before we landed the Rite-Aid account, Gilat was a mere start up; thereafter, we became a cornerstone in the industry. I had personally accompanied Rite-Aid through all the ups and downs with Gilat and had forged personal relationships with Alex and Martin Grass. If we lost the Rite-Aid account during a different period, the damage would probably not have been as serious, but now — when Gilat was suffering setbacks on a daily basis — it was a tough pill to swallow.

No less demoralizing were the conversations with employees. A survey that was conducted by Gilat's human-resources department cast our predicament in an even gloomier light. There were rumors of more dismissals, and the employees complained about the sense of anxiety, anger, and insecurity that had taken hold of them. Although they didn't say it to my face, in closed forums the employees admitted that they had lost their faith in management. "The struggle is being waged by Yoel and Amiram's court", they sighed, "and it is unclear as to what we can do in order to assist them". Another, similar complaint that was making the rounds was that not enough people were involved in the decision-making process. Moreover, many employees argued that the organizational changes were insufficient. Quite a few employees, especially the veterans, yearned for the days when we were more involved in the daily operations and maintained direct relations with the employees. To make matters worse, the political struggles between the various units within the organization reemerged with a vengeance.

To follow is a select group of quotations from that same human-resources survey:

"Amiram and Yoel have to understand that they are managing a big business and not a start up. Most of the company's employees neither served in the Unit nor worked at Barzel Street…"

"We feel as if we are not true partners because we didn't serve in the Unit".

"For the first time, the corridors are teeming with politicking, struggles, and emails that are solely for the purpose of covering people's rear ends…"

Gilat's unique culture, which we were so proud of, was severely shaken. Within a year, the fundamental values, the relationship between the employees and the company, and the level of expectations of both management and staff alike had all taken a dramatic turn for the worse. Sub-cultures and various myths sprouted up, and the original team spirit had become terribly weakened. Consequently, the workers felt that they were losing their identity. The early signs of a change in the employees' attitude towards the company contributed to the feeling that we had lost our way.

Our hardships were hardly limited to the psychological realm. Sales were below expectations, and Gilat was facing its third round of cutbacks within the space of a year. Following another round of management and staff meetings, 300 additional employees were dismissed. Since the publication of the fateful profit warning in March 2001, we had to let go of one half of our workforce: a grand total of 1,200 employees. Heart-wrenching farewells once again returned to the corridors of Gilat. The death spiral had reached a crescendo.

14

The Fight for Survival

When your company is fighting for survival— and over the course of 2002 we were fighting for Gilat's very existence — you have to contend with a string of problems, both large and small. Above all, you have to convince yourself that you can win, or as Zur put it, "Only you decide if you have failed". Faith provides you with the strength to persevere, but once you have run out of belief, the battle is lost.

That said, convincing yourself is a good and necessary part but its not enough; you must also convince your partners, customers, and employees. Everyone has got to know that the hope lives on. You must make it absolutely clear that the situation is under control and that the company has clear strategic advantages. In other words, you must prove that success is a realistic goal. Persuasion is all the more difficult when everyone around you is getting their information from the media and your competitors, not from the company itself. Naturally, a gloomy atmosphere among the company's ranks doesn't make the internal campaign any easier. Furthermore, you will have to fight and win several battles simultaneously. In order to pull off this difficult feat, you must display your technological, marketing, and, not least, your moral superiority in the trenches. This is no easy task for a company in a death spiral.

Throughout the entire crisis, I didn't doubt Gilat's ability to survive for so much as a second, nor did I question my ability to devote myself entirely to one objective: to recover Gilat from its lethal tailspin. The commitment of an entrepreneur to a wounded company can only be compared to the support that the family members afford one of their own at an hour of crisis. Accordingly, I was prepared to do whatever it took to secure the company's survival.

In August 2002, I went through many sleepless nights thinking about new ideas that could perhaps rescue the company from the abyss. As noted above, one of our main problems was the lack of control over the information that was being disseminated about our company. Consequently, I decided to establish what I referred to as the "clarity forum". This group would be comprised of seventy people that were in close contact with our customers: sales and marketing people, the key people in our international offices, customer-service personnel, vice presidents, and several middle level managers. Given the gravity of our situation, the forum would operate in 'crisis mode.' A responsible employee was assigned the job of providing the forum's members with real-time updates on everything that was going on in the company and our industry and saw to it that all the members took part in the weekly teleconference. During the weekly teleconference, we would determine which events were significant enough to warrant special treatment and put our spin on those. This information would also enable us to respond to developments and present our side of the story in a timely manner.

The events were indeed transpiring at a dizzying pace. Newspaper articles, analysts' reports, and developments with our competitors, such as the Echostar-Hughes merger, surfaced regularly. Moreover, customers were constantly requesting clarifications on our financial situation. It was thus encumbent upon us to react, explain, and present our views on a daily basis. The objective was to keep our sales people fully updated on everything that was being published about us in the press. In other words, I didn't want the members of the forum to hear about any developments from the media. Our goal was for Gilat to be the main source of information for both the bad and occasional good news alike. With this in mind, I invested quite a bit of time on managing the forum and planning the agenda of its meetings.

Reports on breaking news items or events would immediately be distributed to all the forum members, with our own emphases and pertinent points of reference. We also decided to put together weekly presentations for the purpose of updating and explaining the situation to the entire forum. During the teleconferences, we would survey the events of the past week, provide updated industry news, and report on the events that were expected to transpire during the upcoming week. Of course, Gilat's managers responded to any questions that the participants had. Targeted presentations were also prepared to assist the marketing and sales people in their daily work. Finally, I instructed all the all executives to tend to the needs of any forum member or customer that approached them with a request for information.

We appointed Tim Perrott to manage the crisis. Tim had replaced Diane as the vice president of investor relations in 2001. He was a sharp, energetic, and efficient executive, with significant expertise in financial matters. Throughout Gilat's darkest hours, Tim kept in touch with all the investors and always did his best, even when the cards were stacked against him. Although Tim really cared about the company and must have been fuming on the inside, he maintained his composure and applied his professional acumen throughout the whole ordeal; extermally, his persona was serene. In contrast, I had a tendency to take things personally and every bit of bad news cut into my flesh, so that I came to admire Tim and rely on his gentle take on events.

Tim organized the teleconferences and ran the entire forum in an exemplary fashion. By dint of his efforts, the forum became the central junction for collecting and distributing information. As the master of spin, Tim always managed to glean the good from the bad and articulate our take on things in a convincing manner. He spent countless hours with reporters and news makers in an effort to present our side of the story. Likewise, Tim invested many long hours with customers that sought information on the financial and general situation of the company.

At the same time, Tim continued to fulfill his duties as Gilat's manager of investor relations in the United States as well as a company spokesman in Latin America and Africa. Within the framework of his duties, Tim flew to various destinations around the world, where he would meet with our local representatives. After getting them up to date, Tim and our local staff would then go to customers and present them with an updated corporate presentation. Moreover, he held press conferences at which he provided the local press with a general presentation of Gilat , its achievements and a detailed explanation of our current status. At times, he occasionally accompanied local television crews out to the field in order to show them our products in action.

The clarity forum was a huge success. The teams out in

the field were no longer caught off-guard by embarrassing news developments, as all the pertinent information arrived directly from headquarters. Moreover, they were given assistance on a wide array of topics, and had an address to turn to for discussing the most painful subject of all: our financial situation and how it would improve going forward. Thanks to the efforts of Tim and the clarity forum, we managed to gradually restore the faith of our employees who dealt with the customers on a firsthand basis as well as the customers themselves. In fact, the forum imbued the entire company with a sense of cautious optimism.

Few are the times in the annals of a company that the labor of a single employee has a decisive impact on the success of the entire organization. Tim was indeed worthy of a medal for his heroic efforts.

While keeping our employees and customers informed was a vital component of our efforts to turn things around, we also sorely needed a high-profile victory to grasp onto and slowly pull ourselves out of the mud.

The largest potential deal was in Colombia, where the government had earmarked $100 million for the construction of 3,000 public telephones and 500 internet centers in small and mid-sized cities that were absent of communications infrastructure. Gilat's asking price was only $67 million, and we were the only company that submitted a proposal for the establishment of internet centers. As a result, we won the deal and were looking forward to getting the project underway. However, as noted earlier, the outgoing government informed us in July — a month before the country's elections — that it was backing out of the project and leaving the decision to the new government.

After the elections, I flew to Colombia in order to try and close the deal. In addition, I wanted to check out some of the sites that we installed and find out how much Colombia was worth to Gilat.

Colombia is a large country with a population of around 41 million. Its vast territory is over a tenth of the size of the United States. However, the central government only controlled about half of the country, as the offshoots of various guerilla movements and drug barons ruled over the rest. The energetic new president swept into office on the wings of a campaign promise to crush the rebels with military force. On account of the rebel menace, Colombia is still a dangerous place for Western business people; and those who dare coming, get around in armored jeeps. In 2002, Colombia was a popular destination for Israelis, but the massive inflow of Israeli tourists came to an abrupt halt when guerilla fighters kidnapped four Israeli hikers in the jungles and held them hostage for several months.

In essence, I didn't know a thing about the Colombian people or their culture. As far as I was concerned, they were Klingons (the peculiar species in Star Trek) — an enigma to all outside observers. This was hardly Gilat's first foray into Colombia. We had already installed and were maintaining over 7,000 public telephones and 700 internet terminals. Our network provided services to about 4 million people, for most of them it was their only way of communicating with people outside their communities. These payphones were very important to the Colombian government because in many instances the communications equipment that we installed in remote villages was the only service that the residents received from the central government.

Likewise, Colombia was an important market for Gilat. Among the governments that purchased our equipment, Colombia was our seventh largest customer.

Fifty people worked for Gilat Colombia as well as hundreds of sub-contractors. Our Colombian crew was a strong and tight-knit group, even though their loyalty to their country was greater than their commitment to the company paying their salaries. Ronaldo, the head of Gilat Columbia, was a typical Colombian. He developed a sprawling network of political ties and was on close terms with the country's entire communications industry. His right-hand man was Juan Gonzalo, an energetic young man with a decent grasp of the international business world who served as the vice president of finance. The technical manager, Janette, was a highly-knowledgeable engineer, but was clueless when it came to the business aspects of our operations. Thrown into the mix was Shai, an Israeli, who was in charge of installing and maintaining the equipment. Shai also served as the contact person between the local staff and our headquarters in Israel. Alexandra, a Colombian living in the United States, was the heart and soul behind Gilat Colombia's business development. Last but not least, was Estrella who served as the chief for all of Gilat's operations in Latin America. In sum, Gilat

Colombia was an aggressive team that put in many long hours and had a burning desire to succeed.

My first meeting in Colombia was on Friday at 8:00 in the morning with Maria Carla, the deputy minister of communications. Maria was thirty-five years old and spoke fluent English. She was an authoritative woman with little patience for small talk. About twenty people took part in the meeting, which lasted about three and a half hours.

At the outset, Gilat's local reps reviewed, in flowing Spanish, the state of the existing network. They reported on the percentage of sites that were in operation and the amount of traffic our network was handling in an attempt to prove to the officials that we were meeting our performance targets. Twenty minutes into the discussion, a crisis erupted. Our people timidly argued that a large portion of the problems that arose in the field stemmed from their inability to reach sites that were under guerilla control. They spoke at length about one incident in which two of our sub-contractors were killed in rebel-held territory trying to complete an installation. However, the government officials, surprisingly for me, rejected this claim as if this is none of their responsibility.

It was disappointing for me to discover the poor relationship and rapport between our people and the government officials. I was particularly offended with the defensive posture our people took during the argument. How could we be held responsible for that? The government representatives were the ones that set the tone, while Gilat's representatives were repeatedly forced on the defensive and were constantly apologizing.

About an hour and a half into the talks, we reconvened in a limited forum: myself, Alexandra, and our lawyer with the deputy minister, the official in charge of the project, and their lawyer. "So as not to build up any false expectations", Maria Carla coldly looked at my eyes, "I am obliged to say that we do not intend on signing any agreements during your present visit. We are unsatisfied with the current state of the network, and we need more time to make a decision".

This time I could have my own direct response without the need for translation. I expressed my surprise and explained to them that I had come all the way from Israel for the express purpose of signing the contract. "I am not a Colombian", I continued, "but in my opinion no other company will do for Colombia what Gilat had. If this is your attitude then we will obviously have to reassess our involvement in your country".

The deputy minister did not expect this sort of reaction, especially the tone. Our transition from defense to offense was instantaneous, and we kept up the pressure until the end of the meeting. Nonetheless, we attempted to conclude the harsh round on a more pleasant and upbeat note: "I have one request of you", she said before we parted. "Give interviews to our newspapers and television. It is imperative that you bring your achievements in the current network to the public's attention".

"No problem", I said.

The weekend was upon us, but the last thing on our minds was rest. We devoted many long hours to a comprehensive review of the existing network, including its technical and financial aspects, and reassessed our expectations for future projects in Colombia. In addition, I gave interviews to three newspapers and embarked on a tour of some of our sites with the country's second largest television network.

We drove to an urban site and met with the elderly women in charge. She was happy to speak before the cameras and had only good things to say about Gilat. In addition, I was filmed talking on the phone to Israel and surfing on the web. Over the course of a lengthy interview, I explained the importance of the project to Colombia: "There aren't many companies in the world that can come to a country like Colombia and lay down telecommunications and internet infrastructure for millions of people. We hope that the Colombian government, which did such a good job on the first network, will also award us the second project".

The television station went all out for us, for it wasn't everyday that the CEO of a major international company — Gilat is indeed considered a communications powerhouse in Colombia — comes to the country, evaluates the company's local operations, and immerses himself in all the details. They were astonished to see me talking with the site manager, Gilat's employees, and even random people who came to make a call, in an attempt to understand the problems and find solutions. The story was aired that very night, and it made an excellent impression on all the viewers.

I then visited a site that was a three-hour ride from Bogotá, the capital. The phone was located in the middle of nowhere in a decrepit house. The entire scene evinced harrowing poverty, as five neglected children wandered about outside. The operator's house consisted of two rooms: a bedroom in which the entire family slept; and the living room, where the phone was located. The film crew gave the operator the royal treatment, and he didn't stop talking. He told the reporters that he made his living selling phone cards, earning about $10 a month from total sales of about $100, which was enough to support his entire family. When they explained to him that I was the head of the company that built the system, he panicked and looked me straight in the eyes. "You haven't come to take away my phone?" he asked in plain spanish.

From the rural lands, we proceeded to one of our laboratories, which was located not far from the airport. I was stunned by the condition of the products that were brought in for repairs: rusty printed circuit boards (PCBs) and boxes; units that, due to the heat, were infiltrated by colonies of cockroaches; and other units that were struck by lightening, the likes of which I had never seen. At long last, I had begun to understand just how difficult the conditions out in the field were.

That evening, I was invited to a glamorous cocktail party that was put for me and was attended by ministers, former ministers, and the country's business elite. The Israeli ambassador and the economic attaché also dropped by, as did a host of other people. I mingled and chatted with several of the local business leaders. For example, I complained to one of the senior managers of Colombia's electric company about the problems we were having with the power grid. He smiled and explained to me that the network was constructed in great rush and that it would take years to improve the situation. The secretary-general of the coffee growers' association enumerated the advantages of Colombian coffee and described the potential gold mine that his associates constituted for Gilat… In addition, the president of a large Colombian communications company complained about the government's condescending treatment of his company, despite the fact that it had already invested over $2 billion in the country. As far as I was concerned, the party was a wonderful opportunity to learn more about this 'Klingon' nation from multiple angles.

Another meeting with the deputy minister was scheduled for the next morning. Eager to make progress, we spared no effort in preparing for the meeting. We had all the performance metrics the financial metrics and people satisfaction measures. We brought summaries from the meetings we had. Alexandra planned to deliver a speech on Gilat's general outlook concerning our Colombian operations, and we went over it several times. I felt like a student before an important examination.

The meeting, which began at 10:00am sharp, pitted Alexandra and myself versus the deputy minister and the government official in charge of the project. To begin with, we held an open discussion in flowing English. I presented my conclusions from the visit, including my thoughts on the condition of the existing network. Maria Carla, the deputy minister, was impressed by the analysis and accepted most of my basic premises. Additionally, I asked that several steps be taken in order to stabilize the situation and she promised to tend to all those matters.

Thereafter, Maria briefly explained her political restraints — what she could and couldn't do — and Alexandra then gave her lengthy speech in Spanish, which we had gone through the night before. "I am a Colombian", Alexandra began. "Despite the fact that I live in the United States, I care a great deal about our country". She then pointed at me and exclaimed: "Yoel, however, is an unsentimental businessman. Besides Colombia, Gilat is active in eighty other countries around the world. Gilat has done much good for Colombia", Maria nodded her head, "but if we are not granted these new projects, which we are legally entitled to, it is unclear whether Gilat will continue its activities. In other words, Gilat may even withdraw from Colombia altogether, with all the implications that such a move entails…"

"But", Carla attempted to defend herself, "there will be many other large projects that Gilat can win in the future…"

Alexandra ruthlessly cut her off: "How am I supposed to explain that to Yoel, if you won't even grant us the project that we have already won fair and square…"

The message had indeed seeped in; within a couple of hours, the project was in our hands. I returned to Israel with the sweet taste of victory on my lips. It felt just like the old days, when we scraped and clawed for every customer and won. I convened our entire staff in Israel and told them all about our adventures in Colombia.

Over the course of my visit, I had grown quite fond of Colombia and felt as if Gilat was truly making a difference there. I was extremely proud of the performance of our technology, service, and staff. Furthermore, it was a tremendous feeling to get away from the daily grind of the reorganization struggles and enter the trenches, leverage our existing networks, and forge ahead. The visit to Colombia was a breath of fresh air that strengthened my faith.

There was yet another reason for optimism: By dint of Amiram's able leadership, we managed to stabilize StarBand.

To begin with, Amiram settled our differences with Echostar. Both StarBand and Echostar agreed to drop the charges against one another. A comprehensive compromise agreement was subsequently signed under which Echostar agreed to hand over all of our subscribers and return part of its debt to StarBand. Furthermore, StarBand prepared a new budget under the protection of the courts, which enabled the company to continue to exist. As a result of the agreement with Echostar, StarBand was finally being compensated for the services it provided to its 40,000 subscribers and the company was out of bankruptcy by the end of 2002. The new business model was predicated on internet technology, which enabled StarBand to work directly with Echostar's distributors. The on-line system covered nearly every element of the business: the receipt of orders from dealers for their customers; the dispatch of equipment to the dealers; acquiring new customers (for example, obtaining their credit card numbers); and servicing them. And all this was accomplished on-line, without so much as a single telephone call! Once again, StarBand's strong and dedicated staff proved that it could quickly adapt to a new business model with all the processes required to master it.

That said, StarBand's turnaround did not substantially improve Gilat's own financial troubles. However, in my estimation, its swift transition from a model that was predicated on subsidizing the customer's equipment (which required a considerable amount of cash) to a model in which customers paid for the equipment upfront was an enormous accomplishment.

As part of the broader organizational reform, Amiram was charged with running StarBand and Spacenet, while I assumed responsibility over the sale of Gilat's equipment. I commanded an army of marketing and sales people that was active in dozens of countries all over the world. This position was tailor-made for me, as there is nothing I loved more than selling our own technology and products. I defined clear targets and reformed both the organizational structure and incentive packages. Moreover, I brought on new managers for different regions and chose to focus on Africa.

Africa was a classic market for Gilat. Not only was the continent bereft of communications, but it was extremely difficult to lay down cables. We put up telephony systems in many countries and established networks that enabled schools and businesses to hook up to the internet. The best example of our superior African operations was South Africa. As the most developed country in Africa — with a communications company that was run according to Western standards — South Africa was quite capable of mounting large-scale projects.

At the outset, most of the deals in South Africa were divided equally between Gilat and Hughes. However, in 1998, we got a colossal project off the ground. Within the span of four months, Gilat connected some 3,000 telephones throughout the country and did so entirely on its own, all. In fact, it was one of the most successful projects that we ever carried out, as it was both quick and highly profitable. Furthermore, we managed to amass a great deal of political capital and bolstered our reputation in the country. In 2001, at the height of our financial troubles, the South African state-owned telecom company decided to launch a high-speed internet program. Despite our predicament, we once again beat out our arch rivals and landed the deal, largely on account of the strong relationships that we had forged in the country. Over the course of my entire visit to South Africa in December 2002, I was given the red-carpet treatment and the topic of our financial situation was not even mentioned.

We also did substantial business in Kenya. Avraham Ziv Tal, Gilat's outstanding sales person for 2002, built a solid relationship with a customer who even asked for, and received, permission to use our name (he subsequently called his firm Gilat Alldean). Avraham sold them telephony and internet systems for the Kenyan army and other customers. The relations with the customer were so good that we were awarded one of the biggest programs in Gilat's history — hooking up 1,000 post offices to a network — solely on the basis of a handshake.

Gilat became a hot name all across Africa, as we also

raked in projects in Angola, Rwanda, and Nigeria. The battles on the Dark Continent always played themselves out in a remarkably similar fashion: Hughes would show up at a particular country and drag our name through the mud, and Gilat would be butchered in the internet and the local press. In response, Tim and Barry, Gilat's vice-president of corporate communications, would rush over to that country and take our local sales persons to a meeting with the customers. In addition, they would hold a press conference and give a slew of interviews in which they would recount Gilat's story. Tim and Barry would then accompany local television crews out to the field in order to show them examples of our service. At the site, the reporters would conduct interviews with satisfied customers. By the next day, complimentary stories on Gilat's contribution to the country would appear in the local press, so that in the end Hughes' approach always worked to our advantage.

The positive momentum carried over to other parts of the world. Following a hard-fought competition, Gilat landed a major deal (1,300 sites) in Tibet. We were elated, for China is considered a tough market to get a strong foothold in. One deal begot another, and we felt as if we were steadily picking up steam.

In January 2003, after what had been a trying year for the entire organization, we assembled all 150 of our sales and marketing people from around the world for an annual sales meeting in Israel. For the first time in quite a while, there was a true sense of hope. Over the course of their stay, we talked abour our financial situation and described the measures we are taking, evaluated the development and launch plans for our various products, and analyzed the depressing losses and big successes. Despite the death spiral, the good sales people managed to get the job done, whereas their less talented colleagues blamed the company's financial situation for their poor showing. The product line managers gave passionate presentations on the products and markets. In one concentrated day, I managed to squeeze in everything that I wished to convey regarding the topics of sales and strategy. An emphasis was placed on the need to execute and the importance of relationships. Together with the sales people, we set targets for the upcoming year and we asked our marketing staff to focus on two topics in particular: Mega deals and follow-on sales to existing customers.

At the time of the sales meeting, the Second Intifada was

at its peak. Despite the never-ending terror attacks, we took all the participants on a full-day tour of Jerusalem. We showed them the Old City — the Western Wall and the tunnels beneath, along with the city's monasteries and mosques — and treated them to an oriental dinner, which was topped off with belly dancers. During the annual sales meeting's emotional closing session, many of the employees declared that, following a long period of doubt, their faith in the company had finally been restored and that the Gilat spirit was alive and kicking.

While I expended all my energy on my work with the marketing people and distributors, Amiram and Yoav handled the matters of the company's reorganization. As noted earlier, $350 million in bonds, which were purchased in 2000, were due to mature in March 2005. The only way to contend with the looming debt was to convert the bonds into stocks, but the bondholders would subsequently possess 90% of Gilat's shares and hence a controlling interest in the company.

After sending home the original batch of financial restructuring consultants, Gilat's management, the bondholders, and the banks chose an Israeli lineup of advisors to spearhead the reorganization process. We prepared presentations and gave them an in-depth survey of the company with the hopes of convincing them that it was in the bondholders' best interests to convert their bonds to a controlling stake in the company. As is our habit, all the company's figures were disclosed to the bondholders and their advisors in a transparent fashion, and we made no attempt whatsoever to sugarcoat the situation. In light of the fact that all the company's primary stakeholders approved of the advisors, we were confident that an accord would soon be hammered out and that we would finally put our troubles behind us.

The bondholders were not the only ones to be hurt by the company's fall from grace, for millions of stock options were held by about 1,500 of our employees, past and present. Before the dot-com crash, Gilat's stock had peaked at $180 and remained above the $100 mark for nearly an entire year. Even though all the option holders were entitled to cash in their option when the price of the stock was over $100, the number of those that actually did so could be counted with on a single hand even though the company never told them not to (I personally signed every employee option that was cashed in). Similarly, not one of the founders had sold so much as a single share since the fourth offering in 1999. Consequently, we were all left with hundreds of thousands of shares whose value had steadily deteriorated as the company's fortunes declined. Gilat's entire staff — its founders, managers, and employees — had wholeheartedly believed in the company's vision.

At that point, all that mattered to us was the company's survival. I was immersed in the wars in Colombia, the United States, and Africa, so that I was less interested — unjustifiably so — in the efforts to convince the bondholders to convert their bonds to stock. Once we had managed to stabilize the company in September 2002, the negotiations with the bondholders, which Amiram and Yoav presided over in the background, dragged on at a lazy pace. The debt was converted into equity in an organized legal procedure that was finally concluded in late January 2003. At the end of the day, Gilat had new owners: Bank Hapoalim (one of Israel's largest banks), Eliezer Fishman (one of Israel's top businessmen), among others. Despite the fact that we had lost control over the company, we hoped that our new owners would let us complete Gilat's recovery process and steer the company back onto the path of growth.

15

Without Us

Our first meeting with the new owners was set for March 2, 2003. Although we sensed that something was up, we treated it as another, ordinary meeting between the shareholders and the company's management. Even before the meeting, the shareholders put out feelers concerning changes in management. We felt as if they were looking for a scapegoat — someone they could line up before the firing squad — and once that person was out of the way, everyone could relax. We tried to find out where we stood *vis à vis* the new owners, but all we got were vague responses. Given my deep sense of commitment to the company, I offered to continue in my current capacity under the title of vice president of sales, while Amiram would assume the position of CEO. They heard our proposal, but didn't respond.

Throughout this period, there was talk of necessary change, but we didn't think that the new shareholders would send us packing. The meeting itself was very brief. Amiram and I sat opposite a lawyer representing Bank Hapoalim and the representative of the new management group. The latter wasted no time before dropping the bombshell: "The new shareholders have decided to ask the two of you to step down after the announcement of the financial reports in mid-April. The new management team will begin training for their new positions immediately. We ask for your complete cooperation in all that concerns the passing of the baton".

Amiram and I looked at one another. We were both stunned and had a hard time digesting the news. Since they were now the owners and we were merely their employees, we realized that such an outcome was a possibility, but nothing prepared us for the blow or the lump in our throats. We were indeed under the impression that they would let us stay on, as there was a sense that

270 • Yoel Gat

things were moving in the right direction: Gilat landed new deals and new customers; and at long last, more money was entering the company bank account than was spilling out. We had generated strong momentum, only to receive a sudden and stinging slap in the face. It was a horrible feeling that was accompanied by enormous sorrow. Why fire us now, after we had already gotten over the two most difficult years? This was not the way I planned to leave Gilat.

We later learned that the new owners had wavered for quite some time over whether to keep us. I didn't blame them for sending us home, neither at that moment nor in the days that followed. I recognized my own mistakes and took full, personal responsibility for the fact that the company had nearly gone under. Although Gilat was still my baby, I had lost control over it and agreed to the bond conversion, which essentially transferred the company to the new parents. Therefore, they had every right to decide that I was not the right person and let me go.

Upon hearing the news, the only thing that we wanted was to be left alone. We asked a few questions for the sake of clarifying matters, but the meeting lasted all of ten minutes. The two of them got up and left us to ourselves. "That's it", Amiram summed things up. "We have to turn over a new page and move on".

"But how?" I thought to myself. "How could we leave a company that was conceived in our very own minds and that we had built from scratch? How could we leave a company whose name shall always be comprised of our initials? What was I supposed to do the next morning? Where was I supposed to go? For the last sixteen years, Gilat was my be all and end all. I woke up with her in the morning and went to sleep with her at night. And there were quite a few nights that I didn't even manage to sleep…"

I left the room and went straight to Simona, who was still working for the company (she was dismissed a half a year later). "You won't believe me", I told her "but I've just been fired".

"It can't be. Why would they do such a thing?"

I was hardly in the mood to see anybody from Gilat, and Simona took me straight home. For the first time in years, I didn't know what I would be doing the next few minutes. As is my custom, I slept on it and showed up for work the next day. I decided that I would continue to run the organization with a firm hand, as if nothing had happened, for this wasn't just another company and I wasn't just another employee. In the two months that remained, I continued to burn the midnight oil. In fact, most of the staff had no idea that these were our final months at Gilat. It took a couple of weeks for the news to percolate down to Gilat's senior executives and from there, by means of a presentation that we put together, to the entire company.

I enjoyed seeing how surprised the new management was by our commitment to Gilat. They had girded themselves for war, as they were certain that we wouldn't cooperate and that the company's operations would be paralyzed during those two months. Of course, they were wrong because you can't overestimate the commitment of an entrepreneur to his company, even when it's no longer his. The passion for the company seeps into every last bone in your body and consumes all your time. The organization is yours; it counts on you and constantly sizes you up. You can't loosen the reins for so much as a moment.

The entire Gilat community was informed of the news: I held conversations with all my friends, sent emails to all the overseas offices, and released an announcement to the press. My friends accompanied me with sullen faces.

In the finest Gilat tradition, Amiram and I did as best as we could during the last two months. We completed the company's financial statements for the year of 2002 and duly put our signatures onto the documents under oath. On April 15, 2003, a meeting was held between the outgoing and incoming boards of directors in which the financials were approved. Later that same day, we raised a toast in the dinning room in honor of Passover. Amiram and I wished the new management the best of luck, and we bid farewell to the employees. After parting ways, I sat down in my office and went over all my email messages for the last time. I then cleaned out my e-mail account and drafted an automatic response to anyone that tried to contact me: "Alice no longer lives here... Please turn to the new management with any request. There is no longer a Yoel at gilat.com".

It was already 11:30 at night. Even on my last day at the company, I failed to come home at a reasonable hour... I closed the notebook, shut down the computer, and collected whatever personal items still remained. Before shutting the door, I took one last look at the place that I had occupied for so many hours and so many years. However, the pain of leaving was accompanied by a new sensation: relief. I felt as if a heavy weight had been lifted off my back. Suddenly, I was free to take off into the great unknown in an attempt to rewrite the history books, one more time.

So long my dear Gilat.

Epilogue

The day after I left Gilat, I met with Yossi Vardi for a quiet lunch. Yossi — the father figure of Israel's high-tech entrepreneurs — wanted to prepare me for life after Gilat: "Learn to sleep in the afternoon and go see some operas in Italy..". As I was about to leave, he also threw me a tip: "Give Jean Frydman a call. He may need your help".

A couple of days later, I paid a visit to Jean Frydman at his luxurious villa in Savyon. I was already acquainted with Jean, an older man who did a lot in his lifetime. Jean is intimately connected to the State of Israel and dedicates most of his waking hours to helping our country. Following a lengthy discussion on the political situation in Israel, the conversation naturally turned to SkyGate, his antenna company, At the time was working on, among other interests, the development of advanced antennae to enable vehicles to hook up to satellite networks. I asked a ton of questions, and Jean answered some of them. Towards the end of my visit, he took me to his study and pointed to a shelf with material about his company's operations. "Take whatever you want, read it, and get back to me", he told me. I took about ten large folders and headed out.

I pored over the material that very weekend. Nestled among the wide range of applications, I also discovered a fascinating sea of products for receiving television in cars and trains. For the most part, the material was technical, but there were also several intriguing business stories. For example, I came across a Bulgaria-based company with a unique technology, but the outfit had its hands in too many things and was suffering from lack of marketing knowhow. In other words, the Bulgarians' most glaring weakness was an utter lack of product focus. They were more like a team of superb engineers at some academic research institute. Their organization was exceedingly different from the place I had come

274 • Yoel Gat

from…

Several days later, I returned to Jean with a startling recommendation: "Shut down the company. It's a complicated field, and it will take an enormous effort to succeed. I'll save you a couple of million of dollars, and you won't even have to pay me a fee for my services…"

He took a moment to mull over my advice before responding: "I am willing to invest more in the company. Look into it and tell me what I need to do". Jean wasn't ready to give up without a fight

His determination made a deep impression on me and piqued my interest in his Bulgarian company. I am the type of person that likes to take responsibility and do things on my own. I am decidedly not a natural consultant. That said, was I ripe for another long-term commitment after having just completed a grueling sixteen-year period at Gilat?

I was fascinated by the new opportunity and decided that the least I could do was look deeper into the matter. So, with nothing else on my dance card, I flew to Paris for a meeting with the company's chief consultant, Dan DiFonzo — an elder American who was a respected figure in the satellite industry — and Emil, the company's head. Dan and Emil arrived with a heap of slides. After a couple of minutes, I realized that they took me for yet another person that Jean had burdened them with. I waited another three minutes before asking them a tough question, which nearly caused the two of them to fall over their chairs. They glanced at each other with a look that seemed to say "beginners luck" and answered my question in a superficial manner. Two minutes later I unleashed another loaded question that hit the nail on the head. They both opened their top buttons and loosened their ties (as usual, I was donning a t-shirt); from that point on, they began to take me seriously. Over the course of two and a half days of meetings, I filled up sheaves of paper in my new notebook — the first of the new era.

I headed back to Israel and Jean's living room in Savyon. "The main problem with the company", I told Jean, "is that nobody is focused on shareholder value. Dan is a strong consultant and is interested in extending his consulting contract, and the Bulgarians would be more than happy to continue developing technologies for the greater good of mankind. From their standpoint, everything is great so long as someone continues to sign the check at the end of the month".

Jean instantly understood. "Go to Bulgaria and tell me what needs to be done".

In Bulgaria, I met a tight-knit band of gifted engineers. They were true professionals with technical skills that were on par with the engineers at the Unit (my select unit in the IDF's Military Intelligence Corps). I enjoyed the discussions and was impressed with the ideas they presented. In addition, I was touched by their warm hospitality. On the other hand, I also realized that they were desperate for guidance. Their main problem was that business and marketing considerations were completely alien to them. Furthermore, as I suspected, the work environment was more suited for an academic research institute than a R&D department of a leading high-tech company. In any event, I was truly excited about the prospects and learned enough about the company to begin charting a new course.

I returned to Jean and my favorite armchair in his living room, and informed him that, "I'm in. Now make it worth my while".

"Tell me what you want", Jean happily replied.

Two meetings later, and less than three months after leaving Gilat, I was the proud owner of a respectable piece of equity in SkyGate , this time around, it cost me a little more than $125 , and in charge of its activities.

Two years after we left Gilat, Gilat was acquired by a hedge fund named York who purchased the majority of the debt and a big part of the equity. I got the first call from them asking if I will be willing to join on board. Since I was already committed to my new company (I changed the name to "RaySat", the topic of my next book), I referred them to Amiram, Joshua and Yoav with the best reference one can come up with. They negotiated a deal with the fund and started to run the company again – this time without all the hassle of the capital structure. Gilat has been doing very well under their tenure and is expected to do well in the many years going forward.

As a final note, I recall a greeting that I received from Idit and Yossi Gal at the end of a sad farewell party that was thrown for me by my Israeli friends at my final meeting in Spacenet:

Yoel,

An ancient Greek myth tells of the wonderful Egyptian bird — the phoenix.

The bird boasts incredible colors and a glorious voice, and its wings carry the phoenix high up into the skies.

When the phoenix reaches the end of the line, she does not die. Instead, she is consumed by a magical fire. She then arises from the ashes and is born anew. She reemerges in brilliant, vibrant colors, and once again ascends high into the clouds, higher than ever before.

We part ways in sorrow, but are sure that, like the phoenix, we will see you take off yet again.

Only the sky is the limit...